Islam, Liberalism and Human Rights

ISLAM, LIBERALISM and HUMAN RIGHTS

Implications for International Relations

KATERINA DALACOURA

I.B. TAURIS
LONDON · NEW YORK

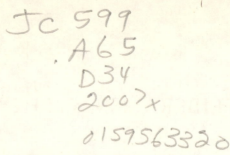
Third edition published in 2007 by I.B.Tauris & Co Ltd
6 Salem Road, London W2 4BU
175 Fifth Avenue, New York NY 10010
www.ibtauris.com

In the United States of America and Canada distributed by
Palgrave Macmillan a division of St. Martin's Press
175 Fifth Avenue, New York NY 10010

Revised edition published in 2003 by I.B.Tauris & Co Ltd
First published in 1998
Copyright © 1998, 2003, 2007 Katerina Dalacoura

ISBN 978 1 84511 382 7

A full CIP record for this book is available from the British Library
A full CIP record is available from the Library of Congress

Library of Congress Catalog Card Number: available

Typeset in Minion by Hepton Books, Oxford
Printed and bound in India by Replika Press Pvt Ltd

To
Spyros

Contents

Acknowledgements

This book originated as a doctoral thesis submitted in the International Relations Department of The London School of Economics and Political Science. I am grateful to Philip Windsor, Michael Donelan, Margot Light and, above all, to Fred Halliday for their help and intellectual stimulation. In Egypt and Tunisia many people took the time and trouble, when they did not have to, to answer my questions and provide insights. I am also especially thankful to my family and friends for their love and support.

My editor, Anna Enayat showed great enthusiasm for the book from the start and I thank her for this. Karin Wermester helped me diligently in the last editing stages. Chapter 4 was written with financial support from the North Atlantic Treaty Organisation in 1993 and Chapter 1 was revised with financial support from the Leverhume Trust in autumn 1997.

Preface to the Third Edition

Since the bulk of the research for this book was completed in the late 1990s, momentous events have rocked the Middle East region and the Muslim world more broadly. The US reaction to the terrorist attacks of 11 September 2001, consisting of the Afghanistan war of 2001, the Iraq war of 2003 and the wider 'war on terror', has been perceived by a growing number of Muslims as an attack on Islam itself. The West, in turn, increasingly sees itself as being assaulted by an undifferentiated enemy, 'Islam'. Despite the frequent protestations in academic and public discourse that you cannot and should not essentialise religions and cultures, since 2001 a 'clash of civilisations' between Islam and the West appears to have become a self-fulfilling prophecy.

This unfortunate turn of events has hardened positions and identities, with Islam and the West frequently described as the antithesis of one other. Because the West is, in Western eyes at least, closely associated with democracy and human rights, the clash strengthens the view that Islam is inherently anti-democratic and violent. Recent developments are used to confirm this view: Islamist extremists have become more active, at both the transnational and the national levels, and have perpetrated attacks in London, Madrid, Morocco, Tunisia, Turkey, Indonesia, Jordan and Egypt, not to mention Iraq. Although it is difficult to measure with precision the attraction of radical Islamist groups, and terrorist attacks could be carried out by a small number of individuals or cells, there is no doubt that the appeal of Islamist extremism has increased over the last few years. This has damaged the prospects for Islamist liberalism and the conciliation of

Islam with international human rights principles, the subject of this book.

However, the growth of Islamist extremism constitutes only one element in a wider and more complex picture. Most Islamist movements in the Middle East have taken steps towards moderation and, in particular, towards incorporating human rights and democratic principles into their ideological discourse.

Developments in Egypt have been fascinating in this regard. Chapter 4 of this book examines Egyptian Islamism until the end of the 1990s. It was around this time that the war between the Mubarak regime and radical Islamists concluded with the defeat of the latter (at a tremendous cost to human rights). Since then the basic contours of the Mubarak regime have remained the same: it is an authoritarian system that allows a degree of controlled liberalisation to counter-balance varied pressures from domestic and international constituencies. The Muslim Brotherhood has continued to seek accommodation within this regime and, indeed, has further evolved towards greater acceptance of democracy and pluralist principles. This does not mean that the Brotherhood has become a liberal Islamist party as I define it in this book. Its social views – especially on women, Copts and freedom of expression – remain illiberal and often reactionary. But the evolution of its political discourse is important and has to be acknowledged, not least because the Egyptian Muslim Brotherhood has such an influence on other Islamist movements in the wider region.

Developments in the Tunisian situation are difficult to gauge because the government of Ben Ali, which has been in power since 1987, continues to rule Tunisia with an iron grip, and the closed nature of the society makes changes in Islamism difficult to follow. However, it is safe to say that although Tunisian Islamism, at least as an active political movement, is lying low in Tunisia after being subjected to severe repression, this has not changed the movement's relative moderation, as described in Chapter 5.

Among Islamist movements in Morocco, Algeria, Jordan, Kuwait and Lebanon we can observe similar trends towards political accommodation, and at least a rhetorical acceptance of democratic and human rights principles. But the movement that has gone further than any other in this direction is outside the Arab world. The Turkish

Justice and Development Party, which has been in government since 2002, can be described as a liberal Islamist party, in that it has proven in practice that it will respect the rule of law and the democratic rules required by the Turkish constitution (those who describe it as a 'post-Islamist' party are implicitly saying that Islam cannot be liberal, a view this book argues against). The other fascinating Islamist case, again from outside the Arab world, is the Iranian one. In this country, the only one to have experienced an 'Islamic' revolution, we are witnessing the thorough secularisation of society and the discrediting of the clerical regime. This has led to the growth of reformism and a robust Islamist liberal intellectual and political movement. But it has also brought forth the reactionary-populist phenomenon of Ahmadinejad.

Tracking the trajectories of Islamist movements in the Middle East region over the last few years has been fascinating, and it has not, it seems to me, undermined the approach to Islam and human rights I propose in this book. On the contrary, it appears to confirm my fundamental thesis, which is that Islam – and hence the relationship between Islam and human rights, and the prospects of an Islamic liberalism – is shaped by the economic, political and social circumstances in which it finds itself, and that it has no independent existence from these circumstances. The growth in the appeal of Islamist terrorism and radicalism in general is an outcome of domestic political developments and a reaction to Western policy. 'Jihadism', as it has come to be called of late, operates transnationally but must be understood primarily within the boundaries of the nation-state. So too does the shift of 'mainstream' Islamist movements towards greater moderation, a result of social transformations but also of changing political circumstances and, in some cases, a measure of political participation and contestation.

Katerina Dalacoura
3 November 2006

Introduction

This is a book on human rights as a value and norm in international relations and of Islam as a constituent of political culture in particular societies. It studies human rights and Islam as two separate issues but also highlights their interaction. It is an attempt to buttress support for the concept of human rights, primarily through discrediting the cultural essentialist thesis.[1] It is also an attempt to dispel the stereotypical image of Islam as inherently rigid and inflexible, an image sadly reinforced by the terrorist attacks of 11 September 2001.

The questions that provided the impetus for this study are many and it is important to list them for the reader. These questions were the driving force behind the work which aimed, if not to answer all of them comprehensively, at least to provide a satisfactory response. The starting point – in matters pertaining to Islam – can be stated simply: What do people in other, and specifically Muslim, cultures think about human rights and why?[2] This gave rise to further questions: How does Islam influence the understanding of human rights in Muslim societies? Is there an inherent antithesis between Islam as a religion and the value of human rights? If there is not, how can we account for the frequently illiberal interpretations of Islam and its authoritarian input into the political process? How do we evaluate proposals for a particularly 'Islamic' conceptualisation of human rights? Is Islam by its nature impossible to separate from politics and if so does this matter? Is secularism the only context in which human rights can be respected? Is Islamic liberalism viable and can it provide an alternative framework to secularism for the respect of rights? What has been

1

the fate of Islamic liberalism in society and history and how can we best explain it?

These questions, relating specifically to Islam and human rights, formed part of a wider attempt at understanding human rights in the international context. In this case, the first question can be again simply stated: How can one support human rights while respecting other cultures? What is the appropriate balance between human rights and toleration? Are human rights a 'Western' value and therefore inappropriate and irrelevant for other cultures and an instrument of imperialism? And finally, what is the relevance of understanding the relationship between Islam and human rights for our understanding of international relations as a discipline? In particular, how can the study of one particular culture shed light on some of the current concerns in international relations such as normative theory, the role of culture and our understanding of the state?

Chapter 1 begins with the broad questions regarding human rights and therefore provides the framework for the rest of the book. It is an examination of the philosophy which underlies the notion of rights and the dilemmas it entails. In the light of these, the chapter attempts to arrive at a consistent normative position on human rights in a multicultural context and argues that there is only one such position.

The rest of the book is *in support* of this position – it is *not* its justification. It is also an attempt to understand human rights in relation to Islam. Chapter 2 surveys the problem at the level of ideas by seeking to establish that Islamic liberalism is a viable option at an abstract level of ideas and laying down the preconditions for it. Chapters 3 to 5 on Egypt and Tunisia examine the same problem in an historical and societal context. The purpose of these chapters is threefold. First, to trace the course of Islamic liberalism within distinct historical periods in two societies. Second, to show that the interpretation of Islam depends on factors other than its supposed inherent nature or an 'Islamic' political culture. And, third, to prove that these factors are political, social and economic. Chapter 6 generalises the findings to the Middle East as a whole and provides some pointers for the analysis of Islamism.

It is necessary at this stage to justify two things as regards Chapters 3 to 5, the choice of the cases to be studied and the time period. Chapter

3 concentrates on Egypt in the 1920s and 1930s, Chapter 4 on the same country from the 1970s to the 1990s and Chapter 5 on Tunisia from the 1970s to the 1990s. The selection was made for a single reason. In all three instances it appeared possible that a liberal interpretation of Islam would predominate in the political culture of the country. This liberal trend was therefore available for study, along with other trends. It was deemed to be more fruitful for the argument (and more challenging generally), to examine such cases rather than, for example, Saudi Arabia or post-1979 Iran. In the latter cases it would be straightforward to argue that Islam is interpreted in an authoritarian way in order to serve as an instrument of power and legitimation for ruling elites. Alternatively, a case such as modern Turkey would not be suitable given the secular constitutional framework and the fact that Islam has not (until recently at least) played such a central role in the political process. The fact that Egypt and Tunisia are part of the Arab Middle East does not signify that Muslim countries which do not belong to this area or ethnic group could not provide useful case studies, although there admittedly exists a strong historical connection between Islam and the Arab Middle East. Egypt and Tunisia were chosen because a general survey of all Muslim societies at all times was obviously impossible and the object of study had to be narrowed down, and because they were deemed sufficient to prove a point or at least disprove one.

The time period for this study is the twentieth century, because it is in our century that human rights as a concept became part of an intense international debate, especially after the promulgation of the Universal Declaration of Human Rights in 1948 and de-colonisation. It is in the second half of the twentieth century, as Chapter 2 will show, that there is an increase in writings on human rights in the context of Islamic political culture. Similar debate occurred in the nineteenth century but under different labels: individual freedom, constitutionalism and democratic government. This overlap in the substance of the relevant issues – despite the use of different terminology – also explains why the choice of Egypt in the 1920s and 1930s was considered appropriate.

The last set of introductory points involves definitions and terminology, precision in which is of vital importance in this study. The term 'human rights' I define on the basis of the Universal Declaration of Human Rights and the various international Covenants and Conventions which followed and expounded on it. 'Human rights' comprise economic and social, as well as civil and political rights, as these rights form an integral whole. I understand human rights as *individual rights*, and collective rights I take to be conditional on individual rights. On the basis of this definition, human rights are closely identified, throughout the study, with liberalism and liberal values and are often used interchangeably with them (as for example in the term 'Islamic liberalism'). Other terms such as liberty, democracy, constitutional government and so on are used when appropriate and allow for a connection with nineteenth century concerns and terminology.

The second set of terms that need to be clarified at this early stage relate to Islam. The term 'Islamism' and 'Islamists' refers to those who argue that Islam must form a part of the political process and indeed provide the moral foundation for society. They are distinguished from secularists who are not a primary focus of this study (although, as we shall see, the distinction is not always sharp). This is not a book on liberalism in Muslim societies but of liberalism in connection to Islam in Muslim societies.[3] In turn, Islamists are divided, for the sake of clarity in the line of argument, into two groups: Islamic liberals and Islamic fundamentalists. The former believe that Islam and human rights can be reconciled, and give equal value to both. The latter are preoccupied with safeguarding the purity of the religion as they understand it and struggle to make its precepts the foundation of social, political and private life, even if that implies a disrespect for rights (although they will not accept that it does). Chapter 2 is in large part devoted to expounding the distinction between those two groups. It is a distinction which is essential for analytic purposes even though, as Chapters 3 to 5 make clear, it does not always neatly correspond to reality. This is because there can exist a range of views between the two groups *and* because Islamists shift and reformulate their positions under the influence of a multiplicity of factors. Various other terms which are constantly employed and are central to the argument – such as authenticity and modernity – will be defined as the study progresses.

Finally, the issues raised by the 11 September 2001 terrorist attacks in the United States, allegedly perpetrated by an extreme Islamist organisation, al Qaeda, need to be addressed briefly in this Introduction. The attacks spurred a vigorous debate, in the West and the Muslim world, on the relationship between Islam and violence. This relationship is not discussed directly in this book. But the approach it introduces in understanding Islam and human rights can also be useful in thinking about the complex links between Islam and violence. Because this approach focuses on context, as opposed to permanent principles, and highlights the ways in which political, economic and social processes shape the interpretation of religion, it is helpful in dispelling the stereotypical representation of Islam as inherently prone to violence.

We know little about al Qaeda, or its leader, Osama bin Laden. But their acts and statements suggest that the organisation can usefully be seen as a product of Saudi Arabian society and politics which are defined by a stern, purist interpretation of Islam. Al Qaeda is also a transnational movement however. As such it is characterised by rootlessness in that it has not interacted with other political forces or with the society it seeks to dominate. It has therefore avoided making the compromises which participation in the political process commonly entails. Its Saudi political origins and the fact that it has subsequently functioned in a political vacuum are plausible explanations for al Qaeda's extreme interpretation of Islam and the violent means it has employed in the pursuit of its goals.

Notes

1. The cultural essentialist thesis is the view that cultures contain immutable and permanent characteristics which are discoverable.

2. When I write 'other' in this instance I mean very simply other than mine.

3. Care has been taken to use the term 'Muslim' society rather than 'Islamic' because the latter seems to have, in various part of the literature and in common parlance, a close connection with Islamism.

1

Human Rights and Authenticity

I

Human rights are the rights people have by virtue of their humanity. They are those rights, essentially to freedom and security, without which any existence would be considered less than human. They are inalienable, independent of obligation, undefined by role[1] and un-conditional on status or circumstance. Rights are legitimate claims or entitlements and as such they imply corresponding duties (although their moral validity does not hinge on these). Since human rights are inalienable they constitute the starting point for political morality in any human society that purports to respect them.[2] Collective or group rights are meaningless if they imply the disregard of individual rights.

The origins of the principles of human rights, as they are concep-tualised in our time, can be traced to at least two strands of Western philosophical and political thought: natural law and the Enlighten-ment.[3] The idea that there exists a higher and more compelling law than that of the princes, which is binding on our conscience, can al-ready be found in Sophocles's 'Antigone'.[4] But it was the Stoic philosophers in the Hellenistic period who introduced the idea of natural law and conceived of the individual as distinct from the citi-zen, worthy of rights and duties because of his human attributes rather than his membership of the city-state. In medieval Christian thought, of Thomas Aquinas in particular, natural law was conceptualised as the rational individual's participation in divine law and consequently the guide to morality and ethics.

Nothing in the Stoic and Christian traditions, however, entailed the rights of the individual as we understand them today, because natural law did not have a specifically political content, in the sense of determining the relationship of the individual to the state.[5] It was the Enlightenment that placed the individual at centre stage and divorced knowledge from revelation. Man, endowed with reason, was henceforth seen as capable of mastering knowledge. This development prepared the intellectual ground for the birth of science and the discovery and exploration of knowledge by the rational individual. At the political and moral level, man, because he is endowed with reason, was ascribed natural rights and the state was conceived of as the outcome of a social contract between the individual and political authority. The Enlightenment helped unleash the potential of human rationality and creativity. Coupled with economic and social developments, such as the birth of capitalism, it constituted an unstoppable force towards ever greater achievements in the accumulation of knowledge and wealth.

The concept of natural rights rested on the (temporarily successful) marriage of the two traditions, natural law and Enlightenment secular rationalism. The former harked back to its religious or metaphysical antecedents (and this is how natural law is understood in this chapter);[6] the latter secularised natural law and rendered human reason sovereign. Without the latter, the concept of human rights would not have emerged. But, I will argue that completely discarding the former has also had a pernicious effect. The empowerment of the individual concealed a contradiction, which was to engulf the tradition of the Enlightenment in the twentieth century. It stemmed from the belief in the human being as the ultimate locus of knowledge and the relation between knowledge and moral truth. If the Enlightenment undermined belief in God and led inevitably to God's death[7] – severing natural law from its origins in divine law – how could the moral worth and the inalienable rights of the individual be defended?

If the first set of problems regarding human rights in our time concerns their moral foundations, the second set, which is related but separable for the purposes of analysis, has to do with their universality. It is again in the twentieth century, when the notion of human rights replaced that of natural rights, that the problem became inescapable. With the abolition of slavery, the recognition of the legal equality of women and the end of colonialism, the concept of human rights reached, in theory, its natural frontiers, those of humanity.[8] The internationalisation of human rights principles in the sphere of law has been remarkable. There are very few states today which do not accede to the Universal Declaration of Human Rights and other human rights instruments. But, beyond this legal level, the transposition of human rights principles from Western to non-Western cultures in the course of our century has been fraught with difficulties.

Before we go on to the discussion of the two major problems for human rights – that of their moral foundations and that which relates to their validity in a multi-cultural world – it is necessary to clarify two points. The first can be summarised as the distinction between the concept of human rights and their conception. The conception of human rights has evolved over time. The debate over whether economic and social rights are of equal importance to political and civil rights is close to being resolved and the present consensus – in academic circles at least – tends to endorse the former as equally inalienable rights.[9] The distinction between 'positive' and 'negative' rights is breaking down.[10] Collective rights, reflecting the concerns of the Third World, have been brought into the debate during and after the period of de-colonisation, and we are currently progressing towards an elaboration of 'third' and 'fourth generation' rights, the right to peace, development and so on. A number of international instruments have spelt out the needs of particular groups (women, children and minorities), and dealt with the protection of rights from especially abhorrent abuses (for example, torture and genocide).

All this is an important development in itself but for the purposes of my argument it is secondary. What I will be considering is not the particular content of human rights at any given time but the idea *per se*. The consensus over the *conception* of human rights – the 'list' of rights – naturally evolves over time but priority lies in the acceptance or otherwise of the *concept* of the human being having inalienable rights *qua* human being, the rights-holding individual.[11]

The second point will be alluded to rather than fully elaborated and it concerns our understanding of the state in relation to human rights. Because the sovereign state is the modern expression of political authority, its ambiguity in relation to human rights is profound. On the one hand, human rights are actualised in the context of state jurisdiction – international human rights legal norms have to be incorporated in and protected by domestic law – and this renders the state their legal guarantor. Concomitantly, given the historical development of international relations, sovereignty and self-determination are an integral expression of the freedom of a people and therefore an expression of their human rights. On the other hand, states have traditionally been violators of human rights, which were indeed developed for the protection of the individual against the state.[12] The ambiguity of the state as regards human rights defies theoretical categorisation and is not to be understood by distinguishing between the state normatively and descriptively.[13] The ambivalence of the state towards human rights is inherent in the concept of the state and their relationship is historically determined and, in any given case, to be empirically discovered. It must therefore be kept constantly in mind and will be highlighted by the rest of this study.

The state is an expression of the society and culture which it governs but at the same time it is an autonomous entity. The corollary of this is that we must question the conventional understanding of human rights, according to which they are held against the state, and argue that they must be understood to be held against *society* also. This view is not tenable, of course, in legal terms but it is important in political analysis. Otherwise, categories of rights such as women's rights are easily sidelined.[14] It is only if we broaden our understanding in this manner that we can meaningfully talk about human rights in a multi-*cultural* (as well as multi-state) world.

II

The debate in the twentieth century regarding the foundations of knowledge, truth and moral values is especially pertinent to the notion of human rights. We need to explore this debate in order to comprehend the predicament of the liberal advocate of human rights in our time. He or she is faced with this predicament because the foundations on which the principles of human rights have rested hitherto, have been undermined.

They have been undermined, I will argue, because these philosophical foundations are in crucial respects contradictory. They are contradictory philosophically and this has begun, in our time, to leave its imprint on historical and social experience. It is quite impossible here to go into a thorough discussion of all the traditions out of which the notion of human rights has emerged. The concept of 'reason' is selected therefore in order to illustrate the argument.

The concept of reason is common to the traditions of natural law and of Enlightenment rationalism. It is because reason is embedded in all human beings that we are capable of discovering the moral law which inheres within us. This law is therefore universal and discoverable by all since we all share a common humanity. Reason will guide us in all paths, those of knowledge, of truth and of morality. The Enlightenment gave rise to the preconditions for modern science and also to the morality of natural rights. Man as the locus of reason became in many respects the master of his own fate and the ultimate arbiter of his existence.

In the *traditional* understanding of natural law, man is seen as endowed with reason by God. It is only as such that man is sacred and, because of that, that his moral worth and natural rights must not be diminished by any other human being. Natural law, however, as long as it was bound up with Christianity, did not evolve into the concept of the autonomous individual, freely exercising his rights and determining his existence. For such a notion to emerge, the Enlightenment was a necessary complement to the natural law tradition. Once, however, the individual became the locus of reason and of the moral law, it was only a matter of time before he would begin to investigate and dispute the traditions of Christianity, and ultimately the existence of God and of divine moral law.

The tension between the two schools can be described in summary form as 'the debate between those who think that men [and states] create morality and thus at the limit may over-ride its rules and those who think that morality is part of our being and that we may not, in short, the debate between Rationalism and Natural Law.' The same author continues that 'this debate, important though it is, is a faction fight within the human rights philosophy.'[15] My view is different – this faction fight is between two ultimately contradictory positions.

The only context in which it could be peacefully resolved would be if common agreement existed on the definition of reason and what it entails for the human condition. If, that is, there was fundamental agreement on values and the demands of reason between people and across cultures. Since this is evidently not the case, as historical reality makes clear, we are left with the question of how we are to reconcile our freedom with our moral worth *qua* human beings. For if we accept only the former as our ultimate standard and value, we are 'free' to denigrate the latter and trample on rights without any censure.

Let us further explore the debate by illustrating the two positions on morality which human rights thinking has tried unsuccessfully to reconcile. The first can be summed up in Dostoyevsky's dictum: 'If there is no God, everything is permissible.'[16] The second is exemplified by the Enlightenment belief that a society can be liberal only if it is a secular society. These antithetical views point towards the question of religion (Christianity in particular), and to historical experience.

The Enlightenment, by elevating the value of human freedom over Christian faith,[17] sought to reduce the hold of religious law and the church over society and thus make the peaceful coexistence of people with different creeds possible. The point was that religion – the belief in the Absolute – rendered people intolerant of other points of view and of one another. That was a perfectly legitimate conclusion given the Christian experience. Religion was of course not detrimental to freedom *per se* – as we have seen, the whole notion of rights rested initially on the religious belief in human worth – but it was to be banished to the private realm and become a matter of personal conscience. In this way, the best of both worlds could be preserved.

But such a compromise was difficult to realise in practice. This is because religion, or at least the Christian religion, is a social affair, as well as a matter of personal belief. Its strength rests on socialisation, worship and the existence of taboos.[18] Religion confined to the private sphere eventually loses its hold on the individual conscience, as the history of the Western world after the nineteenth century clearly demonstrates. If religion is not to guide us in our relationships with one another, it loses its relevance to our existence and therefore withers away.

The Enlightenment also undermined Christian belief through the rise of science. Knowledge and moral truth had been intimately connected in the history of the Christian Church and for good reason. We may be able to distinguish between the two at the intellectual level – leaving the former to the sphere of science and the latter to religion – but the separation cannot really hold: if we can discover truth in other areas, why should we stop short of moral matters?

The Enlightenment, by rendering the individual sovereign and making liberty the primary value of human existence, gave rise to the idea of human rights in the sense of freedoms of which the individual cannot be deprived. Personal autonomy and self-definition – what we can also call the value of authenticity in the personal sense – became ultimate rights and goals in the modern world. (Modernity is, indeed, intellectually defined by those principles among others.) But by opening the way to the death of God, it undermined the beliefs which gave sanctity to human existence. This is because in human society, as we have known it, knowledge and truth, the public and private, could not be rigidly separated. The fusion of the two traditions of natural law and the Enlightenment (or Rationalism), could provide a solid basis for the philosophy of human rights only if such boundaries could be firmly maintained as Locke assumed. We are now faced with their dissolution and this leaves the supporter of human rights in a difficult position.

The aim of the remainder of this chapter will be to throw light on the implications of this predicament by showing what the predominance of Enlightenment thought – because it *has* predominated over the tradition of natural law – has led to. Our concern is not to support one world-view over another for its own sake but to show what the consequences of these developments have been for human rights philosophy; and to bring out what the support of this philosophy entails, if it is to survive the current onslaughts. The argument will be that we cannot be consistent supporters of human rights – if that is indeed the position we want to take – without espousing elements of both traditions, of natural law and Enlightenment rationalism, and without rethinking the separations between knowledge and truth and the public and the private. I will suggest, in the two problems that I will consider – the dispute over the moral foundations of human rights and the position of human rights in a multi-cultural world – that we cannot, in defending human rights, eschew a metaphysical view of the human person and that, if we do, our position becomes self-defeating.

Does this necessarily entail a return to Christian or generally religious values? The answer is in the negative and to support this I need to explain a little further how I use the term 'natural law'. I have not attempted to resurrect the *traditional* use of the term which – in the Christian tradition at least – would integrally link natural law with the revelation or the scriptures. A clear break here is necessary for the principles of human rights to emerge. I do not, however, see the *modern* conception of natural law as identical to secular rationalism either. Natural law relies on and upholds human reason, of course, but also contains an anchor to metaphysics, as opposed to rationalism which treats human reason as the ultimate standard without reference to the transcendental.[19]

Once we have divorced natural law and human rights from the Christian God, it can be seen that they can be accommodated in many different religions, in particular Islam, which will be focused on in this study. It can even be accommodated in an agnostic world-view. Whatever interpretation we give to natural law, however – whether we find our point of reference in Christianity, in Islam, in a belief in a higher Being or in a inchoate metaphysical sense of the sacredness of the human being – we cannot, I argue, escape its necessity if we want to be consistent on human rights.

III

One of the challenges to the philosophy of human rights is the belief that nothing is true, because truth, as such, does not exist. The Nietzschean tradition needs to be examined here because it is one of the outcomes – perhaps the inevitable progression – of the Enlightenment once it becomes divorced from natural law. What I will argue is *not* that this line of thinking is wrong – this is not my task – but, rather, that if we adopt it we cannot consistently defend human rights and we are therefore morally and intellectually powerless against their abuse. Because the belief that nothing is true is one inevitable outcome of Enlightenment thought, to show that it is inconsistent with human rights is a way of defending the necessary complementarity of natural law and the Enlightenment in the philosophy of human rights.

A clear progression can be discerned between the Enlightenment and Nietzsche and ultimately the post-modernists. Once we lose the possibility to resort to the transcendental (and we could, as has been expounded above, if we believe that we can discover truth with our own resources), our appeal to reason-as-endowed by God collapses. We are therefore left with human reason or rationality. But once we start functioning on the basis that we can discover truth with our own resources, one possible argument would be that truth does not exist at all, that it is purely a construct of our minds.[20] Our appeal to human reason (as an absolute standard), and the belief in our cognitive capacities therefore ceases. Belief in human reason depends on its characteristics and benefits being self-evident. When this self-evidence becomes a matter of dispute (as it has), the belief in reason is questioned. Post-modernism is an eminently modern position,[21] since the claim that truth does not exist is again a declaration of the sovereignty of the human subject, the heroic individual of Nietzsche – albeit one that ultimately undermines its own source.

Thinkers in the Nietzschean tradition dispute the positivist distinction between fact and value as well as the idea of truth as representation or correspondence. They believe that the world does not exist independently of us and that our minds are not 'mirrors of nature'. Instead, truth and knowledge are a linguistic affair because every language encompasses a totalising vision of reality. Languages are incommensurate and the task of philosophy to find a 'master-vocabulary' that will make them commensurable is vain. There is no 'truer' or 'better' language than others, because – this is the crucial point – there is no standard independent of us against which they can be judged. This line of thought rejects the notion of reason and rationality advocated by the Enlightenment. It argues that the rational and scientific way of thinking is not a closer representation of reality but is just one way of thinking among many.[22]

For many post-modernists the undermining of theories of knowledge has an emancipatory goal. By pointing out the ways in which theories of knowledge construct and constrain our universe, and the connection between knowledge and power, they seek to free individuals from the shackles of society which controls their minds. Foucault can be read in this way. Other writers, such as Barthes and Derrida, state that reality is not mirrored in texts of human speech but constructed by them – and deconstruction can show how texts and hence truth are self-subverting.[23] The aim is to reveal the radical contingency of our existence and therefore – or at least this is one reading – to liberate us.

But it is doubtful that this goal can be achieved if all discourses (including the post-modernist one), are self-subverting. The view that all texts are self-contained, in the sense that they do not correspond to an outside reality but only relate to other texts, not only subverts the object of knowledge but the subject as well. '"Man" is no longer at the centre of discourse or of anything else.'[24] The only liberation offered is that of self-destruction. This line of thinking is self-annihilating and therefore profoundly anti-humanistic. If we do not share in the view that there is truth 'out there' which exists independently of us and about which we can argue, all conversation must stop. The consistent post-modernist, like the consistent sceptic,[25] has nothing to say about the human condition. The only position that can be thus logically adopted is that of the 'drop-out'. The implications of this position for politics and morality are obvious. If the project of liberation leads to 'dropping out' or self-annihilation, then we cannot talk about liberty at all. One cannot be a liberal and a post-modernist at the same time. One can be either of these things, and each would be self-affirming and perfectly legitimate, but the two cannot consistently coexist.

To further illustrate the point, we can consider in more detail the work of Richard Rorty, a philosopher who describes himself as a 'post-modern bourgeois liberal'. I will maintain that his position is ultimately untenable and that it is erroneous that he be distinguished from other 'extreme' post-modernists (who do not claim to be liberals).[26] Rorty is important because he expresses, in many ways, the 'mood of the times': the collapse of certainties about reality and human rationality, a typically modern condition, coupled with a refusal, on the other hand, to abandon the liberal outlook.

Rorty's work is an attack on correspondence theories of truth and indeed on any theory of knowledge, as summarised above. We can argue against him along the lines that he cannot hold such a view because, by his own standards, he cannot validate it anyway. But what is of interest to us here is his claim that we can dispense with philosophical debate over truth, morality and so on altogether and, moreover, that this will allow us to defend liberal values more effectively.[27] Rorty has been described as 'a liberal without foundations'.[28] He sees himself as a pragmatist and he argues for liberalism on the basis of its being the most 'useful' vocabulary presently available for the things we want to do.

Rorty's argument rests on his assumption that we can be ironists in private – accept the contingency of our beliefs and of our self – and liberals in public.[29] The public and the private cannot be brought together – they simply coexist. But, as has been argued above and will also be argued in the next section, this is a very difficult position to be in, since the private inevitably influences the public. Rorty's view that human rights are worth struggling for, even if we may privately believe that they are contingent, is unconvincing. He defines liberalism as the belief that 'cruelty is the worst thing we do',[30] but fails to show why cruelty against someone who has no intrinsic value should be of profound concern to us (not merely the result of a squeamish disposition). His picture of how liberalism can spread is also self-defeating. The liberal community expands by the usefulness of the liberal language becoming apparent to a growing number of people and by the expansion of the definition of 'we' against traditional dividing lines between us and the 'others'.[31] But this does not leave any room for human agency, for if change is the result of small, purposeless shifts in the vocabularies we use, there is nothing for us to do about changing them.

Rorty's definition of liberalism as the most useful vocabulary for the things we want to do is at best a communitarian proposition, solely appropriate for a particular culture – Western society. As such, it does not tell us anything about human rights which are, by definition, universal. It could not, since the whole thrust of his argument is against the validity of universalist notions and has historicist and relativistic implications. Rorty cannot, on the grounds of the requirement that he himself puts forward – that all arguments must have internal coherence[32] – lay claim to being simultaneously a liberal and a post-modernist. He can separate theories of knowledge and of truth from politics and morality only at the cost of seeing politics and morality as a matter of taste or an accidental condition in which we somehow find ourselves and cannot influence.

The *problematique* of post-modernist thought and the Nietzschean tradition as a whole is a logical extension of the values of the Enlightenment. It leads from a critique of theories of knowledge to a dispute over the existence of the foundation of moral values generally, thus providing evidence for the inseparability of the two. For 'it is vain to hunt for a godless certainty'[33] and the Enlightenment project to establish this certainty (by replacing religion with human reason) was bound to collapse. We are therefore faced with doubts about the existence of reason and about the existence of human nature itself, conceived, as it was, as essentially rational. Post-modernism cuts right through the Enlightenment into the Greco-Judean tradition. All we are presently left with is an appeal to history or pragmatism. We cannot as rational beings discover the moral law that inheres within us. We have therefore two options: a 'leap of faith' – faith in the sacredness of the human being – or dropping the discourse of human rights altogether.

IV

I have argued that if we wish to talk about human rights we cannot consistently and coherently do so unless we agree to debate the philosophical origins of the idea. If we discard the belief that human beings have an inherent moral worth which can be established in relation to some standard which we can all agree to at least talk about, if not commonly recognise, we cannot proceed.

The problem that now needs to be tackled has its source in the concept of freedom. Human rights, whatever the consensus about their content at any given time, have a common purpose: to protect human dignity at a very basic level by safeguarding a minimum standard of liberty and security. In a sense, human rights are the essential grounding without which no existence will be considered human. But they are just that – a grounding, a starting point. Their purpose is to allow the individual, or group of individuals, to live their lives according to what they consider valuable; to do with themselves whatever they see fit; to define themselves in freedom – in other words, to develop 'authentically', in the sense of being true to themselves.[34]

It is for this reason that to believe in human rights is to believe in toleration. Rights are but a means to ensure that we all have the possibility to live our lives as we deem appropriate. No one can maintain a belief in human rights without, at the same time, respecting the choices people make, individually and collectively. The problems become quickly apparent because, the pious hopes of liberal doctrine notwithstanding, we do not all develop in freedom and in reason the same way. We are faced with the possibility that freedom may lead to lack of freedom and the question then becomes how we can prevent the latter without infringing upon the former.

It will soon become clear that this is again a debate about metaphysics – although this time not about whether any absolute standard can exist at all, but about the role it should play in political life. My argument will proceed from the individual level to the societal, from domestic to international society. Once we understand the problem of authenticity at the individual level, we can have a clearer insight about it in international relations. To this end we must examine, first of all, the relationship between state and society, since it is the state which is the embodiment of political authority in our time.

How can the state ensure respect for human rights? How should it protect the freedom of citizens from itself and from each other? In line with Enlightenment and liberal thought[35] there is only one way in which this can be affected. The state must be neutral as regards the choices of its citizens as to how they want to live their lives. The gamut of human rights – political and civil, social and economic – is essential as a means of defending a more fundamental freedom, to choose how we live. If the state defends human rights and protects individuals from each other's transgressions, then freedom will not lead to lack of freedom, because the liberty of one stops where the liberty of the other begins. The state, which is in itself the embodiment of a social contract, therefore 'holds the ring' between individuals and allows each to develop autonomously.

The state, therefore, is concerned with the defence of 'the right' and not of 'the good', in John Rawls's definition. For a society to be just, according to Rawls, it must not embody controversial religious or metaphysical doctrines. Rawls lies in the tradition of liberal thinking which limits religious beliefs to the private sphere in order to secure freedom and tolerance within society. Unlike Rorty, who avoids metaphysical questions because he considers them non-existent and irrelevant, Rawls does so because people cannot agree on them. For the state to adopt one position against the other, even if that position is of the majority, is to divide society and render it intolerant by basing its core values on absolute standards.[36]

I argue, however, following many critics of Rawls, that his position on the neutral state is ultimately untenable and that the liberal state can defend rights only on the basis of a metaphysical position. There is no neutral way of accommodating the various demands of liberty. Liberty is only one among many important values that can claim priority in our lives, personal and political.[37]

Rawls's argument is predicated on his distinction between the right and the good. He relies on the assumption that the liberal society, a society based on his principle of 'justice as fairness', is the only scheme on which individuals can agree, in reason, behind a 'veil of ignorance', regardless, that is, of their relationship with one another, their opinions, assets and their social position. The just is separated from definitions of the good life – which is a matter of individual choice – and it is therefore neutral, ensuring optimal freedom and welfare for all. A necessary corollary of this position is that liberalism need only be political liberalism – in private life the citizen can proceed as he or she wishes.

Such a sharp distinction between private and public is not in fact a common and easy position for anyone to maintain. This is the first objection to Rawls. For citizens to agree to this separation they must already have a view as to what a just society must involve – liberalism in public life – and a willingness to respect it whatever their personal convictions. Why should they? The pertinent example here is that of the religious fanatic,[38] someone whose conception of justice involves the need to make society conform to divine law and who sees the defection of any one member not as a legitimate option but as a negation of this law. If we do not accept Rawls's claim that all would opt for 'justice as fairness' behind a veil of ignorance – if, that is, we fail to see how we could all agree *in reason* to the same principle – then his whole intellectual edifice is shaken. The veil of ignorance is not a useful device if we dispute that this rational side of people would lead to natural agreement and necessarily *predominate* over all others. The just and the good are, in fact, inextricably connected in the human mind.

The logical corollary of the above view is that the state is not and cannot be neutral as regards the good life because it upholds a particular definition of the good life – an autonomous one. Its neutrality is based on one particular conception of the good and is therefore not neutrality at all. This 'purposefulness' of the state is unavoidable. For individuals to be able to make choices as to how to live, these choices would have to be made available to them (because we cannot ensure that some of these options will not disappear if not supported by the state). These choices will have to be made available for future generations. Moreover, the capacity for autonomy is something that has to be developed and continuously supported.[39]

The neutral state thus undermines the conditions for its own neutrality and the criticism that liberals (and Rawls in particular), smuggle a view of the good life through the back door is a valid one. For if a state is to be liberal, it has to be wilfully 'neutral' and actively promote the liberal vision and the institutions that will guarantee its continuation.[40] If the just and the good are not naturally separable, they must be made separable on the basis of a particular doctrine whose justification is the view that the people are ends in themselves.[41] A political system based on the rights of the individual is not a neutral system, as Rawls maintains, because it upholds the liberty and security of the individual at the cost of other values. Rawls himself concedes this, in a way, when he claims that justice as fairness is the result of agreement, behind a veil of ignorance, between 'free and equal citizens'.[42]

We can therefore conclude from this discussion that there is no neutral way of supporting the priority of human rights, even in domestic society, and that the various claims of liberty cannot be harmonised. Toleration is possible only within a society that asserts the primacy of rights and even then it is limited. The liberal society which allows those who seek to abolish it to take over political authority ceases to be liberal. Authenticity is compatible with human rights if it is an individual affair, because each individual is responsible for himself or herself and is free to make choices about his or her life. But it is not acceptable that authoritarian definitions of authenticity transgress the limits of the personal sphere and begin to encroach upon the public domain. In other words, personal authenticity takes priority over societal or cultural authenticity. This scheme of things is of course only a partially satisfactory one – it hinges on a fine balance that can easily tilt towards intolerance – but it is the best available. Once we turn to the international level the dilemmas between human rights and tolerance are much sharper and even less easily reconcilable.

V

International society is primarily a society of nation-states. There is a limited sense in which international society is similar to a liberal society, in that the primary rule of international law is sovereignty. States, that is, cannot interfere in each other's affairs and cannot legitimately and legally use force against each other except in self-defence. This formula is designed to prevent the persistent evil of societies trying to impose themselves upon others, thus curtailing their freedom. It also reflects the belief that it is impossible, even if the best intentions and altruistic motivations of the intervening party could be somehow guaranteed, for a society to be forcibly made to respect human rights.

There, however, the similarity between domestic and international society ends. The difference, for our purposes, is not that international society is anarchic, because the rules of sovereignty and non-aggression perform the same role as government would in a liberal state (the lack of authority becomes problematic only in the case of non-conformity to international law and norms). The difference is that states are not people but are populated by them and in thinking about human rights people are our primary concern. This forces us to enquire about what happens within the boundaries of states.

It is impossible to apply the model of the liberal state to international society because in the philosophy of human rights, as I understand it, the human person is prior to community and authority. If in domestic society the claims of human rights and authenticity can be reconciled – tenuously, as we saw – because government exists to 'hold the ring' between individuals and protect their rights from possible transgressions by others, through the monopoly of the legitimate use of force, the same cannot hold for international society where authenticity is defined at a societal, not an individual level. A society may freely define itself in a way that is not respectful of the human rights of its individual members, or of a group within them. Its development may be an authentic one, yet completely antithetical to human rights principles. What is the believer in human rights to do in such a case, when the various claims of freedom contravene one another? In a nutshell, how are we to reconcile human rights with the principle of toleration between societies?

Before we can proceed to an examination and evaluation of the various attempts to solve this problem, there are two ideas we must clarify and state our disagreement with. The first is the claim that the conflict between authenticity and human rights is in reality a non-issue, because the problem with human rights derives from states, not cultures. Human rights violations are endemic in the state system. Evidence for this can easily be produced by pointing out the remarkable similarity of human rights violations throughout the world. Many claim that violations are a political matter irrelevant to culture, the obvious point being that no culture supports torture or genocide or such other gross abuses of human rights in principle.

This is a powerful argument but it builds on a number of confusions. The first is that the rights of individuals are held against the state only and not also (in a manner of speaking) against society. This is not the case, as I have pointed out. I have already argued that it is very difficult to separate the private from the public in the understanding of the rights-holding individual, because the former will inevitably influence the latter. If we narrow the discussion of human rights to those relevant to the state, we may find it easier to argue that human rights are only a result of state structures, but we will be failing to grasp the problem in its totality.

The second confusion, which is closely related to the first, is that because a culture does not uphold a notion it necessarily abhors it. It is, of course, true that no society or culture advocates torture or genocide *in principle*, but this is not the point. The point is that many societies would place other priorities higher than the sanctity of the individual and not hesitate to sacrifice individuals as a means to achieving those priorities. The issue surely is not that a society upholds torture or genocide *per se*, but that it does *not* uphold the concept of the rights-holding individual.

The state is both protector and violator of human rights. No evidence can be produced to support the contention that it is necessarily the one or the other.[43] On the one hand, power can be abused and people regularly do abuse it. On the other hand, the state protects members of society from each other and lays down the law. What must be clear, however, is that although the state can and often is autonomous from society, it is also part of it and hence an expression of its culture. It is hard to conceive of a society which abhors human rights violations being ruled, for a very long time, by a state that persistently violates human rights. The reverse is also true. No state can decree that a society must respect human rights, although it can take steps to promote them. A state has to have some kind of legitimacy, not necessarily democratic, in order to survive. If a state is not de-legitimised by human rights violations we have to look at the culture of the society over which it rules for at least some of the explanations.[44] Our concern with authenticity and culture and with their crucial role in a normative discussion on human rights then becomes self-explanatory.

The second issue that has led to much confusion is cultural relativism. In very simple terms, cultural relativism is the statement that values are relative to circumstance, in this case culture, and that because it is only culture that validates values we can pass no judgment on them.[45] We, therefore, arrive at the principle of toleration, not through respect for other people's right to define themselves freely, but rather through our disbelief that any moral standard exists against which we can judge values. For the same reasons that were given when discussing post-modernism, such a position is antithetical to human rights – it in fact renders any discussion of human rights meaningless.

If however we only accept cultural relativism in its descriptive guise (which means that it is not relativism at all but a sociological observation of cultural diversity), then it can inform us about the global realities we face in discussing human rights, which involve the discrete expressions and definitions of human nature within communities and the elaboration of different sets of moral priorities in social life.[46]

It must be noted that a principled defence of cultural relativism did originate as a reaction to the arrogance of Western attitudes towards other societies. In the 1920s and 1930s it was a counter-argument, put forward by some Western anthropologists, to the nineteenth-century belief that non-Western societies are inferior to Western societies and would gradually evolve along similar lines.[47] Cultural relativism was thus a reaction to evolutionism and imperialism, and has been described, with some justification, as an ally of liberalism.[48] This may have been the honourable intention, but it could not have the desired effect. The fact that cultural relativists opposed imperialism and cultural arrogance by one part of the world did not make them champions of human rights. If tolerance is based on respect for other people's liberty, then it is a legitimate concern for someone who believes in human rights, and it is worth weighing it against other considerations of freedom. If, however, it is based on a belief that, because everything is defined by circumstance and history, nothing is more or less morally valid, then it stultifies dialogue between cultures.

Once we have clarified the two issues which have bedeviled discussion of human rights, we can begin to tackle our main problem. The world is made up of people who live in different societies and cultures. These cultures give rise to different moralities, not all supportive of human rights.[49] We cannot solve the problem by ascribing all responsibility to the state (if we did there would be no need for a *normative* discussion of human rights), so we cannot in effect proclaim that the solution to all problems regarding human rights is democratisation in the sense of majority rule. How then are we to think about human rights and their universality? How are we to reconcile belief in the sanctity of the individual with the possibility that individuals may collectively reject this principle?

A number of solutions have been offered to resolve this dilemma and we need to examine them one by one. The first proposes that we concentrate on basic rights which can be agreed on universally. These involve the elements of freedom and security which are part and parcel of all human existence and accepted by any culture. It is argued that if we focus on these rights we have a goal to which we can realistically aspire globally but also one that is not morally controversial.

The proposition of basic rights has much to commend it but it does not resolve our problem. This is because, as has been argued here, our primary concern is not whether we can agree on what rights to uphold or reject but whether we can agree on the very concept of the rights-holding individual. It is one thing to say that all cultures provide, in an ideal form, for the basic requirements of humanity and human dignity (they all do) and quite another that they would all recognise the inalienable *right* of any individual to lay claim on them, if these were denied for some reason. Once this distinction becomes our focus, it may be realised that basic rights are not a 'neutral' proposition which can be endorsed by all societies.

The implications of this position can be more fully discussed on the basis of John Rawls's article on the 'Law of Peoples'.[50] Rawls, in line with his general argument that rights are not based on any particular conception of human nature or on a comprehensive moral doctrine, proposes that basic rights can be upheld in all kinds of societies, democratic and hierarchical, because they are neutral.[51] His starting point is that liberalism can also apply internationally and that we must respect what every society decides for itself. The present chapter rejected this position because societies are not persons but are made up of persons. Rawls can only support it on the grounds that basic rights are neutral (the alternative being that he does not care about rights at all). But they are not. To maintain that individuals can claim inalienable rights from government and society, that no one can deprive them of those rights for whatever reason, is a profoundly revolutionary idea. Rawls's disclaimer of metaphysics in the defence of rights in domestic society can be revealed, again, as contradictory and ultimately untenable, when he attempts to apply it across states. Whether we talk about basic rights or the full list of human rights as proclaimed in the Universal Declaration, we cannot do so without assuming a moral position.

A second way in which the justification of human rights can be attempted is through the discovery of cross-cultural universals. According to this line of thought, all cultures share some principles which provide (actually or potentially), a grounding for human rights. They include a universal aversion to death and injury; what has been called the principle of 'retribution tied to proportionality'; some notion of freedom; or of human dignity. It is argued that each culture contains some norms that would be conducive to human rights and that these norms can be discovered through empirical research.[52]

The eclectic cross-cultural approach[53] has much to commend it because it is only 'from within' that a culture can support human rights (as will become evident in the subsequent chapters of this book). But its limitations can be easily pointed out. The obvious point is that even if we accept that universals do exist we cannot take it for granted that they are supportive of human rights. There is a real possibility that there exist universals which are antithetical to human rights. The solution of establishing the lowest common denominator between cultures as regards rights is also unsatisfactory, because even if it could somehow be discovered it would not protect all basic rights (and would certainly sacrifice women's rights).[54] The search for universals therefore, although the most useful way of encouraging global support for human rights, does not resolve the philosophical problem of cross-cultural toleration, unless it could be shown that a universal norm regarding the rights-holding individual did exist.[55]

Similar objections can be raised to the arguments that human rights should be justified on the basis of human needs.[56] We can all agree that humans share a need for security, subsistence, shelter, and some basic freedoms – but this can inform our discussion of what should be the precise list of rights, not prove that people have a right that these needs be fulfilled. Even the very elementary point that the survival of the human race must be secured does not logically lead to respect for universal rights – it smacks of utilitarianism which is a theory that can be conducive to general human welfare but could sacrifice for its sake the rights of individuals.

The next set of arguments which we must consider in attempting to reconcile human rights and the principle of toleration pertain to human nature. Indeed, the belief that there is a universal human nature which we all share and that we can derive the principles of rights from it lies at the heart of a very common (perhaps the most common) conception of natural law and natural rights. But it is not convincing. Deriving the idea of human rights from observing human nature is deriving an 'ought' from an 'is'.[57] To defend human rights one needs to believe that a 'core' of humanness exists beneath and beyond cultural diversity. But this is a necessary, not a sufficient condition.

It must by now be clear that all the above attempts to reconcile the principles of human rights with the value of authenticity (and hence with toleration) between societies and cultures fail. This is because human rights must be based on a moral and metaphysical view of the individual which takes priority over all else. This view cannot be objectively defended. The arguments presented above either implicitly take this view for granted or do not countenance it.

To claim that any of the above arguments is successful is to avoid a dilemma which, in its extreme form, can truly be a tragic one. It is the dilemma of the liberal when faced with a person or society which defines itself in a way that is antithetical to the notion of rights, and which gives priority to other moral values such as solidarity or compassion, or upholds the 'law of God', or the law of communal tradition. Such a person or community can claim a wholly different, authentic existence which is alien to the notion of rights and yet may be a satisfactory and happy one. The tragedy of the liberal is that he or she cannot accept it as morally justifiable without abandoning his or her principles. The liberal position cannot endorse a society which is not liberal just because it is 'authentic' – because this society is comprised of individuals *some of whom* may wish to be free, now or in the future, but may be unable to be so. In that sense, in the liberal viewpoint, personal authenticity must take precedence over cultural or societal authenticity and individual rights are given priority over collective rights.

What I also argue is that, in effect, the value of toleration is subordinate to the value of human rights. For if the latter is interpreted so as to condone any practice, even if it is antithetical to basic freedoms, it becomes contradictory and hence self-defeating. Tolerance is a value which stems from our belief in human rights (indeed it has no other justification but the belief in the inalienable worth of the individual), but if it overwhelms this belief it becomes self-defeating too. The crucial point here hinges on the notion of free choice. The liberal must respect choices which are freely made (so long as they do not limit the freedoms of others), and it is only in this context that toleration makes sense. If a choice is imposed by society and it is antithetical to basic freedoms, the liberal cannot condone it. The choice must therefore be individual choice in order to be free and a society must provide for the conditions for such choices to be made.

Freedom is one value among many. If a person or a society chooses to be free, the costs are high. I am not maintaining that the worth of freedom is self-evident and should take precedence above all else (it cannot be since it is based on a moral proposition which may not be shared by all), but that once it is accepted as the ultimate value it does not serve as a license for any conceivable action or practice, even if that is of the majority. If, that is, we choose to uphold human rights we cannot escape the cost and implications of our choice by arguing that 'anything goes'. The dilemmas are hard and persistent and we cannot evade them by pretending that the various claims of freedom do not contradict one another.

Does all this mean that we become intolerant in upholding freedom? The danger is real but it can be averted once we realise that such intolerance derives from the assumption that no person can refuse to be free once he or she is shown the merits of freedom. The belief in human rights can then become a call to a moral crusade, whose purpose is to provide for unfortunate and unenlightened others the conditions for freedom and point out its obvious benefits.[58]

The fallacy is a double one: that people will prefer to be free, if only given the choice, and that others can somehow make this choice available to them. Once we are rid of these two illusions, we can see that the position of the liberal is not necessarily a contradictory one. Tolerance is reestablished as a very important value in the context of our belief in human rights because it rests henceforth on the proposition that no one, person or society, can or should be *forced* to be free. To divorce human rights from power in this way[59] does not mean, however, that abuses can be morally sanctioned. The believer in human rights would try to point out the merits of freedom and actively support its cause through dialogue and would not rest until it is established, whether in his or her own society or others.[60] But apart from this there is nothing he or she can do. To those who would claim that this is not enough, he or she would answer that this is all one *can* do without again contradicting one's position.[61] It is a wholly different proposition from giving moral sanction to practices which may be authentic but which are not respectful of rights, on the basis of a doctrine of liberty. Once we are clear about our position we can do something about promoting it without falling hostage to those who defend their repressive ideas and practices by appeals to freedom.

VI

A brief conclusion of this chapter on normative thinking about human rights will allow us to connect its core argument with the rest of the book. A problem that we need to pick up again is of the links of natural law with the Christian religion. I argued that the notion of human rights came into existence as a result of the marrying of primarily two traditions, natural law and Enlightenment rationalism. The line of the argument, however, as must be evident by now, inescapably leads us to support the need for the *primacy of natural law*, as I defined it, between these traditions. This involves a subtle yet crucial shift of emphasis which does not deny belief in the existence of human rationality but subordinates it and anchors it in a metaphysical context. I argued along those lines because I find it impossible, on the basis of historical reality, to accept the existence of a standard in 'reason', which is shared by all human beings in similar form and which would necessarily predominate over other concerns. Therefore the conclusion must be that, because the two traditions can be contradictory in some of their constitutive elements, one has to take precedence over the other and provide a framework for it and that if rationalism predominates we cannot, given the disagreement between people and cultures as to what it is to be 'rational' or human, consistently support human rights. Does, then, the connection of the concept of natural law with Christianity mean that the task of the universalisation of human rights is a hopeless one?

Not necessarily. Natural law thinking, as I understand it, is akin to a more generalised notion of the moral worth of the individual. The severance of its links with Christian doctrine is feasible and is already happening. The belief in the moral worth of the individual and its concomitant support of human rights are not an exclusively Western idea and have become part of the collective heritage of humankind. The religious connections of natural law are still useful in bringing out what this chapter has argued, which is in effect that to believe in the sanctity of the human person and of human liberty is not something that can be *proven* as worthwhile or necessary.[62] It is not something that we can all agree on, on the basis of some shared characteristics deriving from reason. It is, like all moral ideals, a matter of *faith*, which we either have or do not. As such it is indemonstrable, self-affirming, independent of the marshalling of proof or disproof and in many ways circular in its reasoning.[63] This is the best we can do with regards to human rights: begin with an axiom that we arbitrarily lay down, while accepting that we cannot prove it. To argue otherwise, to claim that the merits of this faith must be self-evident, is to attempt to impose it on others who may not share in it (such intolerance is contained in some interpretations of the Enlightenment as we have seen). To abandon the notion that the merits of our position must be evident to all does not in any way detract from the belief that this faith is the true and right one.

Such a view of the foundation of human rights principles allows us to break their historical links with Christian doctrine and examine how they have been or can be accommodated in other world-views. It will be evident in the chapters that follow that some interpretations of the Islamic religion have endorsed it. It is also be evident that many interpretations of the Christian religion have not. Indeed, one can go even further and argue that to believe that a human nature does exist and that it implies a set of inalienable rights does not presuppose a religious belief at all, that it can be accommodated in an atheist world-view.[64] No religion or civilisation can claim exclusive right over it. Millions of people throughout the world, in all kinds of societies and of all creeds, defend human rights on the basis of moral belief, and to claim that the idea is exclusively Christian or Western is an affront to them, not a defence of their authenticity.

It was not the intention of this chapter to equate Western with liberal and non-Western with non-liberal. Discussion of human rights has been handicapped long enough by such crude generalisations, which have no foundation in reality, as countless examples in the history of Western and non-Western societies make clear. This book will be concerned with the dilemmas of Muslim liberals more than anything else. For the moment though, suffice it to say that the position and the dilemmas of the liberal are equally stark and potentially tragic in all societies and that all societies include people who uphold human rights. Despite the origins of the idea, which are Western, it has struck universal roots and has found fertile ground in other cultures. The connection with the West has to be broken for another reason, because it is associated with images of imperialism and of cultural arrogance.

It will be the aim of this book to show that the problems and choices faced by societies with very different cultural make-ups have much more in common than is usually assumed. The condition of modernity unites disparate societies in very real ways and has done so since the nineteenth century. The breakdown of traditional communities and the consequent individualisation of society are not exclusive to the West but are a global condition and process. Reactions to it may vary across cultures, though even these reactions often follow similar patterns.[65]

It was necessary here to lay out the dilemmas of the liberal in a stark manner in order to arrive at a consistent position as regards human rights. To be consistent, the liberal will disapprove of choices by individuals and societies which may be authentic but which contravene the principles of human rights. The rest of the book, however, will try to show that cultural authenticity is a very ambiguous concept; that it is not the embodiment of the 'essence' of a culture but the result of choices which are very often individual (though not necessarily individualistic); and, indeed, that the *search* for authenticity is an eminently modern pursuit. If the dilemma of the liberal, on the basis of the discussion up to now, seems to be an impossible one, fraught with hard moral choices, the rest of the book will be an attempt to attenuate this picture and illustrate that in reality the choices are rarely as hard. 'Traditional society' where people have no conception whatsoever of their individuality hardly exists any longer in pristine form.[66] Modern society is of course not liberal society but it is increasingly an individualistic one. Cross-cultural debate is easier than is often made out to be, because our societies have much more in common than is usually assumed. If we aim to promote human rights in the world we must not hold back from engaging in this debate.

Notes

1. Windsor, P. 'Cultural Dialogue in Human Rights', in Desai, M. and Redfern, P. (eds), *Global Governance: Ethics and Economics of the World Order* (London: Pinter, 1995), p. 177. See also Vincent, R. J., *Human Rights and International Relations* (Cambridge: Cambridge University Press, for the Royal Institute of International Affairs, 1986).

2. This is why the philosophy of human rights is identified with liberal doctrine, which asserts the primacy of rights in political morality; Waldron, J. 'Introduction', in Waldron, J., (ed.), *Theories of Rights* (New York: Oxford University Press, 1984), p. 1.

3. The point here is that although other philosophies and cultures do, of course, contain and uphold the notion of rights, they do not do so in the sense of human rights which are unconditional and inalienable: Windsor, op.cit., p. 177.

4. Cranston, M., *What Are Human Rights?*, (New York: Taplinger, 1973), pp. 9–10.

5. In Thomas Aquinas's view the ruler had a duty to be just according to natural law. If he was not, his law ceased to be binding on the conscience of the subjects but this did not allow or compel them to remove him. If not backed by proper 'public authority' such removal could lead to greater social evil than the one which already prevailed. In other words the ruler, for Thomas Aquinas, was answerable to God and to his conscience, not to the ruled. Natural law entailed 'what is right', not 'having a right'. Donnelly J., *The Concept of Human Rights* (London: Croom Helm, 1985), pp. 1–10 and 45–9.

6. Note that many interpret modern (as opposed to traditional) natural law as a completely secular notion. They define natural law thinking as a kind of 'empiricism' which builds a moral system on the basis of the observation of human nature. This is not how I define natural law and later I explain why I find this interpretation problematic. I am grateful to Michael Donelan for helping me to clarify this point.

7. It is a debatable and perhaps a moot point whether secularisation in

Europe was the result of new knowledge or social developments. For a discussion see Chadwick, O., *The Secularisation of the European Mind in the Nineteenth Century* (Cambridge: Cambridge University Press, 1975).

8. The debate is still unresolved, however, about particular cases such as foetuses.

9. Compare Shue, H., *Basic Rights: Subsistence, Affluence and United States Foreign Policy* (Princeton, NJ: Princeton University Press, 1980), Introduction and Chapter 1, with Cranston, op.cit., pp. 65–9. See also Beetham, D., 'What Future for Economic and Social Rights?' in Beetham, D., (ed.), *Politics and Human Rights* (Oxford: Blackwell, 1995). In recent times a strong argument against the need to sacrifice civil and political rights in favour of development and economic and social rights is also made. See Donnelly, J., 'Repression and Development: The Political Contingency of Human Rights Trade-offs' and Forsythe, D. P., 'Human Rights and Development' in Forsythe, D. P. (ed.), *Human Rights and Development: International Views* (Basingstoke: Macmillan, 1989); and Donnelly, J., 'Human Rights and Development: Complementary of Competing Concerns?' in *World Politics*, (Vol. 36, No. 2, January 1984), pp. 255–83.

10. Positive rights are those which require the government to act in order to enforce them, negative rights those that demand that a government refrains from action. It has been recognised, in recent years, that to identify the former with social and economic rights and the latter with civil and political rights is problematic. Famine, for example, is often the result of purposeful action in time of war. To protect civil and political rights, conversely, may require extensive government action in order, for instance, to train the police and army. See Shue, H., ibid., Chapter 2.

11. The distinction between 'concept', what something means, and 'conception', a particular and more concrete specification of that concept is made by Dworkin, R., *Taking Rights Seriously* (Cambridge, MA: Harvard University Press, 1978), pp. 134–6 and p. 226, cited in Donnelly, J., 'Human Rights and Human Dignity: An Analytic Critique of Non-Western Conceptions of Human Rights', *American Political Science Review*, (Vol. 76, No. 2, June 1982), p. 304.

12. For a different view which is indicative of the ambivalence of the state see Boli-Bennett, J., 'Human Rights or State Expansion? Cross-National Definitions of Constitutional Rights, 1870–1970' in Nanda, V. P., Scarritt, J. R., and Shepherd, G. W., (eds), *Global Human Rights: Public Policies, Comparative Measures and NGO Strategies* (Boulder, CO: Westview Press, 1981) The author views human rights as part of the incorporative ideology of expanding state authority. He does not see them as serving for the protection

of the individual. He argues – on the basis of a study of the constitutions of 93 countries in the period 1870–1970 – that the extensiveness of citizens' rights is positively, not inversely related to the level of state authority and centralisation. This work has influenced my study extensively although I do not share Boli-Bennett's negative view of rights.

13. I am grateful to Michael Donelan for pointing out this distinction.

14. Also note that, in a parallel development, human rights organisations such as Amnesty International have expressed concern, in recent years, about human rights violations by opposition groups, as well as by governments.

15. Donelan, M., 'Reason in War' in *Review of International Studies* (Vol. 8, No. 1, January 1982), p. 56.

16. Quoted in Kolakowski, L., *Religion* (Glasgow: Fontana, 1982), p. 82.

17. Windsor, op.cit., p. 178: 'Faith was now [in the Enlightenment tradition] optional but liberty was not. Instead, liberty became the new antecedent to the exercise of reason.'

18. Kolakowski, op.cit., Chapter 5.

19. For clarification see Strauss, L., *Natural Right and History* (Chicago, IL: University of Chicago Press, 1950); Finnis, J., *Natural Law and Natural Rights* (Oxford: Clarendon Press, 1980); D'Entrèves, A. P., *Natural Law: An Introduction to Legal Philosophy* (London: Hutchinson University Library, 1970) and *Aquinas: Selected Political Writings* (Oxford: Basil Blackwell, 1965).

20. This is the theme of Connolly, W. E., *Political Theory and Modernity* (Oxford: Blackwell, 1988), which centres on Nietzsche. See particularly Chapter One.

21. Ibid. p. 3.

22. Rorty, R., *Philosophy and the Mirror of Nature* (Oxford: Blackwell, 1980) and *Contingency, Irony and Solidarity* (Cambridge: Cambridge University Press, 1989) and Marcus, G. E. and Fischer, M. M. J., *Anthropology as Cultural Critique* (Chicago, IL: University of Chicago Press, 1986).

23. Brown, C., '"Turtles All the Way Down": Anti-Foundationalism, Critical Theory and International Relations', *Millennium: Journal of International Studies* (Vol. 23, No. 2, Summer 1994), p. 224.

24. Ibid.

25. Kolakowski, op.cit., pp. 85–6.

26. Brown, op.cit., p. 232. Brown answers his question: 'Is this [a rejection of the main tenets of "bourgeois liberalism"] a necessary tenet of post-modern critical theory?' in the negative, whereas I would argue that it is. For an excellent exposition of this latter view see Geras, N., 'Language, Truth and Justice' in *New Left Review* (No. 209, January / February 1995), pp. 110–35.

27. Rorty, *Contingency, Irony and Solidarity*, op.cit., p. 44.

28. Mulhall, S. and Swift, A., *Liberals and Communitarians* (Oxford: Blackwell, 1992), Chapter 7.

29. Rorty, *Contingency, Irony and Solidarity*, op.cit., Chapter 4.

30. Ibid., Introduction (p. xv): the definition is attributed to Judith Shklar but there is no reference.

31. Ibid., Chapter 9.

32. Geras, op.cit., pp. 123–5.

33. Kolakowski, op.cit., p. 87. See also p. 82: ' ... the legitimate use of the concept 'truth' ... is possible only on the assumption of an absolute Mind.'

34. Taylor, C., *The Ethics of Authenticity* (Cambridge, MA: Harvard University Press, 1991).

35. The justification of liberalism against challenges such as utilitarianism or communitarianism is not within the mainstream concerns of this chapter. The argument rests on the assumption that – by definition – human rights can be realised only within a liberal framework (see note 2 above) and explores only the way in which liberalism is to be defined. It also assumes that liberalism implies a measure of equality within domestic society; and that economic and social rights are full human rights. The debate between liberalism and libertarianism, which revolves around this problem, will therefore not be explored. For a discussion of these issues see Mulhall and Swift, op.cit.; Sandel, M. (ed.), *Liberalism and its Critics* (Oxford: Blackwell, 1984); Avineri, S. and de-Shalit, A. (eds), *Communitarianism and Individualism* (Oxford: Oxford University Press, 1992) and Waldron (ed.), op.cit.

36. Rawls, J., 'Justice as Fairness: Political not Metaphysical' in Avineri and de-Shalit (eds), op.cit.; 'The Right and the Good Contrasted' in Sandel, (ed.), op.cit.; *A Theory of Justice* (Oxford: Oxford University Press, 1972); and *Political Liberalism* (New York: Columbia University Press, 1993)

37. Berlin, I., 'Two Concepts of Liberty' in Sandel, M., (ed.), op.cit., especially pp. 29–34.

38. Mulhall and Swift, op.cit., p. 178.

39. These various points are made, among others, by Kymlicka, W., 'Liberal Individualism and Liberal Neutrality' and Taylor, C., 'Atomism' in Avineri and de-Shalit (eds) op.cit., Raz, J., 'Right-Based Moralities' in Waldron (ed.) op.cit.; Mulhall and Swift, op.cit., Chapters 5, 6 and 8; and Taylor, C., *The Ethics of Authenticity*, op.cit.

40. This is the suggestion of Joseph Raz who stands for a comprehensive liberalism and argues that the liberal state cannot be neutral (see Raz, J., ibid.). Note how in this formulation liberalism begins to accommodate part of the communitarian critique, in accepting the need for a perfectionist state.

41. The communitarians claim that people are not ends in themselves but

are constituted by their ends; that in fact our identity is defined in dialogue with others and in relation to the community. The view that I adopt here is that, indeed, a liberal individual can only emerge from and exist in a liberal state – much like the 'free' market (the other great cornerstone of liberal doctrine) had to be created and did not emerge 'naturally'. But while this position partly accommodates the communitarian critique of liberalism with regard to state practice, the liberal notion that the person is prior to his or her constitutive ends must be reaffirmed as a *normative* principle, if rights are to remain primary.

42. Rawls, 'Justice as Fairness', op.cit., p. 194. Rawls also says that 'justice as fairness is a political conception in part because it starts from within a certain political tradition', ibid., p. 189. It is not clear where all this leaves Rawls – is he committed to his position or does he merely subscribe to and seek to elaborate one particular political tradition? For a discussion of this ambiguity in Rawls . see Mulhall and Swift, op.cit., Chapters 5 and 6.

43. Vincent, R. J., 'Western Conceptions of a Universal Moral Order' in Pettman, R. (ed.), *Moral Claims in World Affairs* (London: Croom Helm, 1979), p. 70. Vincent argues that 'for the moral defence of the state to fall ... it would have to be shown that its affront to justice was systematic, and not merely possible.' The state in this view does not have any intrinsic moral superiority but it is a potential 'framework of order within which justice might be achieved.' This understanding of the state has informed the whole of this study.

44. These points will be reinforced by the discussion on Egypt and Tunisia in Chapters 3 to 5 and will be taken up in Chapter 6.

45. Kluckhohn, C., 'Ethical Relativity' in Ladd, J., (ed.), *Ethical Relativism*, (Lanham, MD: University Press of America, 1985), p. 78, quoting Brandt, R., *Hopi Ethics: A Theoretical Analysis* (Chicago, IL: University of Chicago Press, 1954), p. 11: 'a necessary condition for the tenability of ethical relativism' is to hold in principle that two people may assert 'contradictory ethical views without either being mistaken.'

46. Renteln, A. D., *International Human Rights: Universalism versus Relativism* (Newbury Park, CA: Sage Publications, 1990), Chapter 3.

47. See Benedict, R., *Patterns of Culture* (London: Routledge and Kegan Paul, 1935); Herskovits, M. J., 'Cultural Relativism and Cultural Values' in Ladd (ed.), *Ethical Relativism*, op.cit.; Herskovits, M. J., 'Tender and Tough-Minded Anthropology and the Study of Values in Cultures' in *Southwestern Journal of Anthropology*, (Vol. 7, No. 1, Spring 1951), pp. 22–31 and 'Some Further Comments on Cultural Relativism' in *American Anthropologist*, (Vol. 60, No. 2, April 1958), pp. 266–73; and 'Statement on Human Rights'. Submitted to the Commission on Human Rights, United Nations, by the Executive Board,

American Anthropological Association in *American Anthropologist* (Vol. 49, No. 4, October–December 1947), pp. 539–43.

48. An-Naim, A. A., 'Problems of Universal Cultural Legitimacy for Human Rights' in An-Naim, A. A. and Deng, F. M. (eds), *Human Rights in Africa: Cross-Cultural Perspectives* (Washington D.C.: The Brookings Institution, 1990), p. 339 and Marcus and Fischer, op.cit., p. 20.

49. See Donnelly 'Human Rights and Human Dignity', op.cit., for an analysis of how, even in cases where there is an attempt to marry a particular tradition with human rights principles, the result can be a distortion of those principles. This issue will be discussed in the context of *some* Islamic interpretations of human rights in subsequent chapters.

50. Rawls, J., 'The Law of Peoples' in Shute, S. and Hurley, S. (eds), *On Human Rights: The Oxford Amnesty Lectures 1993* (New York: Basic Books, 1993).

51. Ibid., p. 43: ' … although any society must honour basic human rights, it need not be liberal.'

52. These various views are proposed or discussed in Renteln, op.cit., and An-Naim and Deng, op.cit.; Kluckhohn, C., 'Cultural Relativity' and Duncker, K., 'Ethical Relativity?' in Ladd, (ed.), op.cit.; and Turner, B. S., 'Outline of the Theory of Human Rights' in Turner, B. S., (ed.), *Citizenship and Social Theory* (London: Sage, 1993).

53. An-Naim, A. A. and Deng, F. M., 'Introduction', in An-Naim and Deng (eds), op.cit., p. 8.

54. An-Naim, 'Problems of Universal Cultural Legitimacy for Human Rights', op.cit., p. 354.

55. In such a case, the tension between human rights and toleration would be resolved without of course this implying that the moral standards behind human rights principles would be validated. This is because these standards are 'absolutes', not 'universals'.

56. Donnelly, *The Concept of Human Rights*, op.cit., pp. 27–9.

57. Finnis, op.cit., pp. 33–6.

58. This is why one of the off-shoots of rationalism was nineteenth century evolutionism. The imperialistic implications of the latter have led to the further discredit of rationalism in our time.

59. Windsor, op.cit., pp. 185–6.

60. On the 'integrated liberal', see Dworkin, R., 'Liberal Community' in Avineri and de-Shalit (eds), op.cit.

61. There are some exceptions to this and they include humanitarian intervention in cases of gross abuses of human rights.

62. See also MacDonald, M., 'Natural Rights' in Waldron, op.cit.

63. Kolakowski, op.cit., Chapter 2 and p. 203.

64. Kolakowski would be radically opposed since his argument is that the *validation* of moral rules is possible only within a religious framework (even though atheists may *act* more morally than believers). See Kolakowski, op.cit., pp. 191–2. He is, however, sympathetic to consistent atheists like Nietzsche who, while accepting that 'the universe deserted by God is an absurd universe', are able to 'fearlessly face their freedom' and 'decree a meaning by sheer act of will' – that meaning consisting of a belief in human dignity. Ibid., pp. 210–12.

65. For an example, see Lawrence, B., *Defenders of God: The Fundamentalist Revolt Against the Modern Age* (London: I. B. Tauris, 1990), a study of the similarities between Christian, Jewish and Islamic fundamentalism.

66. Donnelly, J., 'Cultural Relativism and Universal Human Rights', in *Human Rights Quarterly* (Vol. 5, No. 4, November 1984), pp. 410–4.

2

Islam and Human Rights

I

This chapter examines the issues involved in thinking about Islam and human rights at an abstract level, divorced – for the moment – from any social and historical context. One of the principles underlying this discussion (and the study as a whole, as I argued in Chapter 1), is that in considering human rights and liberal principles in general we must shed the assumption of a sharp distinction between liberal Western and other non-liberal cultures. Concealed behind this popular view is the identification of liberalism with a strict secularism. It is more fruitful in thinking about human rights to draw the dividing line elsewhere: not between a secular and non-secular worldview but between one that respects the inherent worth of the individual and his or her inalienable rights, *even if that is encompassed in a metaphysical or religious framework*, and a world-view that does not, be it religious or secular. Only thus can we begin the analysis of the links between Islam and human rights, and the rival discourses they give rise to, with a more open mind. Showing that some interpretations of Islam make room for human rights principles will reinforce the argument that it is *not* necessary to reject religion altogether – and Islam in particular – in order to secure human rights.

A second preliminary point that follows closely upon the first derives from the *problematique* of 'Orientalism' as defined by Edward Said.[1] Said's concern has been to illustrate that knowledge about the

'Orient' in European society has been used as a covert means of sub-jugation. He analyses in detail the ways in which European literature and science have promoted a distorted and biased view of Arab society and a stereotypical picture of Islam. Said traces the development of the 'discourse' of Orientalism and unveils its ulterior motives which are connected with power and political domination through misrep-resentation and – crucially – through the use of cultural terms of reference which are Western and, therefore, inappropriate to the study of Muslim societies.

Said's critique is directly relevant to the subject of this study which is concerned both with human rights (in origin a Western concept) and the interaction between cultures. Chapter 1 attempted to disconnect human rights from power and cultural imperialism, through breaking the link between human rights and a rationalism which, Said agrees, has been used in some of its interpretations as a vehicle for domination by colonising states.[2] Furthermore one aim of this book as a whole is to dispense with stereotypes surrounding Islam and posit a particularist, socio-political approach to problems facing Muslim societies. But if the points that Said makes on imperialism and cultural stereotypes are taken, and have informed this study, it is difficult to address some of the other issues he raises, because – as Aijaz Ahmad has illustrated[3] – they are unclear and contradictory. Said is vague on whether a true representation of Islam or indeed of anything else is feasible (his approach as a whole relies on Michel Foucault). Yet, despite viewing the distinction between representation and misrepresentation as 'at best a matter of degree',[4] he praises the work of a number of students of the Middle East who have eschewed the distortions of Orientalist discourse. Furthermore he is ambiva-lent on liberalism and humanism. On the one hand, he applauds them. On the other, he condemns their underlying philosophy as a set of references used for the subordination of Muslim societies.

We need therefore to reiterate the approach adopted here by using Said solely as a starting point (because his ambivalence on liberalism and representation do not permit either agreement or disagreement). The critique of Orientalism, and doubts about the possibility of rep-resentation, are useful in cautioning us against our own cultural presuppositions and biases. But they must not provide a barrier to an attempt (at least) of communication and understanding. Cultures are not impenetrable worlds to all who were not born and socialised in them. Inter-cultural dialogue is always possible, if extremely precarious. Furthermore the condition of modernity provides common concerns that facilitate this dialogue – as this and later chapters will illustrate – one of these being universal structures of authority as exemplified in the modern nation-state. The concept of human rights in particular, although of European origin, is not exclusive to Western cultures but binds together people from disparate backgrounds. In other words, if terms and concepts that are seemingly 'Western' are used here in the context of another culture this is because they are not alien to that culture but have become part of its concerns, whatever their initial origin and uses may have been.

This chapter will provide the first part of a central argument of the book, by showing that the religion of Islam is not inherently illiberal and that it can be reconciled, at an abstract level of ideas, with the principles of human rights. The remaining chapters will provide the complementary part of the argument, which is that if we want to understand why it is that illiberal interpretations of Islam frequently predominate in historical reality, we have to examine the social and political conditions of Muslim societies, not Islamic doctrine or tradition. In other words, the aim is to defend the proposition that respect or disrespect for human rights is a matter of political will and choice, not of a cultural authentic 'essence' which necessarily shapes and constrains societies.

Section II is a somewhat simplified examination of the basic precepts of Islamic religious doctrine and Islamic law. It is not about traditional Islam *per se* but about how it is conceptualised in our contemporary period. The difficulties these precepts present in allowing for a reconciliation with human rights principles will be contrasted with the ways in which they can be harmonised with them. I will argue that this harmonisation is possible on the basis of a reinterpretation of Islam. Section III is a discussion of various schemes which *purport* to conciliate Islam with human rights but in fact reinforce its authoritarian interpretation. They will be contrasted, in Section IV, with attempts at genuine resolution in order to show that it is, indeed, a feasible option. The texts selected for examination are recent (mostly from the 1970s onwards), because it is during this period that human rights have increasingly become a debated issue in Muslim societies. The chapter will conclude with a clarification of terminology and of vital distinctions.

What we must bear in mind, especially for Section II, is that even if the very broad and generally agreed on principles of the religion are selected for examination, they are not espoused by all Muslims either universally or across time. Also, that the exercise attempted here is not useful except as part of a more general argument because Islam, as such, is not 'something' independent of the societies which give expression to it.[5] The other use which this exercise serves is to explore the intellectual issues which will be subsequently discussed in the context of the politics of Egypt and Tunisia. That discussion will therefore be facilitated.

II

Religion and politics are one: this is the first powerful myth with regard to Islam. It is true that Islam – in some historical periods and in some of its interpretations – has sought to reorganise society by providing guidelines for public as well as private life. But in other instances it has not. It is not the aim of this section to discover to what extent the bond between Islam and politics is historically real or whether Islam is exceptional among religions in this respect.[6] Rather, the argument in this section rests on what is currently *assumed* to be true with regard to the major precepts of the Islamic religion.

The reasons for the close link between Islam and politics are to be found, it is believed, in the story of Muhammad, who combined the roles of political and religious leader for the Arabs, and in the subsequent history of Islam in the Middle East and elsewhere, in which the fortunes of religion and empire were often closely linked. If a religion contains the belief that justice is to be achieved through the institution of an Islamic state (which is what many Islamists maintain), its influence on law and the concept of authority must be considerable and it must also contain a viewpoint on rights, positive or negative. This viewpoint will be examined in subsequent paragraphs.

For the purpose of organising Islamic authority, a set of laws was developed in the early centuries after Muhammad's death, the *sharia*. This was necessary because neither the Prophet in his lifetime nor the divine revelation, the Koran, offered detailed guidance on a range of practical social and political issues. In the event, it was left to political authority and most of all to legal experts to expound the legal doctrine. The emphasis that was placed on the revelation, and its sacred and timeless nature, required that this was done without greatly diverging from the Koran. But at the same time, considerable leeway was allowed in its interpretation. The jurists could appeal to the traditions of what the Prophet did or said (the *hadith*), and use 'independent reasoning' (*ijtihad*) and the consensus of the jurists (*ijma*), in order to construct a workable law.[7]

By the ninth century, however, it was agreed, by the Sunni community at least, that all the necessary interpretation of the Koran had been completed and that the law had acquired its final form. The Shia community dissented, but although *ijtihad* remained central in Shia legal thought in theory (having the status of a separate source of law) in practice it was much limited by the requirement not to stray from the example of the sinless and infallible imam.[8] Over time then, the *sharia* became rigid and unresponsive to social reality.

This is the second major myth with regard to Islam – that the door of *ijtihad* was closed in the ninth century. But the reality was very mixed. Through history a number of ways have been devised to use the law for a variety of social and political purposes and needs. The door of *ijtihad* was never really shut. The law was often pragmatically revised and its unclarified points subject to much debate and interpretation, while the myth that it could not be subject to change was simultaneously upheld.[9]

The above points are important and need to be kept in mind when discussing questions of Islam and human rights. The first of such questions are about the individual. It must be made clear at the outset that the idea that human beings have rights *qua* human beings is absent, in *explicit* form, from the Koran and the *sharia*. Only God has rights, not people.[10] Only God has absolute freedom, human freedom consisting in the complete surrender to divine will.[11] In the Koran submission to God is repeatedly stressed as a cardinal value. The individual's due is not universally the same. It depends on a man's acts and on his relationship with God, on his behaviour and faith, not on his mere being. Rather than rights, it is more appropriate in the Koran and in traditional Islam to talk of man's privileges.[12] Rights, so far as they exist, are ensured through networks of social obligation[13] and duty, not right, is at the centre of traditional Islamic justice.

At the same time, however, Islam stressed the dignity and elevated the status of the individual.[14] In pre-Islamic Arabia, the individual was totally subsumed to the tribe but in the new religion the individual became the vicegerent of God on earth, defined by faith and in reference to Allah, not to the social group. The relationship with Allah was to be direct and intermediaries, such as the clergy, were not considered necessary. The absence of the doctrine of original sin and the conception of death as a natural occurrence – not punishment for sin – meant that a person was not considered inherently evil in Islam.[15] Furthermore the notion of *fitra* (the 'innate disposition created by Allah as a necessary medium to universal guidance'), strengthened the idea of the existence of a common humanity.[16]

If Islam stressed the notion of individual responsibility towards God, there was an ambivalence on this point, which stemmed from the Koran itself. Similar to the Christian belief in predestination there was a tendency to view the course of human existence as determined by God, and a destiny from which the individual could not escape. The tension between predestination and free will has never been resolved in Islam. But despite this ambiguity the individual does have a central place in the Islamic world-view, as in the other monotheistic religions, and this can provide a foundation for the concept of human rights. So can the doctrinal insistence on the equality of all believers. The major distinctions in Islam are between the faithful and the non-faithful and between men and women and they both present major problems for the concept of human rights as we shall see. But, at least between male believers, differences of race, colour, class or nationality are believed to be irrelevant to individual worth.

The position of the individual, the centrality of duty in traditional Islamic justice and the equality of believers, inform the relationship between authority and society. The ruler in traditional Islam holds a sacred trust. He is the one who, by protecting the Islamic order, guarantees the spiritual welfare of the people in this world and the next. The ruler is responsible for the enforcement of the Islamic law and is subject to the law himself. Men are obligated to obey only the good.[17] So the ruler's position is not inviolable, but subject to certain conditions, and this is obviously important for the notion of rights. The ruler is not all-powerful or divinised in any way.

For a number of reasons, however, these prescriptive rules about authority, contained in the law itself, were ultimately thwarted by the very same law. Precisely because a properly constituted authority was supposed to guarantee the welfare of all, the interests of authority and community, not of the individual, became supreme. Because the first centuries after the death of Muhammad were ridden with discord and civil strife (*fitna*), later jurists encouraged allegiance to whatever government was in power, even if it were tyrannical. The ruler was supposed to obey the law and be deposed if he did not, but no institution could really enforce this and no exact legal procedures were worked out to that effect. In extorting confessions the ruler was allowed to use corporal punishment and imprisonment. Outside the *hadd* punishments he had complete discretion over meting out sentences (although it was stressed that the punishment must fit the crime and that he had to be merciful). Authority, in short, was allowed to become absolute by the very law that was meant to restrict it.[18]

None of this is surprising or unexpected in a traditional system of authority. Nor is it exceptionally Islamic. What is important to understand from this discussion on authority, however, is that elements of restricting the ruler do exist in Islamic thought, albeit submerged by a non-democratic historical reality.

Having briefly examined the position of the individual and the relationship between authority and society, we can turn to another set of problems in Islam with regard to human rights: attitudes towards 'unbelievers', religious minorities, women, slavery, the *hadd* punishments and apostasy.

The Koran states unequivocally that unbelievers (or 'idolaters') must be slain.[19] The *sharia* did not contemplate their permanent residence within Islamic society and in theory they could only feel secure there when they were under temporary safe conduct (*aman*). Furthermore, one tradition of *jihad* or holy war was in favour of aggressive expansion and the forcible conversion of unbelievers. But, again, the issue is ambivalent. The same Koran also states that 'there is no compulsion in religion'.[20] Another strand in the religious tradition is in favour of peaceful coexistence so long as Islamic society is not threatened.[21] The ambiguity is revealed by the various meanings of *jihad*. It can be taken to mean aggressive war; purely defensive war; or it can even refer to the personal struggle of the individual to enhance his or her virtue.[22]

The position of Christian and Jewish minorities is different from that of 'unbelievers' dueto their categorisation as 'People of the Book'. Within Muslim society they are ensured certain rights, such as security of person and property, freedom of worship and a degree of communal autonomy. But they are also restricted in many ways. They are subject to a poll-tax (*jizya*), they are not allowed to preach openly and proselytise and are forbidden from holding the highest political offices. Being a non-Muslim in an Islamic state entails the status of a second-class citizen. Minorities enjoy religious tolerance rather than religious freedom.[23] Yet it must be noted that in the history of Islamic empire these minorities have enjoyed relative security during long periods.[24]

The inequality between the sexes is flagrant in traditional Islamic law and doctrine.[25] Certain women's rights are secured. The woman has a right to inheritance; to be a party to a contract in marriage and not an object for sale; to manage her own property; and some rights to divorce. But these, even though important, are only limited rights. A man is allowed to use physical violence against his wife; he can divorce her without explanation; he can be polygamous if he so chooses; he has exclusive rights of custody over the children in case of separation; and the testimony of one male witness is equal to that of two women. Attitudes to women are shaped by the belief that their sexuality poses a threat to social order and must therefore be concealed and controlled.

The issue of women, perhaps more than any other, confirms the view that 'Islam' is not an independent entity but is shaped by social and historical factors. Nowhere does the Koran clearly say that women must be veiled; that stoning is the punishment for adultery; or that women must be secluded or circumcised. As many have persuasively argued, the Koran was either conveniently interpreted or completely ignored, to fit the needs of patriarchal society.[26] In the modern period many liberal and feminist thinkers have gone back to the Koran and tried to interpret it differently or show that many of the restrictions on women are not contained therein. As we shall see, they argue that the 'spirit' of the Koran points towards ultimate equality between the sexes, partly on the grounds that the Koran improved the position of women in many ways, compared to pre-Islamic Arabia.

Arguments of this latter type are today almost universally acceptable as regards slavery. The Koran endorsed slavery as an institution, as of course did Islamic law.[27] But today very few would argue in its favour, even among the most conservative Islamic thinkers. The Koran's restrictions on slavery are seen as pointing, quite clearly, towards its ultimate abolition.

The *hadd* punishments constitute a major problem for human rights. These punishments are prescribed by the Koran and are said to fit a particular set of crimes, those committed 'against God' (unlawful intercourse, highway robbery, alcohol consumption, false accusations). No human legislator is supposed to abolish these laws. But again the issue is ambiguous. There are those who argue that the Koran does not explicitly say that 'the hand of the thief must be cut off' – only that 'it must be stopped'. But even among those who do not question the prevalent interpretation of the Koran the *hadd* punishments are, in our time, largely abhorred and many ways are devised to avoid their implementation.[28]

Islam encourages private property but limits it by strictly prohibiting usury. The law could provide the ground for economic and social rights through the obligation to pay an alms tax (*zakat*) for the poorest members of society. The notion that natural resources ultimately belong to God and that people are merely their custodians could encourage respect for the environment.

The freedoms of conscience and religion, finally, are explicitly denied by Islamic doctrine. Apostasy is punishable by death, and is in fact a double crime, against God and against political authority. But what about the Koranic verse 'there is no compulsion in religion'? One writer can claim, as we shall see, that it is 'inconceivable' that God would prescribe death in matters which pertain to the human

conscience and that the tradition that apostates must be killed originated in the wars of tribal rebellion after Muhammad's death.[29]

To summarise, Islamic religious doctrine and the *sharia* law, in their
traditional understandings, do not contain or uphold the concept of
human rights. The notion of right is not at the centre of Islamic justice. Rather, submission to God and duty are emphasised. The position
of non-Muslims and of women is inherently unequal. In the law, procedures for the protection of the individual against authority and
controls on the government are not worked out.

There are, however, some ideas in the religious doctrine and even
in the *sharia* which can provide building blocks for a conciliation of
Islam and human rights, among which are the equality of believers,
respect for minorities and the belief that the ruler must obey the law.
Duties can imply correlative rights. The position of the individual is
central and the human being is valued, to a degree, for his or her humanity. Even the slave is considered a person in Islamic law, albeit not
a fully responsible one.

It was important to examine these issues because they provide the
staple for many of the contemporary discourses on Islam and human
rights. I do not claim that this has been an examination of traditional
Islam. Rather, it was a glance at how 'Islam' (which often, in effect,
means traditional Islam) is conceptualised in our time. Why does the
past have such a hold in Islamic thought? Here we come to the third
major myth surrounding Islam: that the Koran, being the word of
God, is in its totality unquestionable and lays down the law on everything. This indeed may be so. But, as any examination of Islamist and
generally Islamic discourse makes clear, there are many, sometimes
contradictory, readings of the Koran. This means that we are not really constrained by the text, even though it and the injunctions it
contains cannot be set aside. Which interpretation we adopt is a matter of *choice*, not predetermined by the text itself. This section has
shown that, on every issue which is related to the question of human
rights, there is profound ambivalence in Islam. The next section will
concentrate on those who have interpreted this ambivalence in an
illiberal fashion.

III

During the 1970s and 1980s human rights became a more prominent subject in the Middle East, among governments, political activists, intellectuals and ordinary people. This development is not new – like the rest of the world, Muslim societies have engaged with the notions of democracy and constitutionalism since the nineteenth century – but it does represent a renewed interest in those issues, its reference point now being the Universal Declaration of Human Rights. As such it testifies to the increasing prestige of the notion but does not necessarily imply that respect for rights or – what is equally important – a proper understanding of what they mean has also grown. The idea of human rights has been disseminated and has been picked up by various groups in the service of various causes, some pernicious to rights. As for the compatibility of human rights and Islam, the views expressed range from the assertion that Islam was the first historically to introduce the notion of rights and is therefore their best guarantee, to the claim that Islam is absolutely incompatible with rights and always will be.

The position of Chapter 1 was that the concept of human rights is an absolute, even though its conception may change and develop *over time*. The pertinent question now is whether the conception of human rights can vary *among cultural settings* and still retain its substance. The answer is that it can, but we must guard against the following. First that the notion of human dignity may be confused with the notion of human rights.[30] Second that, in facile attempts to transpose the notion of human rights in a particular cultural setting, which do not really resolve the relevant contradictions, the notion will be distorted. This is what occurs in the various schemes which purport to reconcile Islam and human rights which will be examined next.

Three texts have been selected in the first instance:[31] the 'Universal Islamic Declaration of Human Rights' issued by the Islamic Council in 1981; Abul A'la Mawdudi's *Human Rights in Islam;* and Sultanhussein Tabandeh's *Muslim Commentary on the Universal Declaration of Human Rights.*[32] Each represents a different strand of thought. The first is a declaration of semi-official status, enjoying governmental approval. The second is the work of an Islamist thinker who has inspired opposition movements in the Middle East and beyond. The third has been written by a traditionalist religious thinker. The first and second have much more in common in their approach than the third. Governments and opposition compete with one another for the definition and appropriation of a 'modern' Islam while the traditionalist opinions Tabandeh stands for are those of a dwindling minority.

The tone of the 'Universal Islamic Declaration of Human Rights' is set in the first sentence of the foreword: 'Islam gave to mankind an ideal code of human rights fourteen centuries ago.' The preamble states a belief in the 'Vicegerency (*Khilafah*) of man who has been created to fulfil the Will of God on earth'; that 'rationality by itself without the light of revelation from God can neither be a sure guide in the affairs of mankind nor provide spiritual nourishment ... '; and that ' ... our duties and obligations have priorities over our rights ... '. The Declaration calls for an Islamic order, wherein the *sharia* would be respected.

In the list of 'inalienable' rights that follows the term 'the Law' refers to the *sharia* law. This is a major source of difficulties for the compatibility of the Declaration with the concept of human rights. Article 1, for example, states that human life is sacred and inviolable and that 'no one shall be exposed to injury or death, except under the authority of the Law'. What this – or the injunction that 'the sanctity of a person's body shall be inviolable' – mean in relation to the *hadd* punishments is left unclear. The rights to freedom, equality, justice, a fair trial and protection against torture are affirmed. The Koranic principle 'there is no compulsion in religion' guarantees the rights of minorities, but the Koranic injunctions that contradict this are not mentioned. The next article (11), states that 'every individual in the community (*Ummah*) ... ' is eligible to assume public office – therefore excluding non-Muslims. People have 'the right to choose and remove their rulers in accordance with this principle [process of free consultation (*shura*)]' but no explicit mention is made of the exact mechanisms of this process, a serious omission given the contested meaning of *shura*.

Articles 12 on the 'Right to Freedom of Belief, Thought and Speech' and 13 on the 'Right to Freedom of Religion' are also indicative of the problems. 'Every person has the right to express his thoughts and beliefs so long as he remains within the limits prescribed by the Law'. The issues of apostasy and blasphemy, however, are not openly confronted. Economic and social rights are secured, as is the right to property. But the next stumbling block is article 19 on the 'Right to Found a Family and Related Matters'. Among other problematic statements are the following: 'Every spouse is entitled to such rights and privileges and carries such obligations as are stipulated by the Law', 'Motherhood is entitled to special respect ... ' and 'Within the family, men and women are to share in their obligations and responsibilities according to their sex, their natural endowments, talents and inclinations ... ' The problems of inequality between men and women are clearly avoided or papered over and this becomes more evident in the following article 20, on the 'Rights of Married Women' (not, note, of women as a whole). A married woman can 'seek and obtain dissolution of marriage (*khul'a*) in accordance with the terms of the Law'. She also has the right to seek divorce through the courts and she can 'inherit from her husband, her parents, her children and other relatives according to the Law'. Given that the *sharia* gives extensive rights of divorce to the husband and not to the wife and imposes unequal distribution in inheritance between men and women, it is obvious that the matter is wilfully avoided.

Mayer has pointed out that the Arabic text, which is the original and therefore the more authoritative version of the Declaration, suffers even more from omissions and inconsistencies than the English translation.[33] The Declaration glosses over the most thorny issues of Islam and human rights: apostasy, equality between Muslims and non-Muslims, and between men and women. The problems with Mawdudi's text are similar.

Mawdudi begins by analysing the concept of *tawhid*, unity of God and creation, which 'negates the concept of the legal and political sovereignty of human beings'. He next explains the concept of *khilafa* which refers to man as the representative of God on earth. Democracy in Islam begins here and this concept makes it 'abundantly clear' that 'no individual or dynasty or class can be *khilafa* but that the authority of *khilafa* is bestowed on the entire group of people, the community as a whole, which is ready to fulfil the conditions of representation after subscribing to the principle of *tawhid* and *risala* (prophethood).' Further, 'Every person in an Islamic society enjoys the rights and powers of the caliphate of God and in this respect all individuals are equal'; 'In this respect the political system of Islam is a perfect form of democracy.' What distinguishes it from Western democracy, according to Mawdudi, is that it is not based on popular, but on divine sovereignty. This, what the author describes as 'the essence of Islamic political theory', opens the way for his analysis of human rights principles.[34]

Mawdudi's text, as Mayer has pointed out, is most telling in what it omits.[35] In the section on 'fundamental rights' the author states that 'every Muslim is to be regarded as eligible and fit for all the positions of the highest responsibility in an Islamic state without distinction of race, colour or class' – the distinctions based on sex or religion are not mentioned. The *sharia* would not be modified in such a polity but 'an advisory council comprising men learned in Islamic law' will 'ascertain the real intent of the *sharia*' in cases where two or more interpretations of the injunctions are possible.[36] The contradiction with the principle of majority rule is blatant. By denying popular sovereignty and identifying the law of the land with the *sharia*, supreme power is automatically handed over to 'learned men'.

Mawdudi's assertion that all citizens have the same rights, be they believers or unbelievers, is belied by his own list of rights. The right to life is treated in a superficial and patchy way, through a mixture of Koranic injunctions and polemical counter-examples of the West's abuses – which permit the author to maintain that 'only' Islam guarantees the right to life. It is followed by 'respect for the chastity of women' (a circumscribed notion of a right), which is also allegedly solely guaranteed by Islam. The 'right to freedom' is relevant to slavery only. After an attack against Western slave practices, Mawdudi claims that 'the problem of the slaves of Arabia was solved in a short period of thirty or forty years' and the 'only form of slavery which was left in Islamic society was the prisoners of war'. He does not condemn slavery in principle.[37]

Mawdudi distinguishes basic human rights from the rights of citizens in an Islamic state which he then discusses. Are these human rights? The categorical confusions are constant. The rights to life and property are followed by 'the protection of honour' and the 'right' not to be insulted by nicknames. Under the 'right to protest against tyranny' (which is a partial right) there is a sudden reference to the Pakistani Penal Code, a parochial slip. Freedom of expression is limited by the condition that 'it should be used for the propagation of virtue and truth', as is the right of association. A brief reference to freedom of conscience and conviction wholly evades apostasy. Equality before the law does not, apparently, mean full equality for non-Muslim citizens. Their lives and properties may be protected but it is not plainly stated whether they are equal in all rights. The 'right to avoid sin' is baffling. It turns out that it refers to the obligation of citizens to disobey the law of the state if it contravenes divine law. Finally democracy is to be expressed through *shura* – but no attempt is made to reconcile this institution with the functions of 'learned men' mentioned above.[38]

In contrasting Mawdudi with Tabandeh, a traditionalist Islamic thinker, it will become evident that the latter is quite unequivocal about the irreconcilable points between Islamic law and the Universal Declaration of Human Rights. On article 1, for example (Tabandeh takes the articles of the Declaration one by one and comments on them), he states that although Islam does not recognise distinctions based on race or class it does recognise those based on religion, faith and conviction. Details of the inequality between Muslims and non-Muslims before the law are expounded in his commentary on article 2 and they are quite stark, to the point that the punishment for murder is different depending on whether the victim is a Muslim or not. On slavery he is more circumspect. The conditions that permitted the existence of slavery at the time of the Prophet no longer exist and the aim of Islam was clearly to limit slavery. He therefore states his opposition to it without, however, condemning it outright in principle. He is forced to admit that if the conditions for slavery did exist today it would have to be legalised, but takes great pains to prove that this cannot be so. Tabandeh's views, although seemingly less progressive than Mawdudi's, are in fact more conducive to human rights principles because he does not deny the contradictions but tries to reconcile them with his belief that 'freedom is an innate principle of humanity'.[39]

In his comment on article 16 he is explicit, men and women are unequal. A Muslim woman is not allowed to marry a non-Muslim because that would mean subordinating Islam to other religions (since women are inferior to men); a woman does not have equal rights to divorce, because she is unreliable by nature; the consent of her parents is necessary for her marriage (although her consent is needed also); and she is not allowed to take part in politics (here Switzerland, 'one of the most civilised countries and most perfect societies of the world' according to Tabandeh, is brought in as living proof of the benefits of this policy). He affirms the need for chastity and veiling. Finally he lists the rights of husband and wife. As many other writers on Islam and human rights he translates 'right' as the 'other's duty'. He also asserts that because women are to be protected and supported by men their welfare is more secure, thereby implicitly denying the need for women's rights. He affirms the inequality of women in inheritance and in legal testimony, as well as polygamy, although he disapproves of the latter given that men cannot treat all wives equally.[40]

On freedom of conscience and religion, Tabandeh states that only Muslims can hold public office and that apostasy is unacceptable. He accepts freedom in political but not in religious thought.[41] He concludes by reiterating the view that the Universal Declaration of Human Rights 'had not promulgated anything that was new nor inaugurated innovations' and that 'every clause of it, indeed every valuable regulation needed for the welfare of human society ever enacted by the lawgivers, already existed in better and more perfect form in Islam'.[42]

All the elements of the above three works on Islam and human rights recur in various contexts, governmental, oppositional or among ordinary people. Some additional examples will help to elucidate the problems. The frequent assertion by Muslims, who may even be apolitical, that their religion has best safeguarded human rights since its inception, is similar to governmental declarations to the same effect. Former President Rafsanjani of Iran stated, for example, that 'human rights are among the most important jurisprudential/historical issues inspired by the verses of the Holy Koran' and 'That which the international community is trying to draw up nowadays has been under discussion in Islam for a long time, and in the Islamic country of Iran, many of the individual and social rights from which the Muslims benefit also hold good for [religious] minorities; a clear example of this is the presence of deputies representing those minorities in the *Majlis* with the same rights as the deputies of the Islamic *ummah*.'[43] In a similar vein, the Foreign Minister of Iran in 1993, Ali Akbar Velayati, contrasted Islam's respect for rights with the Western equation of human rights with 'unbound freedom' [sic]. He claims that 'Western-ers endeavour to impose their own beliefs and Western values on the world' whereas human rights are variously implemented in different countries.[44] The Islamic Republic is quite aggressive in propounding 'Islamic' human rights against the West.

Popular literature and propaganda reflect similar views. A recent translation, in booklet form, of *The Treatise on Rights* by Imam Zayn al-Abidin Ali ibn al-Husayn, who lived in the early period of Islam, illustrates the confusion surrounding the term 'right'. Although the translator does note in the introduction that the term '*haqq*' might better be translated as duties, obligations or responsibilities, he nev-ertheless proceeds to translate the word as 'rights' in order to show that 'in considering human rights primarily in terms of responsibili-ties, Islam diverges profoundly from most modern Western views'. The argument is as a result nonsensical at various points. It states, for ex-ample, that acts have rights against the person; that 'the right of him who asks your counsel is that you give him your counsel' or that (in addressing the ruler) 'the right of your subjects through authority is that you should know that they have been made subjects through their weakness and your strength'.[45]

In another booklet on *Women's Rights in Islam*, the author claims that 'The role designated for a Muslim woman by Islam is the clearest proof of the equality and rights that she enjoys within the faith.' She repeats a frequent argument of Muslim apologists in relation to women (and religious minorities), that because the roles of men and women are different this does not mean that they are unequal. She refers to Allah's 'natural division of labour' which is part of the 'natural bal-ance' and according to which 'the male is obliged to bear a greater part of the economic responsibilities, whilst the female is equipped to shoulder the greater part of the childbearing and rearing responsibil-ity'. The booklet is a tortuous attempt to prove that unequal rights and responsibilities, which cannot be doubted because 'to find fault with this natural ordering of things is to question God's wisdom', in fact corresponds to equality between the sexes.[46] In similar though cruder form, the pamphlet entitled *Why Two Women Witnesses?*, which defends the Koranic principle that the testimony of two women is equal to one man's, asserts that 'the intellectual status of a Muslim woman is neither marred nor degraded by the Commandment'.[47]

Scholarly research is not immune from such arguments. Abdul Aziz Said's 'Islamic Perspectives' on human rights fails to come to grips with theoretical problems and contradictions. He states for example that 'the Islamic state combines elements of theocracy with democracy', a perplexing proposition on which no light is shed by the subsequent attempt to elucidate: 'The state is democratic since the right to govern derives from counsel among the believers ... However the rights of the people to change the law and the state are limited' and 'In the Islamic state, sovereignty belongs to God alone'.[48] In another article the same author makes comments such as 'While in the liberal tradition freedom signifies the ability to act, in Islam, it is the ability to exist or, more accurately, to become' – and leaves it at that.[49] A semi-scholarly article entitled 'Human Rights: Towards an Islamic Framework', claims that 'What is at issue is not whether or not human rights should be respected in the Arab world – this is not questioned – but rather the form which these human rights should take.' It proceeds to make a case for human rights based on the *sharia* law which safeguards the rights of all, including women, as exemplified in the Saudi Arabian Basic Law.[50] *The Iranian Journal*'s special issue on human rights is similarly replete with evasions and distortions.[51] One instance is the argument that, in contrast to Christianity, Islam has not suffered from a struggle between church and state because it recognises no clergy. This suggests that in Islam secularism and secularisation are not an issue.[52]

Finally, Hassan Turabi of Sudan, claims that in the whole of Islamic history, the attempt has been to limit the powers of government; that despite anti-Muslim prejudices plurality and diversity is an ideal in the Islamic civilisation; and that Islam respects sexual equality.[53] In his analysis of the Islamic state, he states that 'an Islamic order of government is essentially a form of representative democracy' – in which, however, the majority/minority pattern would not be appropriate,[54] the role of the legal profession would be minimised and in which 'Christians in particular who now, at least, do not seem to have a public law, should not mind the application of Islamic law as long as it does not interfere with religion'.[55]

The problems with the proposed solutions for a conciliation between Islam and human rights described above are fairly evident but can nevertheless be listed here for the sake of clarity. First, in arguing that Islam from its inception introduced human rights, they make an ahistorical claim which fails to distinguish between 'having a right' and 'what is right' and between human rights and human dignity. The Koran contains, as I argued in section II, some general principles that may be conducive to respect for the human person and his or her rights but it does not explicitly propound the notion of inalienable rights, as no traditional text would. Rather, it stresses duties. This is the second point, the confusion, in the texts described above, between rights and duties. The question whether the notion of duty contains within it the notion of right is complex. A right does imply a duty, but it is of crucial importance to the idea of human rights that the right exists independently of and prior to its correlative duty. The centrality of duty in Islam is not a mere difference in emphasis but a judgment that rights are less important than duties. This, and the categorical confusion that stems from too close an attachment to the literal Koranic word, is evident in some publications where, under the heading 'the rights of' children, women and so is found a list of the duties others have towards them.[56]

The third problem in some of these texts is that 'the community' is exalted above the individual. There is a failure to distinguish between atomism and individualism and to see individual rights and the well-being of the community as complementary. This is usually the result of a desire to distance Islam from the West and its excessive individualism. Fourthly, and crucially, there is confusion between people having equal rights yet different roles, and people having different and therefore unequal rights. In this context, which is relevant particularly to women and non-Muslims, exhortations for 'protection' and special 'respect' are a means for the diminution of rights.[57]

Last, but not least, these texts betray a serious misunderstanding of the notion of freedom. On the grounds that freedom does not mean license for everything and anything but needs guidelines and rules – an obvious point for anyone who cares to think about liberty in society

– they define freedom, perversely, as restriction. The preoccupation is not to impose rules that will allow individuals to be protected from abuse by authority and their fellow citizens (therefore allowing them to participate freely in social and political life), but rather to protect people from themselves and from each other, through separation and stringent moral prohibitions. This lack of faith in the innate goodness of the human person and in his or her capacity for responsibility and freedom is typical of a traditional religious ethic which – as in other interpretations of monotheistic religions – relies for its proper functioning on the fear of God and the threat of punishment. In this respect this ethic is profoundly anti-humanistic.

It is evident that the concern of these authors is to defend Islam, not human rights. With the growing prestige of the concept of human rights internationally during the twentieth century and particularly from the 1970s onwards, many thinkers and political activists have felt compelled to take the notion on board.[58] This may or may not be a positive development. What is certainly negative is the facile incorporation of rights into an interpretation of Islam which is profoundly inhospitable to any notion of human rights.

It is the purpose of this chapter to show that this negative development is not inescapable and to produce evidence of the compatibility of Islam and human rights. This means a redefinition of what Islam consists of, not a reinterpretation of the concept of human rights that will render it an empty shell. Section II briefly described the points of difficulty but also of potential compatibility between Islam and human rights. What will now follow is an examination of how some thinkers have used this potential to argue for a true and valid conciliation, or the beginnings thereof. They achieve this only by raising the level of discussion from the detailed and particular points, of what the Koran says here and there, to broader concerns.

IV

Let us start from a brief and concise text entitled 'Human Rights in Islam' by Majid Khadduri. Its author notes that inequality of men and women and the institution of slavery stand in opposition to the concept of equality and brotherhood of man propounded by Islam. His explanation is that the Prophet preferred gradual over revolutionary methods but that 'his ultimate purpose was clear: he intended to eliminate slavery and put women on an equal footing with men'.[59] On apostasy, he claims that its punishment by death originated in the wars that followed the prophet's death; and claims that 'in matters which pertain to human conscience, it is *inconceivable* (my italics) that God would prescribe death'.[60] Islam and human rights are compatible because the author's conception of the religion is *tantamount* to a respect for human rights principles.

Abdulaziz Sachedina, who will be used as a second example, confronts the question of freedom of conscience in the Koran. He starts by discussing the two opposed schools of Koranic exegesis, the 'Mutazilite and the Asharite'. The former argued that 'human beings, as free agents, are responsible before a just God' and that 'good and evil are rational categories which can be known through reason, independently of revelation'. The Asharites believed the opposite, concluding that 'God alone creates all actions directly, but in some actions a special quality of "voluntary acquisition" is superimposed by God's will that makes the individual a voluntary agent and responsible'.[61] The latter set of views have predominated in Islamic history, though the influence of the former has not been completely eradicated. The author also discusses the idea of *fitra* and, through an analysis of the Koran, concludes that the 'fundamental moral equality of all human beings at the level of universal guidance' has parallels to the notion of natural law.[62]

Sachedina tackles the ambiguities of the Koran on responsibility and conscience and uses the views of various Muslim theologians to illustrate his points. He then takes up apostasy and states – as Khadduri – that there are no Koranic passages that specifically prescribe the execution of apostates. By disentangling matters of conscience from politics and bringing out the ambiguities of the Koran on this, he proposes a fresh understanding of Islamic precepts and concludes that they are not categorical on this matter. He does not, in contrast to authors examined in section III, deny that the contradictions do exist, but attempts to resolve them; he does not discard the opposite point of view but constructively engages with it, and he does not try to project on to the Koran the notion of human rights, only to find therein ideas that would be potentially conducive to it.

Another author who can be considered an Islamic liberal is Asghar Ali Engineer. In his book on the *Rights of Women in Islam* Engineer points out that nowadays no one invokes the scripture to justify slavery and that the question of women is comparable to that of slavery.[63] He discusses the influence of sociological and historical factors upon Koranic interpretation and the *sharia*. He claims that 'there is a general thrust towards equality of the sexes in the Quran' and that 'Biological otherness, according to the Quran, does not mean unequal status for either sex. Biological functions must be distinguished from social functions'. He says that 'when the Quran gives man a slight edge over woman it clarifies that it is not due to any inherent weakness of the female sex, but to the social context'.[64]

Engineer carefully examines the language of the Koran and the verses from which each particular ruling regarding women has been derived. He disputes traditional understandings and contrasts them with the Koranic text seen in a different light. His method is typical of an important trend in Muslim feminist writings, which he draws on extensively (as he does on medieval theologians and jurists). He finds fault in all the points of inequality between men and women which have been justified by the Koran and various traditions. He concludes that women 'enjoy all their rights as individuals, not merely by virtue of being a mother, wife or daughter though such status would be considered for purposes of their inheritance'.[65] He attempts, in short, to separate Islam from patriarchy and enjoins Muslims to reform Islamic law by breaking the links between the two.

His account is not altogether without problems. He does not, for example, stress that even though the Koran may have shown a disapproval of certain institutions such as polygamy it did not prohibit them in principle. He also underplays the blatant inequality between the sexes that the Koranic verses – whatever one's understanding of the spirit of the holy book – in fact propound. This discredits his cause. In general, however, his methodology is convincing, and useful in defending women's rights and human rights in general in the context of Islam, because it is rooted in the historicity of the text of revelation and in the distinction between what may be perceived as the 'essence' of the religion as opposed to its particular injunctions.

A major contribution to the debate over reformism is by Abdullahi Ahmed An-Naim. He states, succinctly: 'Although it can easily be shown that certain aspects of *Shari'a*, traditional Islamic law, are inconsistent with some universal human rights, the purpose [of this chapter] is to illustrate that Islam itself can be consistent with and conducive to the achievement of, not only the present universal standards, but also the ultimate human right, namely the realisation of the originality and individuality of each and every person.'[66] The author here brings into the debate the concept of authenticity (on a personal level), and also makes the distinction between historical tradition and the Koran, which provides the framework for his analysis. The *sharia* 'violates most of the crucial civil and political rights provided for by the Universal Declaration of Human Rights'.[67] Even if *ijtihad* is applied, the problem of inequality of women and non-Muslims will not be solved because some texts in the Koran and *hadith* are explicitly discriminatory. The solution which An-Naim suggests is that of the Sudanese Ustaz Mahmud Muhammad Taha (executed by the Nimeiri regime in 1985): the Koran was revealed in two stages, the first, in Mecca, dealing with general moral and religious principles and the second, in Medina, being more specific and legalistic, because it was responding to a concrete situation. Only the first, according to An-Naim, must be taken as authoritative for all time. Apart from this most crucial point, which is the cornerstone of his argument, he states, secondarily, that the *sharia* was not expounded until the second and third centuries of Islam and was therefore influenced by the practices of generations of Muslim. It needs therefore to be reinterpreted to fit new circumstances.[68]

An-Naim develops his arguments in his major work *Towards an Islamic Reformation* by taking each of these issues in turn. First, he shows that 'the public law of *Shari'a* is not really divine law in the sense that all its specific principles and detailed rules were directly revealed by God'.[69] He restates his doubts about the adequacy of *ijtihad* in achieving reform within the framework of the *sharia* and describes this attempt as 'wishful thinking' for 'given the fundamental conception and detailed rules of the *Shari'a*, it is clear that the objectionable aspects cannot possibly be altered through the exercise of *ijtihad* as defined in historical *shari'a* for the simple reason that *shari'a* does not permit *ijtihad* in these matters because they are governed by clear and definite texts of the Qur'an and Sunna'. He is, however, concerned to find 'an Islamic way out of this deadlock', and his answer is the distinction between the two messages of Islam. It is urgent that this be done because, he argues, 'the founders of Islamic modernism [Afghani and Abduh] are somewhat disappointing in their attempts to generate concrete results for public law purposes'. He gives examples of the unconvincing methodology of attempts at reform pointing out that their fundamental methodological flaw is that they refer to those aspects of the Koran which are conducive to rights and ignore its opposite injunctions. He proposes taking these opposite injunctions into account and explains their existence by the need to serve the conditions of the time of the Prophet and of early Islam.[70] This author, in short, does not prescribe, like Engineer, a rereading of the Koran in its totality on the basis of a liberal spirit but suggests distinguishing between two parts of the Koran (the general and the particular), and accepting the perpetual legitimacy only of the former. This, he maintains, will give the force of law to reformed precepts (banning polygamy for example), because they would not be a matter of opinion in interpretation but of fact.

An-Naim proceeds to examine, on the basis of his proposed methodology, constitutional issues, criminal justice and international law and concludes by considering basic human rights. He bases his belief in the universality of human rights on the principle of reciprocity – a principle which, in his opinion, is shared by all major cultural traditions – which implies equal rights for all members within a society and in relations with other societies. The *sharia* did not apply this principle and 'denies women and non-Muslims the same degree of honour and human dignity that it guarantees to Muslim men'.[71] It should therefore be discarded. He emphasises this again in his discussion of Ayatollah Khomeini's *fatwa* against the writer Salman Rushdie: 'Although I know this [punishment, possibly by death, of apostasy] to be the position under the *Shari'a*, I am unable *as a Muslim* to accept the law of apostasy as part of the law of Islam today' [italics in the original].[72]

Various other thinkers have confronted the question of reform in

Islam, with similar aims and mixed results. Mohammed Arkoun's paper *Rethinking Islam Today* attempts to deal with the connections of Islam and modern culture. He asserts that 'historicity is the unthinkable and the unthought in medieval thought'[73] and argues that these boundaries, which still exist, must be brought down and a new exegesis attempted, on the basis of new knowledge. Jacques Berque, in his book *Relire le Coran,* discusses a broad range of issues in rereading the text of revelation – his comments on *fitra* and its relationship with human freedom being particularly pertinent to our subject.[74] I will refer to other such reformist thinkers in the chapters on Egypt and Tunisia, and must postpone further discussion until then.

This examination of thinkers who attempt a genuine resolution of the contradictions between Islam and human rights principles indicates that such an exercise must not concentrate narrowly on the Koranic text or the *sharia* but take on board broader issues. We need to summarise these essential prerequisites for a liberal Islam.

First is the distinction between two perspectives on Islam. One, of the religion as a sacred, unchanging, eternally determined body of rules. The other, of Islam as capable of development and transformation through time without this incurring a violation of its essential 'spirit'. The tension between the two approaches runs through Islamic thought in modern times (the consciousness of 'change' being inherent in the very definition of modernity). Without adopting the latter view Islam cannot be reconciled with international human rights principles. If the literal word of the Koran and the traditional *sharia* are accepted as prescriptive, there is no room for conciliation. Similarly, if society at the time of the Prophet is posited as the ideal, the outcome is sterility in liberal thought, even if that ideal is described as democratic. In general terms, despite being anathema to many Muslims, the historicity of Islam and of the revelation must be accepted if a convincing conciliation of Islamic and human rights principles is to be achieved. This means a recognition that the revelation was appropriate for the time of the Prophet and not, in its literal form, for all time.

It in turn necessitates a reinstatement of the right to interpret the Koran and the recognition that the 'door' of *ijtihad* was never really closed. *Ijtihad,* however, is a necessary but not sufficient condition for a liberal interpretation of Islam. Some of the world's most ardent Islamic fundamentalists – Hassan Turabi primary among them – have endorsed it and proceeded to interpret Islam in an illiberal way.[75] For *ijtihad* to result in a liberal interpretation of the Koran it must be coupled with a liberal impulse.

A third crucial prerequisite for a liberal interpretation of Islam is that the law must have the purpose of serving humankind and must therefore be adaptable to its needs. This is very different from the traditional view of the law as existing in order to 'serve God' so to speak, through realising the divine will on earth. But, again, this condition is necessary but not sufficient for a liberal interpretation because serving the public interest can be used as means of control. Khomeini, for example, argued in 1988 that the state has the right to 'destroy a mosque' if the public interest (*maslaha*) requires it.[76]

Intolerance does not principally stem from the details of Islamic law and the Koran – whether this point is compatible with that universal human right or not; nor from the domain and scope of Islamic law – whether it should cover some or all aspects of life, personal and public.[77] Rather, it hinges on the perceived *purpose* and *source* of law. If the law is seen as an immutable divine imperative – serving God, not man, and coming from God directly, without human intervention – the law becomes intolerant, whatever its particular rules, partly because those who execute the law cannot be held accountable. This is what happened in Iran after 1979.[78] Once respect for an Islamic humanism becomes the driving force, however, Islamic law can be vested with divine sanction without becoming intolerant.

The Manichean way of thought that juxtaposes 'Islam' and 'human rights' as two opposing absolutes is only one viewpoint. An alternative consists of human rights principles being encompassed in and informing the understanding of the *essence* of Islamic religion (given that human rights principles are indeed absolutes). This eliminates the juxtaposition between the divine and the human being by resting on a belief in the innate goodness of the individual (the absence of the notion of original sin in Islam, noted above, could strengthen such a conception). The latter becomes the true vicegerent or *khilafah* of God on earth. Adopting such a viewpoint would place the debate on authenticity, which is currently raging in the

Muslim and especially the Arab world, on quite a different basis. Because of the historical connection between Islam and Arab civilisation, the concept of authenticity often involves the defence of Islamic and/or Arabic identity in opposition to the West, and the values it represents. Once these values (among which are human rights) are dissociated from the West, the debate can assume quite a different form. Authenticity in the Muslim world can be reconceptualised once a humanist Islam provides its foundation.

Chapter 1 argued that belief in human rights – in the sanctity and freedom of the individual – involves an indemonstrable set of principles which either one shares or does not share. Chapter 2 argues that these principles do not necessarily contradict a faith in the God of Islam, but only some understandings of this faith and of this God. If my argument is persuasive, and if such conciliation is a possibility at an abstract level, our next question must be what has happened to it in the historical reality of Muslim societies – and why. In other words, what we must look for is the existence – or not – of a *liberal impulse* in specific Muslim societies, that would inform the understanding of the Islamic religion. One of the cornerstones of this book is that the causes for the existence of this liberal impulse, or lack thereof, must be sought, not in the text of the Koran or in the *sharia*, but elsewhere. This will be the purpose of Chapters 3 to 5.

V

Before proceeding to those chapters, however, we need to clarify some key terms. One argument that is often brought to bear in discussions on Islam and liberalism conerns the weight of the religious and political intellectual tradition in the Muslim world. More specifically, it is argued that the reason why illiberal interpretations of Islam have been the rule rather than the exception in the Muslim (and in particular the Arab) world is because 'reason' did not become predominant over revelation at any time during Islamic intellectual history.[79] The marginalisation of the Mutazila is seen as the result (or cause), of the banishment of reason in religious matters and is often lamented as a lost opportunity for a rational culture to arise from within the

Islamic world. Similarly, the lack of a tradition of constitutionalism in Islamic societies is believed to be the reason why a liberal political culture has not developed.

These developments were important but they only beg the question. If that was the way legal, religious and political thought did develop, it must have served a purpose and constituted a necessary 'rationality' for the proper function of Muslim societies. We cannot judge whether a particular legal system or set of religious rules served a society well through the lenses of our own time.[80] Such a view would be quite irrelevant because it would mean transposing our terms of reference and our concerns to a pre-modern age, whose links with and influences on the present time are quite indirect.

In seeking answers to modern concerns, especially on the individual and his or her rights, we must focus on the period from the nineteenth century onwards, when the advent of modernity presented an inescapable challenge to Islamic thought and to Muslim societies as a whole. Through colonisation, wars, trade, its increasing incorporation into a world capitalist system, the emergence of the nation-state and, crucially, the spread of ideas, the Middle East was tightly integrated into a global network.[81] It was forced to respond and engage with the two principal, defining notions of modernity: the inescapability of change and the centrality of the individual.[82] As the aspects of life defined by tradition narrowed, the intellectual heritage underwent transformative permutations.

In modern times insistence on respect for 'tradition' and its prescriptions is often not the direct outcome of a continuum with a pre-modern world which weighs heavily upon Muslim societies and determines their thought and institutions. Rather, 'tradition' is reconceptualised and reinvented and only as such does it play a central role in current debates. Its centrality in such debates is not, that is, evidence of the potency of a traditional world but rather one of the many elements which define modernity. Pre-modern history has a role but is mediated through current societal concerns. It may therefore be more useful to refer to 'traditionalist' rather than 'traditional' political or religious thought[83] – and even that is being increasingly displaced and marginalised (as in the case of Tabandeh's ideas). Centre stage in twentieth-century Islamism belongs increasingly to two prototypical trends: Islamic modernists and later liberals – and Islamic fundamentalists.[84]

The two are closely connected and this is why the central figure of Islamic modernism, Muhammad Abduh, is seen also as a precursor of fundamentalism. Both trends seek to reform Islam. Both are scripturalist, in the sense of advocating a return to the text of revelation to answer all questions – therefore by passing tradition. Both advocate *ijtihad* (and *ijtihad*, as I stressed above, can be both a reactionary and a progressive tool). Both, that is, engage with the notion of change and perceive the individual as the medium for a redefinition of Islam.

Where they diverge is on the purposes they seek to serve. Islamist liberals, feminists, modernists – all the terms are relevant here – accept the need for change and view it as a positive development: change means progress. They also seek, in tune with a liberal impulse, to liberate the individual and give him or her a central place in religious and political thought. They view the law as a means of serving the needs of humankind and of society and divine revelation as accessible to human reason. The fundamentalist impulse is the reverse. Change is seen as a negative development and there is an urge to reverse it. The individual must be subsumed to the collectivity or to the will of God even though he or she is the vehicle of reform (in the sense that social reform comes through personal regeneration).[85] This is different from a traditional outlook which has no conception of or interest in either the notions of change or the individual.

Nothing exemplifies more clearly the profound ambiguity of modernity. For the fundamentalists' reaction to it, their anti-modernism, is as much a modern phenomenon as its approval.[86] It can be placed in a universal context of Christian, Jewish, Hindu and other fundamentalisms. It is part of a global response, even revolt, against modernity, rather than an inevitable outcome of Islamic history.[87] The two Islamist trends battling over the fate of society and Islam in the Middle East constitute the parallels to the two children of modernity in the Western world: liberalism and totalitarianism.

The ambiguities between the two trends and their close links have been illustrated in Leonard Binder's reading of Sayyid Qutb, the Islamist writer who provided the inspiration of extremist fundamentalists in Egypt and beyond.[88] According to Binder, Qutb advocates the anarchy of believers. For him the individual is the medium of a reformed society and has a direct relationship with the text of revelation through an aesthetic rather than legalistic experience. But Binder, in arguing that a convergence of fundamentalism and liberalism may be Qutb's eventual contribution, forces his point and fails to grasp the deep gulf separating Qutb from Islamic liberalism. Qutb's idealism, which discards the practical working out of individual freedom, is more conducive to a repressive than to a liberating ideology.

Section V has made these distinctions for their own sake but also as a prelude to the discussion of Egyptian and Tunisian politics. They provide a justification for the choice of historical periods for this study and explain the choice of nation-states as case studies. The response of the Middle East to the advent of the modern world has been chaotic, as it has been in all cultures and societies. Everything is up for grabs, including the definitions of Islam and human rights, modernity and authenticity. New groups and individuals continuously add their voices to the debate, each pronouncing a different opinion on what these terms entail. The outcome of this debate is open-ended. Political and social change ensures that the views that predominate at any one time are constantly shifting. To understand this process and its implications will be the aim of subsequent chapters.

Notes

1. Said, E., *Orientalism* (London: Penguin Books, 1978).

2. Ibid., pp. 122–3.

3. Ahmad, A., *In Theory: Classes, Nations, Literatures* (London: Verso, 1992), Chapter 5.

4. Said, op.cit., p. 272.

5. See Geertz, C., *Islam Observed: Religious Development in Morocco and Indonesia* (Chicago, IL: University of Chicago Press, 1968) and Rodinson, M., *Islam and Capitalism* (London: Allen Lane, 1974, translated by B. Pearce), for cogent examples of the malleability of Islamic doctrine and evidence of the transformations and permutations religion undergoes when adopted by particular societies.

6. For examples of contradictory views on this issue compare Lewis, B.,

The Political Language of Islam (Chicago, IL: University of Chicago Press, 1988), with Piscatori, J. P. (ed.), *Islam in the Political Process* (Cambridge: Cambridge University Press in association with the Royal Institute of International Affairs, 1983); Halliday, F. and Alavi, H., 'Introduction', in Halliday, F. and Alavi, H. (eds), *State and Ideology in the Middle East and Pakistan* (Basingstoke: Macmillan Education, 1988); Ayubi, N., *Political Islam: Religion and Politics in the Arab World* (London: Routledge, 1991); and Mozaffari, M., 'Islam and Civil Society' in Ferdinand, K. and Mozaffari, M. (eds), *Islam: State and Society* (London and Riverdale, MD: Curzon Press and the Riverdale Company, 1988).

7. Schacht, J., *An Introduction to Islamic Law* (Oxford: Clarendon Press, 1964) and Coulson, N. J., *A History of Islamic Law* (Edinburgh: Edinburgh University Press, 1964).

8. Bannerman, P., *Islam in Perspective: A Guide to Muslim Society, Politics and the Law* (London: Routledge for the Royal Institute of International Affairs, 1988), pp. 46-9. On the Shia see Enayat, H., *Modern Islamic Political Thought: The Response of the Shi'i and Sunni Muslims to the Twentieth Century* (Basingstoke: Macmillan Education, 1982), Chapters 1 and 5.

9. Piscatori, J. P., *Islam in a World of Nation-States* (Cambridge: Cambridge University Press, in association with the Royal Institute of International Affairs, 1986), pp. 3-10 and Bannerman, P., op.cit., Chapter 2 and especially pp. 32–3. I am grateful to Robin Ostle for emphasising this point and its importance.

10. Piscatori, J. P., 'Human Rights in Islamic Political Culture' in Thompson, K. W. (ed.), *The Moral Imperatives of Human Rights: A World Survey* (Washington D.C.: University Press of America, 1980) p. 142.

11. Tamadonfar, M., *The Islamic Polity and Political Leadership* (Boulder, CO: Westview Press, 1989), p. 128.

12. Piscatori, 'Human Rights in Islamic Political Culture', op.cit., p. 144.

13. Rosen, L., *The Anthropology of Justice: Law as Culture in Islamic Society* (Cambridge: Cambridge University Press, 1989), p. 74.

14. Khadduri, M., *The Islamic Conception of Justice* (Baltimore, MD: Johns Hopkins University Press, 1984), p. 233. See also Piscatori, 'Human Rights in Islamic Political Culture', op.cit., pp. 139–42.

15. Esposito, J. L., *Islam: The Straight Path* (New York: Oxford University Press, 1988), p. 31.

16. Sachedina, A. A., 'Freedom of Conscience and Religion in the Qur'an' in Little, D., Kelsay, J. and Sachedina, A. A., *Human Rights and the Conflict of Cultures: Western and Islamic Perspectives on Religious Liberty* (Columbia, SC: South Carolina University Press, 1988), p. 57. This work will be discussed in section IV below. Mortimer, E., in 'Islam and Human Rights' in *Index on Censorship*, 5/83, p. 5, argues that 'Indubitably Islam contains within it the

concept of natural law, and hence of natural rights.' And he continues: 'Like the American constitution and many other Western authorities it interprets these rights as God-given.'

17.   Piscatori, 'Human Rights in Islamic Political Culture', op.cit., p. 143.

18.   Coulson, N. J., 'The State and the Individual in Islamic Law' in *International and Comparative Law Quarterly* (Vol. 6, Part 1, January 1957), pp. 49–60.

19.   'Slay them wherever you find them'. *The Koran*, translated with notes by Dawood, N. J., (London: Penguin, 1990), 2:190, p. 29.

20.   Ibid., 2:255 , p. 38.

21.   Malik, M. I., 'The Concept of Human Rights in Islamic Jurisprudence' in *Human Rights Quarterly* (Vol. 3, No. 3, Summer 1981), p. 58.

22.   Nasr, S. H., *Traditional Islam in the Modern World* (London: Kegan Paul International, 1987), pp. 27–33.

23.   Hollenbach, D., 'Human Rights and Religious Faith in the Middle East: Reflections of a Christian Theologian' in *Human Rights Quarterly* (Vol. 4, No. 1, Spring 1982), p. 106.

24.   See An-Naim, A. A., 'Religious Minorities under Islamic Law and the Limits of Cultural Relativism' in *Human Rights Quarterly* (Vol. 9, No. 1, February 1987), pp. 1–18, for minorities in general.

25.   The literature on women and Islam is extensive. For an introduction, see: Kandiyoti, D. (ed.), *Women, Islam and the State* (Basingstoke: Macmillan, 1991); Hijab, N., *Womanpower: The Arab Debate on Women at Work* (Cambridge: Cambridge University Press, 1988); Beck, L. and Keddie, N. R. (eds), *Women in the Muslim World* (Cambridge, MA: Harvard University Press, 1978), especially Chapters 1 and 2; *La non-discrimination à l' égard des femmes entre la Convention de Copenhague et le discours identitaire* (Colloque Tunis 13-16 Janvier 1988, UNESCO et CERES, Université de Tunis, 1989); and Boullata, I. J., *Trends and Issues in Contemporary Arab Thought* (Albany, NY: State University of New York Press, 1990), Chapter 5.

26.   Keddie, N. R., 'The Rights of Women in Contemporary Islam' in Rouner, L. S. (ed.), *Human Rights and the World's Religions* (Notre Dame, IN: University of Notre Dame Press, 1988), pp. 81–3. Keddie makes the further point that when Islam spread outside the Middle East the position of women, traditionally freer, remained so.

27.   Islam did however regulate or even limit slavery. Owners of slaves were urged to emancipate them, to treat them well and to avoid enslaving free men. See for example 24: 33 in *The Koran*, p. 249.

28.   Bannerman, op.cit., pp. 25–6.

29.   Khadduri, op.cit., p. 238. The views of Sachedina, op.cit., are similar.

30. See Donnelly, J., 'Human Rights and Human Dignity: An Analytic Critique of Non-Western Conceptions of Human Rights' in *American Political Science Review* (Vol. 76, No. 2, June 1982), pp. 303–16.

31. These three texts are critically examined (among others), in Mayer, A. E., *Islam and Human Rights: Tradition and Politics* (London and Boulder, CO: Pinter Publishers and Westview Press, 1991). The approach and comprehensive critique contained in Mayer's book have informed parts of this section.

32. *Islamic Council: What It Stands For* (pamphlet), pp. 25–43. The Islamic Council is, strictly speaking, a non-governmental organisation but its views reflect official positions closely. Note that, as this is a pamphlet, no page numbers will be given for quotations in subsequent paragraphs. Mawdudi, A. A., *Human Rights in Islam* (Lahore: Islamic Publications, 1977). Tabandeh, S., *A Muslim Commentary on the Universal Declaration of Human Rights* (Iran: 1966, translated by F. J. Goulding).

33. See Mayer, op.cit., pp. 104–7 for examples.

34. The quotations in this paragraph are contained in Mawdudi, A. A., op.cit., pp. 5-7.

35. Mayer, op.cit.; see pp. 114, 117–120, 158–9 for examples of such omissions.

36. Mawdudi, op.cit., pp. 8–10.

37. Ibid., pp. 14–21.

38. Ibid., pp. 22–34.

39. Tabandeh, op.cit., pp. 15–25.

40. Ibid., pp. 35–67.

41. Ibid., pp. 70–4.

42. Ibid., p. 85.

43. *Summary of World Broadcasts* (1174 A/6, 11 September 1991).

44. *Summary of World Broadcasts* (1821 MED/5, 16 October 1993).

45. Ibn al-Husayn, Zayn al-Abidin Ali, *The Treatise on Rights* (Qum: Foundation of Islamic Cultural Propagation in the World, 1411 Hijri Year, translated by W. C. Chittick,), pp. 5–18.

46. Sherif, S., *Women's Rights in Islam* (London: Ta-Ha Publishers, 1989), pp. 2–3.

47. Khan, S. M., *Why Two Woman Witnesses?* (London: Ta-Ha Publishers, 1993), p. i. The author tries to show through 'logical explanations' and 'scientific evidences' that 'In woman deception is almost physiological ...' [sic].

48. Said, A. A., 'Human Rights in Islamic Perspectives' in Pollis, A. and Schwab, P. (eds), *Human Rights: Cultural and Ideological Perspectives* (New York: Praeger, 1979), p. 87.

49. Said, A. A., 'Precept and Practice of Human Rights in Islam' in *Universal*

Human Rights (Vol. 1, No. 1, January–March 1979), p. 73.

50. Cooper, J., 'Human Rights: Towards an Islamic Framework' in *Gulf Report* (No. 34, October 1993), pp. 17–23.

51. *The Iranian Journal* (Vol. 3, No. 4, Winter 1991/92).

52. Pirzada, S., 'Concept of Islamic State and Human Rights in Islam', in ibid., p. 681.

53. Turabi, H., lecture at the Royal Institute of International Affairs, London, 28 April 1992.

54. Turabi, H., 'The Islamic State' in Esposito, J. L., (ed.), *Voices of Resurgent Islam* (New York: Oxford University Press, 1983), p. 244–5.

55. Ibid., p. 250. Only a few texts have been selected here for discussion but the list of publications on human rights and democracy in Islam which distort the meaning of human rights or fail to resolve the pertinent contradictions is quite long. Some examples include: Hussain, S. S., *Human Rights in Islam* (New Delhi: Kitab Bhavan, 1990); *Human Rights in Islam. Report of Seminar Held in Kuwait, 1980* (International Commission of Jurists, 1982). Bani-Sadr, A. A., *Human Rights in Islam* (Arab Encyclopedia House, no date) is a half-way house. He papers over many of the problems and this subtracts from the clearly liberal spirit of the book. See also Hirsch, E. (ed.), *Islam et droits de l'homme* (Paris: Librairie des Libertés, 1984) for a collection of essays from various standpoints.

56. See Donnelly, op.cit., especially pp. 306–7.

57. In the case of women 'equality before God' is used as a roundabout way to dismiss inequality on earth. Simone de Beauvoir in *The Second Sex* (London: Picador-Pan Books, 1988, translated by H. M. Parsley), has expressed this eloquently in the context of the Catholic religion but her words are relevant to some views of Islam too: 'On the human plane she [the woman] thus appears to draw her grandeur from her very subordination. But in the eyes of God she is a perfectly autonomous being.' (p. 259); 'In modern civilisation, which - even for woman - has a share in promoting freedom, religion seems less an instrument of constraint than an instrument for deception. Woman is asked in the name of God not so much to accept her inferiority as to believe that, thanks to Him, she is the equal of the lordly male.' And 'although subordinated to the law of men by the will of God Himself, woman none the less finds in Him a mighty refuge from them ... Why remodel this world which God Himself created?' (p. 633).

58. Hjarpe, J., 'The Contemporary Debate in the Muslim World on the Definition of "Human Rights"' in Ferdinand and Mozaffari (eds), op.cit., p. 37. Hjarpe makes the point that some of these human rights schemes are apologetic and seek to present an alternative to 'Western' ideas, but in fact

testify to the prestige of the Universal Declaration of Human Rights by mirroring its pattern.

59. Khadduri, op.cit., p. 234.

60. Ibid., p. 238.

61. Sachedina, op.cit., pp. 55–6.

62. Ibid., p. 64.

63. Engineer, A. A., *The Rights of Women in Islam* (London: C. Hurst, 1992), p. 2.

64. Ibid., pp. 44–5.

65. Ibid., p. 144.

66. An-Naim, A. A., 'A Modern Approach to Human Rights in Islam: Foundations and Implications for Africa' in Welch, C. E. and Meltzer, R. I. (eds), *Human Rights and Development in Africa* (Albany, NY: State University of New York Press, 1984), p. 75.

67. Ibid., p. 81.

68. An-Naim, 'Religious Minorities under Islamic Law and the Limits of Cultural Relativism,' op.cit., pp. 15–16.

69. An-Naim, A. A., *Towards an Islamic Reformation: Civil Liberties, Human Rights, and International Law* (Syracuse, NY: Syracuse University Press, 1990), p. 11.

70. Ibid., pp. 50–63.

71. Ibid., pp. 162–4.

72. Ibid., p. 183.

73. Arkoun, M., *Rethinking Islam Today* (Washington D.C.: Center for Contemporary Arab Studies, Georgetown University, Occasional Paper Series, 1987), p. 11.

74. Berque, J., *Relire le Coran* (Paris: Albin Michel, 1993), p. 98. There are many authors who reinterpret Islam along the liberal lines described in this section. See, for some further examples: Laroui, A., *Islam et modernité* (Paris: La Découverte, 1987); Nazir-Ali, M., *The Roots of Islamic Tolerance: Origin and Development* (Oxford Project for Peace Studies, Paper No.26, 1990); Green, A. H. (ed.), *In Quest of an Islamic Humanism: Arabic and Islamic Studies in Memory of Mohamed al-Nowaihi* (Cairo: The American University in Cairo Press, 1984); Amin, H., *Le Livre du Musulman désemparé* (Paris: La Découverte, 1992, translated by R. Jacquemond); Cherfils, C., *L'Esprit de modernité dans le monotheisme islamique* (Saint-Ouen: Centre Abaad, 1992); Ferjani, M. C., *Islamisme, laïcite et droits de l'homme* (Paris: L'Harmattan, 1991). See also Boullata, op.cit., Chapters 3 and 4 for a discussion.

75. Sidahmed, A. S., 'Sudan: Ideology and Pragmatism' in Sidahmed, A. S., and Ehteshami, A., (eds), *Islamic Fundamentalism* (Boulder, CO: Westview

Press, 1996), p. 189. Note that Turabi also distinguishes between the 'eternal' and the 'changing' elements in Islam but again this does not render his discourse more liberal.

76.   Kazemi, F., 'Civil Society and Iranian Politics' in Norton, A. R., (ed.), *Civil Society in the Middle East* (Leiden: E. J. Brill, 1996), Vol. 2, pp.123–4.

77.   Even if Islam is banished from the political sphere, this could conceivably leave family law untouched, condemning women to perpetual inequality.

78.   Binder, L., *Islamic Liberalism: A Critique of Development Ideologies* (Chicago, IL: University of Chicago Press, 1988), pp. 156–7, makes this point forcefully: 'The insistence that Islam unites religion and politics and that Islam is freedom, justice and equality by definition, even if intended to break down the barriers between traditional Islamic political practices and the modern European political ideal, can result in an illiberal regime'. And: 'The gravest danger to liberal government arises when the application of a general *Shari'a* rule to particular circumstances is given the sacred character of the word of God. The Iranian experience suggests that this is more likely to be the case when the state fears opposition and is anxious to consolidate power.'

79.   See for example, Lewis, B., *The Arabs in History* (London: Hutchinson, 1970), pp. 139–43.

80.   See for example Kedourie, E., *Politics in the Middle East* (Oxford: Oxford University Press, 1992), who does exactly that.

81.   See Hodgson, M. G. S., *The Venture of Islam* (Chicago, IL: University of Chicago Press, 1974), Vol. 3, especially Book 6 on 'The Islamic Heritage in the Modern World', for a fascinating account of this period. My views have been greatly influenced by Hodgson, and particularly by his analysis of the 'Great Western Transmutation' and its universal impact.

82.   'Modernity' of course implies a host of other ideas but, in my view, these are the two most important ones.

83.   Hodgson does not use these particular terms but notes that advocates of what he calls 'neo-*Shar'ism*' in the nineteenth and twentieth centuries rejected or lost touch with the Islamic heritage and concentrated on the *Sharia*, the one focal point with which they could identify and through which they could dissociate themselves from the West. Islam was thus 'reconceived'. See Hodgson, op. cit., pp. 386–92.

84.   For the interrelatedness of these developments see Keddie, N. R., 'Ideology, Society and the State in Post-Colonial Muslim Societies' in Halliday and Alavi (eds), op.cit., especially p. 16: 'Islamism is not as strong in states which are *really* largely traditional and have not experienced a major Western cultural impact, though such states are increasingly rare as Westernisation impinges almost everywhere.'

85. There is a parallel here with the social composition of fundamentalist movements: membership may result in the subjugation of the individual to the group and to God but it is a result of *individual choice* by people who are far removed from traditional life. This is why these movements tend to be principally urban phenomena. On this point see Chapters 3–5.

86. Berman, M., *All That Is Solid Melts into Air: The Experience of Modernity* (London: Verso, 1982), p. 15, defines being modern as 'to be part of a universe in which, as Marx said, 'all that is solid melts into air'. According to Berman 'this feeling has engendered numerous nostalgic myths of pre-modern Paradise Lost'.

87. Lawrence, B., *Defenders of God: The Fundamentalist Revolt against the Modern Age* (London: I. B. Tauris, 1990).

88. Binder, op.cit., Chapter 5.

3

Egypt, 1920s–1930s

I

After critically examining a number of attempts to reconcile Islam with the principles of human rights at the intellectual level, and arriving at the conclusion that such a project can indeed be viable, given certain conditions, we turn to three historical cases. It is not possible to bring the history of Islam as a whole into the picture, because that would entail the detailed study of a great number of disparate societies over a period of fourteen centuries. I propose, nevertheless, that to examine three cases is sufficient to disprove two commonly held views. Firstly, that once Islam is allowed a part in the political process its contribution will be necessarily detrimental to human rights. Secondly, that Muslim societies tend to be illiberal societies is due to the essential nature of the Islamic religion.

In all three cases that I have selected the conditions for the rise of an Islamic liberalism were favourable. In throwing light on the reasons why these conditions did not bear fruit – in the sense of giving rise to a fully-fledged Islamic liberalism that would become deeply rooted in the social conscience – the three chapters that follow will show that an approach which gives primacy to social, economic and political factors in explaining the emergence of political culture, in discrete Muslim societies, is more beneficial for our understanding of Islamic issues than generalisations about Islam. The thesis against cultural essentialism will thus be strengthened. The exposition and defence of the anti-essentialist thesis is important for our understanding of Islam as religion and culture – but even more vitally so for our understanding of international relations in general.

The international dimension is crucial in explaining the reasons why human rights principles became relevant to societies which did not have a pioneering role in conceiving and elaborating them. This does not entail the simplistic proposition that Egyptians, for example, 'adopted' European political and philosophical ideas or that these ideas were 'exported' by Europe to the Middle East (which in any case fails to explain why, among a host of ideas, these and not others were adopted). The processes were much more subtle. It was the spread of the concept of the nation-state, the structures of state authority, and of capitalism, which made the principles of human rights relevant to political reality in the Middle East. At a more fundamental level, changing conceptions of space and time, of the individual and of the notion of change, created the mentalities or frames of mind that could accommodate human rights principles. Ideas which were European in inspiration interacted with political realities and *choices* by political actors in the Muslim societies under consideration. Disparate societies were thus brought into the universal context of modernity, which cannot be claimed as the exclusive product or property of any single culture or civilisation. To bring these processes into the discussion of international politics, and recognise their importance, could contribute towards a reordering of the questions that international relations prioretises as a discipline.

The reasons for the choice of Egypt in the 1920s and 1930s as a useful example in support of my argument are many. During the nineteenth century, the Egyptian state began to be transformed into a modern machine of administration and control, first by its own rulers and later by them in conjunction with the British colonisers. During the same period (or even earlier, in the eighteenth century), the country became integrated into a world capitalist system, mainly through the export of cotton. Nationalist and democratic constitutionalist ideas were gradually coming to the fore, as they did in other parts of the Ottoman Empire at the time. Towards the end of the nineteenth century and the beginning of the twentieth, Egypt was the centre of a major intellectual movement towards a modernist reformist Islam in the Arab world. These developments provided the setting for a limited yet important experiment in constitutional democracy in the 1920s and 1930s, on which this chapter will focus. During those years, it appeared that a liberal polity – encompassing a liberal vision of Islam – was beginning to emerge. By the late 1930s and especially in the 1940s, however, this potential had waned and Islamic fundamentalism seemed to be gaining ground over Islamic liberalism. At the same time, liberal democracy as a whole became discredited.

In short, Egyptian society at the time under consideration contained all the factors which are deemed to be important for the argument. The interaction of all these elements and their role in explaining the birth and viability (or otherwise) of Islamic liberalism will be considered. The aim will be to explore ideas surrounding human rights and authenticity, even though at the time these notions may not have been considered under these precise labels. While pursuing the anti-essentialist argument, and drawing attention to the growing pervasiveness of a way of thought accompanying the spread of modernity and modern state structures, we will shed light on many of the points made in Chapters 1 and 2 above. For example, on the close interconnectedness of the private and the public and the impossibility of separating the two in instituting a political liberalism; on dispelling the notion that the existence of secularism or secularist ideologies is the only safeguard for the protection of human rights; on the distinction between understandings of Islam that merely purport to respect human rights and others that adequately do so; on the non-traditional nature of both Islamic liberalism and Islamic fundamentalism, and on the ambivalent role of the state as regards the promotion of rights. These questions will be addressed not only in this chapter but in Chapters 4 and 5 as well.

II

To understand the 1920s and 1930s in Egypt we must look as far back as the mid-eighteenth century. It was then that various new forces of were beginning to affect Egyptian society. Here it will be usefull to look at two books which deal with the beginnings of modernity and capitalism in Egypt during the eighteenth and nineteenth centuries:

Islamic Roots of Capitalism by Peter Gran and *Colonising Egypt* by Timothy Mitchell.[1] Gran's aims are multiple, but primary among them is to prove that the stark juxtaposition between a vibrant European culture and a stagnant Islamic world, passive recipient of ideas and material influences, does not hold. He disputes the conventional picture of eighteenth century Egypt as a period of 'chaos and anarchy in which little happened of historical interest' and shows that 'internal forces were pushing the country towards a capitalist transformation long before the advent of the Western entrepreneur'.[2] This indigenous development was thwarted by the forcefulness of Western capitalism, which relegated Egypt to a position of dependency in the international capitalist system. Gran, however, argues that the Third World was, through its dependent position, an indispensable part of the global, and therefore Western, capitalist transformation. He states, 'the industrial revolution was a global event, and I question the strong tradition in the West to assume a proprietary relationship to it.'[3]

Gran's analysis illustrates the view that there are many ways for a society to relate to its past and that the notion of authenticity is a fluid and indeterminate one. It is impossible to test his hypothesis regarding the Egyptian capitalist transformation but it is nevertheless useful as an intellectual challenge. Would the notion of authenticity be as starkly defined in opposition to the West if certain developments, specifically capitalism, had arisen indigenously? How is authenticity to be defined in the context of a global system that is so tightly interdependent and in which social and economic developments interact with intellectual traditions or the selective choice of such traditions?

The theme of Timothy Mitchell's book is the captivity engendered by capitalism and modernity. This is a fascinating book, inspired by the work of Michel Foucault. It describes the subtle processes by which Egypt was colonised and controlled, by the British and more abstractly by capitalism itself. The strength of the book lies in its detailed analysis of how this was achieved through changing ideas of space in architecture, and the use of maps and plans; by changes in pedagogical methods; novel notions of truth as representation; a sharp shift in the conception of language and the written word, expressed in the introduction of the printing press, newspapers and books, and the 'capture' of the individual body through the promotion of hygiene and health. Accompanying these subtle changes was a new conception of politics which sought to strengthen authority by atomising society and controlling individuals, each to be 'separately cared for, schooled, disciplined and kept clean in an economy of individual order and well-being'.[4] A new type of political authority – embodied in the modern state – thus arose, meticulous and continuous, seeking to reorder and dominate.

Mitchell brings into relief the profound changes brought about by colonisation and capitalism, whose vehicles were both foreign and local actors. He also emphasises the international dimensions of the revolutionary transformation of Egyptian society from the nineteenth century onwards, and analyses the process of its introduction into the modern world, and its corresponding modes of thought. As an indictment of liberalism, however – and this has been the normative position of Chapter 1 – it fails to convince. Liberalism is not a means of control and domination but the necessary shield of an individual, his or her *only* protection, in a society which has already been radically transformed into a modern one, by other forces. A second point of disagreement is with Mitchell's implicit view of a society which (except for its ruling classes) was passively being shaped by outside forces. My position, by contrast, is that the society's participation in the transformation was essential and indisputable. Such reappropriation of the Egyptians' active participation could allow for a redefinition of authenticity that is no longer in stark and sterile opposition to the West.

It is important, therefore, to be more precise on this last point of the Egyptians' role and we can begin with the economic sphere. Although the position of Egypt in the international market did seriously constrain economic realities, it did not wholly determine them, for it interacted with the history and conditions in the country itself and with the political decisions of its rulers who sought to safeguard the de facto, though not formal, independence it had acquired from the Ottoman empire. Thus, after the initial impact of market forces in mid-eighteenth century, the situation took a different turn under Muhammad Ali in the first half of the nineteenth. Muhammad Ali undertook to strengthen the state apparatus and the economy. He centralised both by reappropriating and redistributing land, promoting industry and monopolising trade. He and his successors, however, failed to make Egypt economically self-sufficient. The concentration of landed property in constantly expanding estates and the conversion of agriculture into a near monoculture may have contributed to the rise of living standards during the nineteenth century. But it also exposed Egypt further to the vagaries of a volatile international market in which it had a vulnerable position as an exporter of a single raw material, cotton.

Because of pressure, from the mid-nineteenth century onwards, from a Britain intent on free trade policies, Muhammad Ali's trade monopolies were dismantled. Industrialisation never took off in any major way because of the lack of essential managerial skills, investment, technology and raw materials; but also because cheaper European manufactures swamped the local market. Thus, the Egyptian economy in the last part of the nineteenth century was shaped by a combination of international pressures and later colonisation, the attempt by Egyptians to resist these (industry under Muhammad Ali served this purpose), and local conditions and limitations.[5]

Capitalist transformation – of a non-industrial kind – was initially undertaken by the state in the service of political ends. It was thereafter primarily continued by large landowning interests that cultivated and exported cotton. Non-Egyptian minorities rather than local merchants became the link with international markets. This is not to say that Egyptian Muslim merchants were non-existent or unimportant, nor did the importation of manufactured goods mean that local artisans and small scale industry no longer played a part in the economy.[6] The point is, rather, that because of Egypt's particular position in the international market and a constellation of domestic factors, the class that undertook to transform the economy and which became politically dominant was a landowning one.[7] Furthermore, because the majority of the population was a largely illiterate peasantry subject to a complex system of domination and control, and industrial workers were few and, until the early part of the twentieth century, politically unorganised, there was before 1919 no systematic pressure from these groups for economic and social rights and political representation. This is not to claim that liberalism and liberalisation in political life must necessarily follow the European pattern, only to note that in the case of Egypt it did not. It will be shown that political change in a liberal direction did take place, but was promoted by other social actors in the framework of a nationalist movement.

The second important point to note at this stage of the argument relates to state formation. Throughout the nineteenth century the administrative and extractive capacities of the Egyptian state were greatly enhanced.[8] Muhammad Ali started its 'Egyptianisation', which subsequently acquired greater momentum as Egyptian landowners supplanted the Turkish elite in key economic and administrative posts. Conscription, taxation, planning, schooling – as Mitchell discusses them – bound society ever closer to the state. State formation in nineteenth-century Egypt was as brutal and violent an affair as any other, but societal resistance in the first stages gave way to gradual integration, thus creating a potential for eventual political liberalisation and governmental accountability.

III

Rapid economic transformation, state formation, social changes and the threat and later reality of European imperialist domination, provided the framework for intellectual and political developments in Egypt. They influenced and stood in dynamic interaction with religious and political thought, which this and subsequent sections will analyse. This body of thought must be situated in two contexts. The first is of nationalist ideology in its broadest sense, as a desire for independence from a power, Britain, perceived as increasingly threatening. In its first stages, nationalist sentiment was not necessarily focused on the Egyptian nation-state but had pan-Islamic and pan-Ottoman connotations. It was only after the turn of the century, and in particular after the dissolution of the Ottoman Empire and the abolition of the caliphate by Atatürk in 1924, that it gradually became focused on Egypt as a separate entity.[9]

The second context was provided by the changing role of Islam.[10] Here the work of M. G. S. Hodgson (as partially expounded in the last chapter), is particularly useful because it describes the radical break experienced by the Muslim world with the advent of modernity in the nineteenth century. As a result of the challenge, many Muslims rejected their immediate past in favour of a distant and glorious future and became attached to the *sharia* as 'the one point at which they could clearly identify themselves as Muslims and dissociate themselves from the West.'[11] Islam was thus transformed, and the concern of its reformers became to improve society and withstand the European onslaught. It is in this way that nationalism and Islamic reformism were, from their inception, intimately connected in Egypt as complementary elements in the search for authenticity within the radically new parameters of the modern world.

This is the context within which we can trace novel conceptions of politics and of the individual and his or her rights. The body of political and religious thought (to be examined shortly) did not deal directly with 'human rights' in the twentieth-century terminology of the Universal Declaration. It nevertheless studied and pronounced on the principles underlying their philosophy: for example the concept of reason, the limitations on political authority, the conflict between individual freedom of thought and divine authority, the role of science and independent enquiry as opposed to revealed texts and the position of women and minorities in society.

The beginnings of reformist thought can be traced to the work of Rifa'a al-Tahtawi (1801–73), a major thinker and reformer. But the modern tradition of Islamic reformism firmly begins with Jamal al-Din 'al-Afghani', (1839–1897), a political activist and Islamic reformer who spent the years between 1871 and 1879 in Egypt.[12] Despite his pan-Islamic or pan-Ottoman appeals, Afghani was one of the first links in the chain of nationalist thought in the Middle East. But his even greater contribution was to show that resistance had to be carried out through political action and that such action could lie within the bounds of Islamic political tradition (a reformed tradition to be sure). This did not prevent him from viewing many Western ideas as worthy of emulation. The ambivalent relationship with Europe, its ambiguous impact on the notions of Muslim self-definition and its multifaceted links with Islamic reformism, as first expressed in Afghani, were from his time to become characteristic of all Islamic reformist trends.

The dual goal of strengthening religion and society, Afghani argued, was to be achieved by returning to the rationality of the Koran, to the sciences which thrived within Arab civilisation at its peak (and which were given thereafter to Europe), by reaffirming independent reasoning, *ijtihad*, in interpreting religious injunctions, by emphasising the notion of free will as opposed to predestination[13] and through constitutional government, in the sense of restricted autocratic rule. But he was also intent on emphasising that reason in itself was not sufficient as a social and moral guide unless complemented by religion, though in Islam, which was by its nature a rational religion, this would not be a contradiction.

The attempt to find a balance between the concept of reason and religious belief is not theoretically problematic as a foundation for liberal thought within Islam. It was other problems that bedeviled Afghani's thought in terms of its liberal potential (and the whole of reformist tradition as it later developed, partly on the foundations he constructed). For one thing, his position did not rest on a basis of trust in the innate goodness of the individual, but rather on a 'pessimism about human nature',[14] which had to be controlled and restricted. In the second palce, and as a partial corollary, Afghani insisted on religion providing a source of social cohesion and control, and in doing so showed himself to be bound by a fundamental social elitism. Thirdly, Afghani's progressive and innovative ideas, which could potentially ensure a respect for individual rights, were combined with a number of traditional concepts in a haphazard way.

The influence of Afghani on Muhammad Abduh (1849–1905), the central figure of Islamic modernism in Egypt at the turn of the century and beyond, will become apparent.[15] The two men collaborated closely but Abduh was more of a writer and thinker than a political activist. His thought was an attempt to reconcile Islam and modernity, reason and religion, the sovereignty of God and of the individual and human freedom with social strength and solidarity. The possibilities of a reconciliation between liberalism and Islam were discussed in Chapter 2. In Abduh we have one such attempt, which will be examined in subsequent paragraphs, although this examination is secondary to the main purpose of this chapter which is to describe the fate of his reformist legacy *in society and history*.

One of the starting points in Muhammad Abduh's thought was

the juxtaposition between Islam in society (a society in apparent decline), and modern ideas and culture, reflecting the European world. He perceived this duality in Egyptian law and education and in the attitudes of the people around him, who seemed increasingly to belong to two incommensurate worlds. He was intent on bridging the gap between those two worlds but not by denying the irreversible (as he saw it), march of modern ideas and institutions, nor by rejecting its many beneficial implications and values. Rather, he sought to prove that Islam was compatible with, and in fact encouraged, these modern values – reliance on human reason and its concomitant promotion of human welfare and respect for science and progress.

Abduh argued that in Islam reason and revelation are in harmony, and that the two could not contravene one another. 'If there appears to be a contradiction one or the other has been incorrectly understood.'[16] There are some matters – mostly metaphysical – which are beyond human understanding, but it is largely inability of individuals to correctly make use of their reason which prevents them from understanding. Abduh supported the notion of free will as opposed to predestination and put forward the elements of a natural law position. The individual can discover, through his faculty of reason, what is right and wrong. Reason and revelation are two alternative routes to truth.

Abduh distinguished between individuals in themselves and in groups, arguing that groups are guided much more clearly by 'considerations of collective self-interest rather than collective moral duty.'[17] Groups must follow the moral law, but this law is in keeping with reason and with the long-term advantage of the group and can be learnt from the study of history. Abduh accepted the notion of change and evolution in society and saw it as beneficial and necessary. He did not view political organisation as determined in all its details by Islamic doctrine but believed that it should evolve in accordance with the group's needs and in the light of reason, discovered and agreed on through consultation. He therefore advocated the merits of constitutional government, of individual rights and liberties and of limitations on political authority, which is essentially civil authority.[18]

The problematic element in Abduh's view of the political relevance of Islam was its preoccupation with unity in society – unity among citizens and between rulers and ruled – and the assumption that 'in the light of right reason conflicts of interest simply dissolve away'.[19] Such an assumption allowed Abduh to favour despotic, albeit just, rule (including British rule) as preparation for representative government because, before the latter could be introduced, the public had to be politically educated. The implicit elitism of this viewpoint was to be one of the major weaknesses of Islamic reformism, as I already mentioned in the case of Afghani. It is interesting that this attitude stemmed in no small measure not from traditional Islamic concepts, but from Abduh's faith in reason, whose 'light' would have to be provided to a populace steeped in ignorance. The parallel with European colonial attitudes in general is inescapable, and it must have had a role in Abduh's later career during which he became integrated in the British system of occupation.

The second reason why Abduh failed to insist on a comprehensive protection for the individual and citizen – what we would today term his or her human rights – was because he did not fully break with traditional reasoning. This, in part, explains the contradictions which characterise his and his successors' thought. For he may have made general statements on reason and individual freedom, but he did not expound in detail what they would entail in public life. He often used traditional terminology and showed a reluctance to draw a sharp line with past ways of reasoning. He also failed to make explicit the fact that some changes – in law for example – had to be instituted on the basis of principle rather than of expedience or past practice. This, it has been argued, constituted a lack of clear direction by the father of Islamic modernism and led to great confusion among his successors.[20] It allowed his mixed legacy to be appropriated by all kinds of people, from Westernising secularists to Islamic fundamentalists.

It may be that the quality of Abduh's thought was lacking in some respects and that it was timid in others. But Abduh represented the beginnings of a trend of thought which depended on those who followed in order to progress along reformist and ultimately liberal lines. Whether this happened or not may be related to the quality of his thought and its shortcomings. But it is, more importantly in my view, the result of what his successors *chose* to do with this legacy, how they used it in interaction with the society in which they lived.

IV

Abduh's career and thought developed in the context of the British occupation of Egypt or, as it came to be called, the 'veiled protectorate'. The British in Egypt after 1882 continued with the restructuring of the state administration and the transformation of the economy (except for industry and education which they neglected). Indebtedness and fiscal imbalances were remedied and the system of justice reorganised. Prosperity in the country as a whole increased, in a context of growing integration into the international economy. The British maintained the khedive in power – indeed khedive Tawfiq was restored to his throne with the support of the British in 1882, after the defeat of Urabi's proto-nationalist revolt – and, given that their occupation was at the time considered temporary, undertook to prepare Egyptians for self-rule. This, and plans for their eventual withdrawal, were not pursued with any vigour and by 1914 the reaction was becoming increasingly vehement.

The reaction followed two paths.[21] The first was represented by Mustafa Kamil, Muhammad Farid and the Nationalist Party, created in 1907, which – within the limits of the limited participation of the Egyptian population in the nationalist movement prior to 1914 – was by far the most popular movement.

Mustafa Kamil (1874–1908) was uncompromisingly opposed to British occupation and initially sought the help of the French and later the Ottomans to bring it to an end. He looked to the sultan and the preservation of the Ottoman Empire as a counterweight to the British but without implying that Egypt should fall under Ottoman rule again. In Kamil's thought, the land of Egypt was a higher object of devotion than anything else. The bonds of *wataniyya* (nationhood) were not restricted by language, religion or status; they were something other and stronger, which united ruler and ruled and Muslims and Copts.[22] He believed that Egypt must remain true to Islam, but an Islam correctly interpreted: 'the real Islam is patriotism and justice, activity and union, equality and tolerance.'[23]

Despite Kamil's emphasis on Islamic solidarity, and the ways in which the Nationalist Party after his untimely death in 1908 became associated with traditionalists and conservatives, he is considered the founder of modern Egyptian nationalism. Even if we concede that 'political sentiment in this period was of the kind that hardly distinguished religious belief from national consciousness,'[24] this trend in nationalist thought represented the true patriotic position at the time, of unconditional opposition to the British. The second trend, which is important not because of its popularity – limited before 1914 – but because it provided the nucleus of the post-1919 nationalist movement after the demise of the Nationalist Party, was not unambiguously opposed to the British occupation. This second trend was associated with Muhammad Abduh, Sa'd Zaghlul, Qasim Amin, Lutfi al-Sayyid, the Umma Party, created in 1907, and its newspaper *al-Jarida*.

The views of the *al-Jarida* group and of its intellectual continuation in the inter-war period, the Wafd, are often described as having centred on three concepts: secularism, nationalism, liberalism. This trend is said to have drawn in part on the legacy of Muhammad Abduh (one of the forms that this legacy took, the other being that of Rashid Rida and the Muslim Brotherhood, which will be examined in Section VI). The argument is that Abduh's position, resting on an ultimately untenable compromise between reason and religion, had the inevitable consequence of the secularisation of political thought, and that it unwittingly the grounds for its justification. This alleged eclipse of Islamic modernism as a potent intellectual and political force, and its replacement by a liberal nationalist position as the major vehicle for intellectual and political change in the 1920s and 1930s, is used as evidence of the unworkability of the intellectual marriage of liberalism and Islam and the intellectual failure of Islamic modernism.[25] The sharp division between Islam and secularism implies that nothing can occupy the space between the two, in other words that Islamic liberalism is unviable. Muslims can either be secular or obscurantist. Islam, in other words, is unreformable.

It is true, as I will show, that the major thinkers of the nation and the political forces they represented in the inter-war period were nationalists and liberals. It is also true that for them the Egyptian nation became the object of highest devotion and that Islam was not their primary concern, as it had been for Abduh (although he, as well, had been devoted to the Egyptian nation), and that in this sense they stood their mentor's ideas on their head. The emphasis in the inter-war period was on popular sovereignty, not on God's law or the Islamic *umma*. The dissolution of the Ottoman Empire and the abolition of the caliphate in 1924 further removed any concrete objects for Muslim supra-nationalist loyalties. Furthermore, the struggle against the British and the mushrooming of popular participation in the political process after the revolution of 1919, made democratic representation in a national framework appropriate and useful.

It is not true, however, that Islamic modernism failed *and* disappeared from the political scene, or that the cause of this lay in its *intellectual* weaknesses. It may be the case that, with the Wafd, Egypt entered the age of modern nationalism and that, within the concept of the modern nation, religion was to occupy a restricted space. But the struggle over what *kind* of religion was to occupy that space was still a crucial one, and Egyptian nationalism contained a place for the Islamic reformist message. In the 1920s and 1930s, that is, we can observe that secularism and Islamic reformism coexisted, and that nationalism and Islamic reformism continued to jointly inform the evolving understanding of identity in Egypt.

The values of the Wafd and its leader, Sa'd Zaghlul (1857–1927), centred during their heyday in the 1920s and 1930s on the need for national independence from the British and, within that context, a belief in popular, democratic government. The Wafd saw itself as the party of the Constitution (specifically the Constitution of 1923 which was promulgated after partial independence in 1922), and as the legitimate representative of the Egyptian people against the claims of the khedive. Its stress on equality of rights among Egypt's citizens and its unifying role in the political process contributed to the overwhelming support it enjoyed among the country's religious minority, the Copts. Its ideological make-up also allowed for the mobilisation of Egyptian women for the nationalist cause. This emphasis on the equality of rights, the rule of law, and democratic representation, together with the Wafd's enormous popularity in the early 1920s – in the context of nation-wide popular mobilisation after and in part because of World War I – gave the 'liberal experiment' an enormous potential for success.[26] The Wafd in its early years illustrated the fertile ground that nationalism can, in certain circumstances, provide for human rights, within a context of collective rights.

The predominance of nationalism in the inter-war period meant that the Egyptian nation, not religion, became a primary intellectual and political focus. But Islam continued to be important, and the debate over its appropriate role in public life and between its modernist and traditionalist interpretations raged on. The one side in this debate represented liberals of all hues, for the struggle for independence had brought nationalism and Islamic reformism together in a liberal framework.[27] Sa'd Zaghlul had started his career as a disciple of Abduh. When holding public office he had attempted to put his mentor's teachings into effect. Zaghlul studied in al-Azhar in 1871 when Afghani was there. He was a lawyer, a judge and later a minister of education (1906–10) and justice (1910–13). In association with Abduh, Qasim Amin and Lutfi al-Sayyid he tried to reform education and the legal system – the latter on the basis of enlightened Islamic jurisprudence – and to apply Abduh's principles in secular courts while also founding a school for *sharia* judges. After the revolution of 1919 and his rise to leadership other concerns pressed on him, but he did not abandon the ideas of his mentor.[28]

The public debates of the 1920s and 1930s on the reform of religious institutions and Islamic law also show that the struggle over the meaning and scope of Islam continued to be a contentious issue in public life. These debates can only be fully understood if placed in their political context, for they were not purely intellectual controversies. Thus, the questions of the reform of al-Azhar and the employment of its graduates in the legal system partly reflected the power struggle between the king and the Wafd (the Azhar were staunch allies of the former, not only on ideological grounds, but also because both Fuad and Faruq defended their autonomy). In trying to reform al-Azhar, however, the Wafd, irrespective of whether it was involved in a power struggle or not, acted as the medium for the promotion of liberal and modernising values.[29] The highest achievements in this respect were in 1920, 1923 and 1929 when family law – the last remaining domain in which Islamic law was exclusively applied – was partially reformed along modernist Islamic lines inspired by Abduh.[30]

The liberal nationalist values that Sa'd Zaghlul and the Wafd stood for, and their close connection with the school of thought of Muhammad Abduh, are reflected in various forms and degrees in the major liberal intellectual figures of the first half of the twentieth century – above all in Ahmad Lutfi al-Sayyid (1872–1963) whose imprint on the national consciousness was enormous. Lutfi al-Sayyid began his intellectual career under the influence of Abduh. He cooperated with Zaghlul and others to form the Umma Party and was editor of *al-Jarida*. He was associated with the Wafd but broke with it shortly after 1922, thereafter being informally linked with the Liberal Constitutionalist Party. For al-Sayyid religion had ceased to be a primary concern, but his understanding of Islam lay firmly within the reformist school.[31] It was the same for the other major thinker whose liberal ideas left an imprint on Egyptian society – Taha Husayn (1889–1976). Taha Husayn had been influenced by the ideas of Abduh. The publication of his work on pre-Islamic poetry in 1926 created a furore because of its challenge to conservative religious dogma. Religion played a secondary role in his thought, which centred on the Egyptian nation (connected with Europe rather than the East), but the relevant point here is that his conception of religion was a modernist one. In his work on pre-Islamic poetry he questioned the ulama's rigid interpretation of the Koran and the *hadith* and argued for the introduction of rational methods into the study of the religious texts. He claimed that the Koran was a historical document, understandable in the light of its own era, but to be discarded in the modern age and that Islam was not, in essence, opposed to free thought.[32]

Lutfi al-Sayyid's and Taha Husayn's world-view was very much that of nineteenth century liberalism, characterised by a confidence in the concept of reason, an almost deterministic belief in the natural laws of progress, respect for individual rights (the latter being interpreted as civil and political rights in the context of minimal government) and a devotion to the nation as the expression and culmination of the above values. These ideas were the dominant mode of thought among the Egyptian elite and within the political system during the 1920s and 1930s, thereafter being challenged for reasons that we shall examine. Within this context, Islam was given a subordinate but important position; and, more crucially, it was conceptualised in modernist and reformist ways so that it could play a positive role towards the improvement of society and respect for individual freedom and responsibility. In other words, Islamic modernism did not fail but was incorporated within a broader, hospitable framework.

There also existed, during this period, a parallel trend of liberal thought which centred more exclusively on Islam. Its principal exponents were Qasim Amin and Ali Abd al-Raziq. Qasim Amin (1865–1908), was a contemporary of Abduh and died shortly after him, but his ideas played a role in the nationalist movement later. Indeed, it has been noted that 'since Qasim Amin feminism had formed part of the content of nationalist thought.'[33] Amin introduced a reasoning on women's rights which became characteristic of feminist Islamic thought throughout the century, as we saw in Chapter 2. He argued, for instance, in his book on women published in 1899, that the lack of women's emancipation was not due to Islam itself but to its corruption, and that rules such as the seclusion of women are not prescribed by the Koran. Although he was not a feminist in the full sense he argued that no society can be truly based on freedom if such freedom is not practiced in family relations (indeed he went so far as to say that the cause of social malaise was the lack of freedom for women), and that a woman's freedom depends on her education and her ability to earn a living. [34]

Ali Abd al-Raziq (1888–1966) argued, creating a furore in the 1920s, that Islam, by contrast to its conventional understanding, prescribes a separation of religion and politics. Islam, he claimed, did not impose a particular political system and Muhammad was never a king. The caliphate was not a religious institution and its existence was not necessary for worship or public welfare. God had therefore left the field of civil government and worldly interest to the exercise of human reason, according to the requirements and needs of the time. It was not even necessary, according to Abd al-Raziq, that the *umma* be politically united, for mankind had to remain diverse and the state constructed on rational and natural grounds.[35]

Abd al-Raziq lies within the boundaries of Islamic modernism despite the fact that he was perceived at the time as attacking the fundamentals of the religion; for it is through an examination of religious precepts that he arrives at the conclusion that religion and politics must be separated. He represents what Leonard Binder terms the 'rejected alternative', namely the view that liberalism is Islamic not because Islam itself *is* reason, science and democracy but because it allows humankind to live according to the rules of reason and freedom as it sees fit, at any given time. When Abd al-Raziq's views were published they were furiously attacked by the Azhar and Rashid Rida. But he was defended by the Liberal Constitutionalist Party, with which he had links, and other members of the political establishment. It is no small matter, as a testament to Egyptian liberal political culture in the early part of the century (especially in comparison with the present situation in the Middle East), that although a furious debate and a governmental crisis did erupt upon the publication of Abd al-Raziq's views, there was no violence or executions.[36] In fact it is significant that a debate took place at all. What bode ill for the future, and was indicative of the weaknesses of the political system as a viable liberal polity, was that Sa'd Zaghlul did not lend him his support – because Abd al-Raziq was associated with a rival political party.[37]

V

The complex interactions and mutual influences between liberal Islamist and liberal secular thought must by now be evident. The preceding section has argued that in the historical period under consideration the two trends, far from representing mutually exclusive worldviews, in fact influenced and reinforced one another. It follows that, in attempting to understand the trajectory of the liberal impulse in Egypt, *we can examine Islamic and secular liberalism in tandem*. This liberal impulse appeared on the verge of becoming predominant in Egyptian political culture in the 1920s and 1930s. This section will examine why it did not. It will show that the reason why Islamic modernism did not carry the political day was not its intellectual inadequacy and inconsistency but the fact that *liberalism in general* did not carry the political day. The causes of this, in turn, were eminently social and political and stemmed neither from an inherently illiberal nature of Islam nor from the entry of 'the masses' – as the vehicles of this supposed nature – into the political arena.[38]

With nominal independence in 1922 and the Constitution of 1923 – outcomes of the popular nationalist revolt against the British in 1919 under the leadership of the Wafd – a constitutional system was introduced in Egypt. That system was to be based on shared power between the king and a democratically elected parliament and it enshrined individual citizen's rights. The beginnings of a modern democracy were thus established, and on a number of solid foundations at that: popular mobilisation brought about by the effects of World War I and aversion to British rule; a nationalist movement, the Wafd, which riding on its enormous popularity united various social groups and brought in women and the Coptic community,[39] and on a liberal political outlook represented by the Wafd and the thinkers examined earlier. There were also a series of underlying factors which gave solidity to the undertaking: a centralised state which, despite its oppressive roots, had developed organic links with society over the previous century and an economy which, despite its dependent position in the international market, was working reasonably well and had brought a substantial rise to the standard of living of the population as a whole.

So what went wrong? The first weakness that we must consider was political and it lay in the system since its inception. The constitution itself gave considerable powers to the king which Fuad (who became khedive in 1917, and king from 1923 until 1936), and later Faruq (1936–1952), abused. A struggle for power between the king and the Wafd ensued. The former drew on his legitimacy and popularity whenever available, on the support of various political parties and politicians such as Ismail Sidqi, on the frequent collaboration of the British and the support of the conservative religious establishment represented by al-Azhar.[40] The continuous interference of the king, and the intrigues and the suspensions or violations of the Constitution that accompanied it, caused serious malfunction in the political process and made a mockery of democratic rule. The polity could not function as a constitutional monarchy with a monarch who did not respect its founding principles. But he was allowed to do this by politicians who did not hesitate to collaborate with him if it was in their interest. The undermining of the constitutional system by the king must therefore also be seen as a failure of the whole body politic.

An equal share of responsibility lies with the British. The unilateral Declaration of 1922 had given Egypt nominal independence but reserved four points to British discretion: the security of Imperial communications, the defence of Egypt against foreign aggression, the protection of foreign interests and minorities and the question of the Sudan. This truncated sovereignty did not allow for full Egyptian responsibility in political matters and gave the British a continuous foothold and cause for interference in the country. The British lent their support to Fuad and later Faruq, but also occasionally bullied them into submission. But their most heavy-handed tactics were reserved for the Wafd. Apart from covert involvement, the numerous failed attempts by Egyptian governments to negotiate a final treaty of independence with the British created public frustration and diverted attention from pressing domestic problems. When agreement was finally reached in 1936 it was again a partial resolution. It ended the Capitulations and abolished the Mixed Courts and Egypt entered the League of Nations as a sovereign state; but it left Suez and the Sudan in British hands. This arrangement, and above all the outbreak of World War II, perpetuated the British presence.

Interference by Britain was due to considerations of its own interests and international developments but was also partly due to the ambivalent attitude of the Egyptian elite who depended on the British for the export of cotton and whom they courted, despite their desire for Egyptian independence.[41] This same elite, whose social origins and attitudes will be examined later, was also largely responsible for the way the parliamentary process developed in this period, a process punctuated by elections whose results were unrepresentative of public opinion, and continuous splits and realignments among politicians.[42] Political parties used the trappings of democracy when it brought them power but discarded them when it did not, and in that both the Wafd and the Liberal Constitutional party were particularly adept. The latter, despite the impeccable liberal credentials of their ideology, undermined the constitutional system out of a belief that they were best suited to govern, an antipathy for the Wafd's populist stance and an elitist attitude towards what they perceived to be a populace in need of tutelage. They therefore did not hesitate to restrict constitutional rights or collude with the king in preventing duly elected governments from assuming office.[43]

But the party that had the greatest responsibility for the fragmentation of the political process was the Wafd itself which, because of its overwhelming popularity, acquired a contemptuous attitude towards all other parties. The frequent deprivation of its legitimate right to govern by the king, the British and other parties or individual politicians further hardened such attitudes and created a vicious circle. When the opportunity arose the Wafd restricted political liberties and muzzled the press, took part in intrigues and finally in 1942 colluded with the British against king and prime-minister to overthrow the government and take power. By then the movement had lost its aura and legitimacy.

The Wafd's assumption that it alone represented the collective will of the people and that the national interest was tantamount to its own party's interest is indicative of the precarious balance between collective and individual rights which characterises all nationalist movements, a balance which can tip either way. But it also stemmed from the fact that the experience of constitutional rule in Egypt prior to 1923 had been brief and haphazard.[44] This lack of precedent was reflected not only in the behaviour of political actors but also in the way the political system as a whole was structured. Patronage and the division of spoils was what tied the parties to the electorate. In rural areas, parties relied on local notables and landowners to 'direct' the *fellahin* vote. Leaders of student activists, whose role in the political process had been central since the early part of the century, were bribed. The habit of replacing bureaucrats at all levels with those loyal to whichever party came to power soon became established.[45] The result was fragmentation and discontinuity not only in the political process but in state structures themselves.

In sum, the lack of an educated and politically aware electorate and hierarchical relations of domination and control in rural but also urban settings, deprived the political system of the necessary checks and balances, despite the existence of a vibrant press and a relatively independent judiciary. Such lack of liberal political culture was not surprising given the way the political system had developed up to that point. The 1923 Constitution and the polity it established were supposed to eventually remedy this situation. This did not happen, for the political reasons examined above, but also because of social and economic factors to which we must now turn.

The history of Egyptian liberalism, from Abduh through the *al-*

Jarida group to the Wafd and the Liberal Constitutionalists contains one unifying thread: disregard for social and economic inequalities. A social elitism characterised the thought of Islamic reformers – as Section III above shows – and a similarly patronising attitude towards 'the people' characterised the liberal thinkers and politicians of a secular bend. For Lutfi al-Sayyid – who, unlike the religious reformists, did advocate democracy – national strength derived mainly from national consciousness, not changes in the economic sphere. Taha Husayn did not consider economic issues except in the most general of ways and Muhammad Husayn Haykal, another prominent liberal of the time, was constantly torn between respect for individual freedom and the necessity of social order. The social and political elites were characterised by contempt for the ignorant and poverty-stricken masses of the *fellahin* and urban poor. Although there was some concern to better their lot through education an improvement through concrete social and economic changes was not envisaged.[46]

The dominant elites in Egypt were fundamentally landowning elites. The process by which the economy had been transformed into an agricultural, export-oriented one had begun, as we saw, in the previous century and had continued under the British. Economic structures and the accompanying legal system were modernised – in the sense that private property was legally recognised and producers were taxed by a central government on an individual basis – but there was no substantial industrialisation. The landowning elite and the urban *effendiya* (professionals and civil servants) were the mainstay of the Egyptian political classes, in the sense that they, predominantly, wielded political power.

Two significant points must be noted in the description of these classes. First, their interpenetration. The urban *effendiya* retained, throughout this period, connections with their rural origins. It was the sons of middle and large landowners who entered the professions and the high or low echelons of the bureaucracy.[47] Secondly, the financial and industrial bourgeoisie was small and primarily of foreign extraction. It attempted to promote Egypt's industries and private enterprise in cooperation with its Egyptian wing – organised around Bank Misr which was established in 1920 – but the results were not impressive.[48] The petty merchants and small industrialists, on the other hand, who were primarily Egyptians, lacked close links with the higher bourgeoisie and therefore the strength to affect a transformation of the economy in themselves. As a consequence, even as late as 1952, industry constituted only a small part of the economy and it remained mostly in the hands of non-Egyptians, as did the bulk of foreign trade.[49]

The ambiguity in this state of affairs was profound, for all the social groups that wielded political power at elite level had both common and antithetical interests with non-Egyptian elements, foreign minorities and Britain. The country had suffered during World War I and this, among other things, had contributed to the national movement of 1919. But thereafter, although all groups stood to gain from independence – landowners, professionals, civil servants, industrialists and financiers – they were also organically tied to the international market, which in turn constrained the Egyptian economy and worked increasingly to its detriment. This explains, in part, the continuation of the British presence, with its disastrous political implications as discussed above. It also explains the lack of social and economic transformation in the country which would have allowed an inclusionary democratic regime to strike root.

We can elucidate the problems further if we examine the social composition of the main political parties and their economic and social programmes. The Wafd represented an alliance between the *effendiya* classes and middling landowners, as well as some large ones.[50] Even though it was a predominantly urban movement its links with the countryside were equally vital, for the *effendiya* retained, as we have seen, multiple rural connections. Furthermore, the interests of the middling landowners who supported the Wafd were not fundamentally different from those of larger landowners.[51] Because of these intricate links with rural interests, and whatever its aspirations for national independence and its plans for economic and social reform, the Wafd did not deliver economic and social change. Its attempts at land reform did not ultimately make an impact. Its labour legislation, despite its links with the labour movement, was timid and belated. It did not – and arguably could not – transform the economy in the direction of industry, development and growth.[52] The inadequacy of its social and economic programme was one of the major causes of the discredit of the party and its decline from the mid-1930s onwards.

What had started off as a movement of change became, even more markedly after World War II, the mainstay of the status quo.[53] The emergence of a radical leftist wing within the party by that time debilitated it further rather than steering it towards a reconsideration of its aims.[54]

Other parties had an even greater attachment to the established order, none more so than the Liberal Constitutionalists who had come into being as a result of a split with the Wafd in 1922. The party of large landowners *par excellence*, as had been the Umma Party before it, it counted amongst its supporters the most prominent liberal intellectuals of the period and its programme centred on individual rights and democratic liberties. But it lacked any specifics on social and economic development or the way to achieve them. Other parties as well failed to become the spearhead for change. Some represented specific interests or individual politicians, like the party of Ismail Sidqi or the palace Union party, and lacked a proper constituency. The Saadist party, which split off from the Wafd in 1937–38, comprised large financiers and industrialists, whose activities were too closely tied to foreign interests to make a substantial impact.

In addition to pointing to the inadequacies of the political classes, we need to examine why substantial change did not come from below. The gap separating petty traders and industrialists from the higher bourgeoisie has already been noted. The former did not carry sufficient economic or social clout to make their demands felt, for their role in the economy was small and they lacked representation at an institutional level. The emergent labour movement on the other hand, although increasingly militant (with some results), was from the start part of the wider political game. Its close association with the Wafd brought it some benefits but on the whole delayed the rise of a class consciousness.[55] The socialist and communist groups, which were linked with the labour movement, were small and mostly of foreign extraction. The *fellahin*, finally, though the majority, were impoverished and unable to force land reform. Illiterate in their greatest numbers and having suffered the dissolution of their communal structures such as the village unit, they relied on the landowners to direct their vote or protect their interests.[56] Overpopulation and pressure on the land, already a problem at the time, caused the landless and poorest among them to swell the ranks of the urban unemployed.

In sum, no class or political formation was able to become the vehicle for the necessary social and economic changes which would provide the foundation for the success of a liberal constitutional system. And these changes had become imperative. For the steady rise in the standard of living in Egypt during the second half of the nineteenth century and the first two decades of the twentieth had ended and the inter-war period was already one of stagnant incomes and little growth. Cotton yields ceased to increase as they steadily had done in previous decades, and the price of raw materials in the international market fell.[57] Boom and bust abroad violently affected the domestic situation which reached a nadir in the Great Depression of the late 1920s and early 1930s. Population growth and pressures on the land were becoming alarming and hence the need for land reform which was not, however, carried out. The failure of Bank Misr to engender industrial development (despite the imposition of tariffs in 1930), and the multiple ties of the financial and trading world to foreign interests, blocked an alternative way of development for the country as a whole and added to the social pressures which eventually tore the system apart. It is against this background of growing constraints due to the domestic structure of the economy and the multiple links forged with economic interests abroad that the failure of the political classes to institute change must be understood. Many of these constraints were by their nature insurmountable because of the dependent position of Egypt in the international capitalist system. But the political classes had the option, as all elites do, to reform themselves, an option which they failed to take up.

VI

The strains in the system resulted, from the 1930s onwards, in growing popular involvement in non-electoral politics and increased violence, either planned (in paramilitary organisations within political parties for example) or spontaneous. The liberal constitutional system and the values it represented – among them individual rights –

were discredited by their association with a class that seemed increasingly obsolete and unreformable. The demise can be observed most clearly in the Wafd and its supporting classes: for the *effendiya* class of professionals and civil servants, as well as the petty bourgeoisie, became the recruitment ground for the emergent Islamic fundamentalism of the Muslim Brotherhood and of the fascist Misr al-Fatah.[58] Civil servants faced growing threats to their position because they depended for employment not on a vibrant sector of the economy but on a state whose ability to deliver was becoming increasingly restricted. The professions, similarly, were becoming an overpopulated sector by the 1930s.[59] The oscillation of the emergent middle classes between one type of nationalism (the Wafd's) and one version of Islam (the Muslim Brothers') was to become an important characteristic of Egyptian politics for decades to come.[60] As the Wafd's prestige and power declined, the appeal of liberal nationalism and Islamic modernism similarly declined, and a new group emerged to contest the interpretations of nationalism and Islam from a radically different standpoint on modernity and its implications.

The Muslim Brotherhood represented the second route taken by the reformist legacy of Muhammad Abduh through the person of Muhammad Rashid Rida (1865–1935), his disciple and biographer.[61] Rida fleshed out the political aspect of Abduh's thought, which had been relatively undeveloped. He can be seen as 'in many ways the founding theoretician of the Islamic state in its modern sense.'[62] The setting for his thought was the crisis over the caliphate in the 1920s and the quest for the institutions that would provide for its continuation. Rida did not believe that the caliphate as such could be resuscitated. Instead, in expounding the prerequisites for its replacement, he made 'a subtle, almost imperceptible transition' from the caliphate to the Islamic state.[63]

In such a state, popular sovereignty would be an important source of law and would be expressed through the institution of *shura*. On this and on many other points – the necessity of *ijtihad*, the need for law to conform to public interest (*maslaha*), the promotion of women's rights, the opposition to the death penalty for apostasy – Rida's ideas were relatively liberal. But he did not expound these views beyond a level of generality and this was detrimental to Islamic reformism which, by that stage, required that its practical relevance be made explicit.[64] Rida's general injunctions and mere assertions that Islam is coterminous with reason and democracy, his use of 'traditional' political terminology and his conservative tenor served as a stepping stone from Islamic modernism to the Islamic fundamentalism of the Muslim Brotherhood.

In Rida's thought the religious and the political spheres had remained distinct. In the Muslim Brothers' the latter was subordinated to the former.[65] Armed with the concept of the Islamic state introduced by Rida, they proceeded to give it an authoritarian bent. Although their ideology retained many of Abduh's elements, the polity they propagated was not conducive to a respect for rights, for they argued for the form not the substance of those rights. On the one hand they asserted the need for *ijtihad* and proclaimed that the specifics of the political system would be determined by the time and place of its application on the basis of a democratic system and the public interest, a respect for political liberties, popular sovereignty and a social contract between rulers and ruled. But on the other hand they emptied these ideas of democratic content by the assertion that the *sharia* would be dominant and politics would be subjugated to religious dictates. Their authoritarian tendencies were evident in their rejection of multi-partyism (they were not unique in this, given the way multi-partyism had degenerated), in their opposition to equality for women, in their support of the *hadd* punishments in penal law and other such views.

The Muslim Brotherhood is the prototype of the Islamic fundamentalist movement in the Middle East. In its ideology and organisation and in its social composition we can trace the unmistakable contours of a very modern movement – predominantly urban, relying on propaganda and individual recruitment. But it rejected the values underlying modernity, including individual freedoms. Its plea for individual reform contrasted with its subsumption of the individual in a collectivity greater than its parts. It was preoccupied with change but resolved this preoccupation by aspiring to return to an idealised past. It used the 'instruments' of modern technology and methods of political organisation, but rejected their underlying values. The phenomenon of the Brotherhood revealed the extent to which the concepts of modernity had permeated Egyptian society by the 1920s and 1930s.[66] The processes of modernity combined with the growing social and economic crisis caused the modernism of the turn of the century to be replaced by the Muslim Brotherhood's virulent anti-modernism.

In the 1930s and more pointedly in the 1940s, the Muslim Brotherhood and the Wafd emerged as the two main rival mass movements in the Egyptian political arena. In the face of a discredited liberalism, which had failed to tackle the country's mounting economic and social problems, the Muslim Brothers forcefully introduced a concern for the people's welfare and organised self-help at the popular level; they advocated the nationalisation of natural resources, land reform, labour legislation and became involved in the trade union movement, its strikes and demonstrations; they criticised the evils of capitalism and condemned it as a tool of domination of both local and foreign elites.[67] This last concern was becoming more pressing with the failure of the Wafd and the dominant classes generally to wrestle independence from Britain, a failure made acutely poignant by the debacle of the Arab armies in Palestine in 1948–49.

With the Muslim Brothers we come full circle from Afghani. For despite Banna's rejection of nationalism as a foreign ideology, and his protestations for Islamic unity, the Muslim Bothers were battling for Egypt, whose national boundaries coincided with the Islamic state and on which they were intent on imposing the *sharia* – a law that was to be 'the law of the land' despite its sacred character. The Wafd and the Muslim Brothers fought over the fate of the nationalist movement in Egypt and its backbone, the middle classes. Within this context of a triumphant nationalism they contested the role and interpretation of Islam.

The liberal intellectuals and the existing parties had failed to prevent the rise of conservative Islamic feeling in the country at large, for they had failed in their role as social reformers and as nationalists. Now, in an attempt to shore up popularity, they abetted this reactionary conception of Islam. Intellectuals such as Muhammad Husayn Haykal and Taha Husayn introduced Islamic subject-matters in their writings in the 1930s and political parties, such as the Liberal Constitutionalists and the Wafd, resorted to religious slogans.[68] Islam had become a pawn in the political and ideological game, used by establishment and opposition to serve conflicting purposes.

VII

The aim of this chapter has been to trace the development of a proposed reconciliation between Islam and liberalism in Egyptian history and society. It has argued that the partial failure of this attempt, the rise of illiberal political movements from the 1930s onwards and the eventual replacement of a constitutional by an authoritarian regime in 1952, were not the results of either the intellectual inadequacies of Islamic reformism or of the people's instinctive attachment to a traditional Islam. Instead, it attributes the causes for this development to the identification – in the popular mind – of liberalism (religious and secular), with a dominant class which remained profoundly elitist despite its democratic pretensions.[69] To support this argument, we have shown that Islamic and secular liberalisms can coexist and that they are yoked together in their trajectories. Islamic reformism was discredited because of the discredit of liberalism in general. The reasons for this were social and political and would apply to any society, not only to specifically Muslim societies.

Throughout the period studied in this chapter, the debate centred, in fact though not in name, around the understanding of identity and authenticity – on questions such as who were the Egyptians, how should they define themselves in relation to their past and to European culture, and what were the highest values they should adhere to? This debate was carried out in the context of a profound transformation of Egyptian society by the forces of modernity (which affected most, if not all areas of life, though this is not to say that Egypt became a 'modern' society), a transformation accomplished through the spread of market forces which pulled the Egyptian economy into international capitalism, the introduction of novel concepts and ways of understanding society and self and of new structures of authority, primarily the centralised nation-state. 'Islam' also changed profoundly from an integral part of social existence to an object of study and/or an ideological programme. As such it took two forms: liberal modernist and authoritarian anti-modernist. Within the framework of a rising nationalist sentiment and its twin concern of what 'authenticity' must mean for Egypt (and here the ambiguous relationship with Europe provided the central nexus), the proponents of these two conceptions of Islam and their allies fought over the soul of the country.

Nowhere can the impact of this struggle, and partial defeat of Islamic liberalism be seen more clearly than in developments regarding the nation's religious minority and its women. The limited headway in the reform of family law has been noted above. It reflected the limited headway of liberalism in general. Among the country's Copts, the enthusiasm for the inclusionary nationalism of the Wafd subsided by the 1930s and even more so thereafter while inter-communal strife replaced the harmony of the initial phase of the nationalist movement. One may explain developments on the women and Coptic issues in terms of 'tradition' ('Islam' included), not having been eroded by 'modernity'. This certainly was so in large parts of Egyptian society, for example in many rural communities. But the fact that the greatest strains, on women and Copts, occurred in urban areas and among classes that had ceased to inhabit a traditional world, point to a more persuasive explanation. A society in the grip of a tremendous transformation focused on women as the principal repositories of 'authenticity' and on the exclusion of non-Muslim 'others' as the affirmation of identity.

Even so, the headway in questions of religious and sexual equality was limited, not non-existent. In many other ways Islamic liberalism had achieved extensive progress by 1952. Civil and penal codes had already been introduced at the end of the nineteenth century in Egypt.[70] The bifurcation of the legal system between the *sharia* and national courts, and between local justice and capitulatory rights was extensive, but it had meant a complete reconceptualisation of legal notions and the widespread acceptance of the principle of the rule of law. The *jizya* on religious minorities had been abolished as early as 1855. And with the Constitution of 1923 equality of all citizens, whatever their religion, was introduced.

Reforms of Islamic law continued throughout the first half of the twentieth century and culminated in the promulgation of the Civil Code of 1948. The established view on the Code has been that its author, Abdarrazaq al-Sanhuri, 'relegated Islamic law to a minor place ... while praising its adaptability and relevance to modern needs in his published writings.' This is perceived as evidence of the failure of Abduh's reformism.[71] The argument is intelligible if one takes the view that Islamic reformism can only be deemed successful if it covers all aspects of life and law. Against it, I have posited the view that such universality need not be a prerequisite. Al-Sanhuri's formula is evidence of the success of Islamic reformism and its accommodation within a national, liberal framework.[72] It successfully sustained the legacy of Abduh and is evidence that Islamic liberalism had not been, by the end of the period, wholly crushed between two inhospitable extremes.

On the parallel question of liberal culture in general, moreover, the achievements cannot be underestimated. Egyptian society, despite the ultimate erosion of the parliamentary system, had been implanted with the values of individual rights and democratic representation to some degree. The Wafd may have suffered eventual decline and yet, until Nasser, it (and therefore the values it represented) had been the single most popular party in the history of Egypt – more popular by far than the Muslim Brothers at any period. The continuous agitation by the people of Egypt for the Constitution, national independence and for their rights in general cannot be written off and one has to agree with al-Sayyid Marsot that, given the circumstances, it is impressive that liberal institutions developed as far as they did.[73] The fate of these institutions, and of liberalism and Islam in general, will be examined in the context of Egyptian history after Nasser, in the next chapter.

Notes

1. Gran, P., *Islamic Roots of Capitalism: Egypt, 1760–1840* (Austin, TX: University of Texas Press, 1979); Mitchell, T., *Colonising Egypt* (Cambridge: Cambridge University Press, 1988).

2. Gran, op.cit., Foreword, p. vii.

3. Ibid., p. xii.

4. Mitchell, op.cit., p. 103.

5. Mustafa, A. A. R., 'The Breakdown of the Monopoly System in Egypt after 1840' in Holt, P. M., (ed.), *Political and Social Change in Modern Egypt: Historical Studies from the Ottoman Conquest to the United Arab Republic* (London: Oxford University Press, 1968) and Owen, R., *The Middle East in the World Economy, 1800–1914* (London: Methuen, 1981).

6. Owen, op.cit., p. 291.

7. Baer, G., 'Social Change in Egypt: 1800–1914' in Holt, (ed.), op.cit.

8. See Goldschmidt, A., *Modern Egypt: The Formation of a Nation-State* (Boulder, CO: Westview Press, 1988), pp. 16-22 and al-Sayyid Marsot, A. L., *A Short History of Modern Egypt* (Cambridge: Cambridge University Press, 1985), Chapter 4.

9. Too much has been made of the supposed antithesis between Islam and nationalism. My view is closest to Zubaida, S., *Islam, the People and the State: Political Ideas and Movements in the Middle East* (London: I. B.Tauris, 1993) who does not see any essential contradiction.

10. By the end of the nineteenth-century state control over religious institutions in education, law and charitable endowments (*waqf*), had been greatly extended as noted in Vatikiotis, P. J., 'Religion and State' in Warburg, G. R. and Kupferschmidt, U. M., (eds), *Islam, Nationalism, and Radicalism in Egypt and the Sudan* (New York: Praeger, 1983), pp. 57-8. The subordination of religion to the state, rather than the separation between the two, deepened in the twentieth century.

11. Hodgson, M. G. S., *The Venture of Islam: Conscience and History in a World Civilization* (Chicago, IL: University of Chicago Press, 1974), Vol. 3, Book 6, p. 387. (This passage was also used in Chapter 2 above but it was necessary to repeat it here.) The advent of the modern world, furthermore, transformed the *sharia* into the 'law of the land' and this process was aided by the colonial administration: 'In areas under Western rule, the *Shari'ah* law was commonly enforced by Western authorities at the expense of local customary law, in the name of 'law and order'. This was done partly out of a desire to govern according to the best indigenous norms and partly in the hope of achieving common legal standard throughout a given territory ... The *Shari'ah*, so extended in jurisdiction, was not exactly the old *Shari'ah*.' (p. 386).

12. On Afghani's life and work see Hourani, A., *Arabic Thought in the Liberal Age, 1798–1939* (Cambridge: Cambridge University Press, 1983), Chapter 5; Keddie, N. R., *An Islamic Response to Imperialism: Political and Religious Writings of Sayyid Jamal ad-Din 'al-Afghani'* (Berkeley, CA: University of California Press, 1983) and Kedourie, E., *Afghani and 'Abduh: An Essay on*

Religious Unbelief and Political Activism in Modern Islam (London: Frank Cass, 1966). The following paragraphs draw on these works.

13.   Enayat, H., *Modern Islamic Political Thought: The Response of the Shi'i and Sunni Muslims to the Twentieth Century* (Basingstoke: Macmillan, 1982), p. 135.

14.   Keddie, op.cit., p. 79.

15.   The following paragraphs draw primarily on Kerr, M. H., *Islamic Reform: The Political and Legal Theories of Muhammad 'Abduh and Rashid Rida* (Berkeley, CA: University of California Press, 1966), Chapter 4; Hourani, op.cit., Chapter 6; and Abduh, M., *The Theology of Unity* (London: George Allen and Unwin, 1966, translated by I. Musa'ad, and K. Cragg).

16.   Kerr, op.cit., p. 110.

17.   Ibid., p. 122.

18.   Hourani, also notes that Abduh made a central distinction between 'what was essential and unchanging [in Islam] and what was inessential and could be changed without damage' (Hourani, op.cit., p. 145); and that since the Koran and *hadith* did not lay down specific rules on relations between men reason, exercised through the procedure of *ijtihad*, could be the guiding principle in this sphere (p. 148). But – Hourani argues – although Abduh identified certain traditional Islamic concepts with European political ideas – *maslaha* with utility, *shura* with parliamentary government, *ijma* with public opinion – (p. 144) his ideal government was still that of medieval jurists: 'the just ruler, ruling in accordance with a law and in consultation with the leaders of the people' (p. 157).

19.   Kerr, op.cit., p. 134.

20.   This is one of the main themes in Kerr, ibid., and in Sharabi, H., *Arab Intellectuals and the West: The Formative Years, 1875–1914* (Baltimore, MD: Johns Hopkins Press, 1970).

21.   Hourani, op.cit., p. 199.

22.   Ibid., pp. 199-208. It has been noted that Kamil gradually moved away from advocating unity between Muslims and Copts. This became a more pronounced tendency in his movement after his death. It contributed to rising inter-communal tensions in Egypt which worsened in 1907–1911, culminating in the holding of rival Muslim and Coptic Congresses in 1911. The attitude of the Copts towards the British was ambivalent until after 1919.

23.   Hourani, op.cit., p. 202.

24.   Vatikiotis, P. J., *The History of Modern Egypt: From Muhammad Ali to Mubarak* (London: Weidenfeld and Nicolson, 1991), p. 190.

25.   Vatikiotis, ibid., p. 216. Vatikiotis only concedes that Abduh introduced a 'questioning spirit' in a generation of liberal thinkers.

26. The term is taken from the title of Al-Sayyid Marsot, A. L., *Egypt's Liberal Experiment: 1922–1936* (Berkeley, CA: University of California Press, 1977). On the Wafd see Deeb, M., *Party Politics in Egypt: The Wafd and its Rivals, 1919–1939* (London: Ithaca Press, 1979).

27. Al-Sayyid Marsot, *Egypt's Liberal Experiment*, op.cit., pp. 218–19.

28. Hourani, op.cit., pp. 209–17, Vatikiotis, *The History of Modern Egypt*, op.cit., pp. 257–60.

29. Crecelius, D., 'The Course of Secularization in Modern Egypt' in Smith, D. E. (ed.), *Religion and Political Modernisation* (New Haven, CT: Yale University Press, 1974), pp. 67–94 and 'Nonideological Responses of the Egyptian Ulama to Modernization' in Keddie, N. R. (ed.), *Scholars, Saints and Sufis: Muslim Religious Institutions in the Middle East since 1500* (Berkeley, CA: University of California Press, 1972), pp. 167–209. In the second article Crecelius describes the ulama's resistance to reform and their increasing marginalisation, especially after 1922.

30. Anderson, J. N. D., 'Law Reform in the Middle East' in *International Affairs* (Vol. 32, No. 1, January 1956), pp. 46–8. The reform was carried out through selective appeals to various schools of Islamic law or early Muslim jurists, but also occasionally through a virtual (though unofficial) exercise of *ijtihad*. The limited nature of the reforms and the frequent inability to justify them on principle indicate the sensitivity of the issue and the slow pace with which the reformist message was spreading.

31. Al-Sayyid Marsot, *Egypt's Liberal Experiment*, op.cit., pp. 219–28; Hourani, A., op.cit., pp. 170–83, and Vatikiotis, *The History of Modern Egypt*, op.cit., pp. 240–5.

32. Smith, C. D., *Islam and the Search for Social Order in Modern Egypt: A Biography of Muhammad Husayn Haykal* (Albany, NY: State University of New York Press, 1983), pp. 90-6 and Hourani, op.cit., Chapter 12. Husayn's book set off a vehement response among conservatives, who branded him an apostate and helped having the book withdrawn.

33. Hourani, A., p. 215.

34. Ibid., pp. 164–70. In a second book in 1900 Amin renounced reformism in favour of a fully fledged secularism. But his ideas on women and Islam remained very influential.

35. Ibid., pp. 183–92 and Binder, L., *Islamic Liberalism: A Critique of Development Ideologies* (Chicago, IL: University of Chicago Press, 1988), pp. 128–46.

36. Al-Sayyid Marsot, *Egypt's Liberal Experiment*, op.cit., pp. 249–50.

37. Hourani, op.cit., p. 216.

38. This is one of the central themes in Zubaida, op.cit. and Al-Sayyid

Marsot, *Egypt's Liberal Experiment*, op.cit. The identification of 'the people' with traditional and conservative Islam, which this chapter disputes, is exemplified by Safran, N., *Egypt in Search of Political Community: An Analysis of the Intellectual and Political Evolution of Egypt, 1804–1952* (Cambridge, MA: Harvard University Press, 1961), pp. 102–5. In answering the question 'did the uprising [of 1919] mean that Liberal Nationalism in any meaningful sense had been accepted by the country at large?' Safran makes a distinction – in the case of 'dependent countries' – between 'positive' and 'negative' nationalism, and links the former with the middle classes and the latter (religious-xenophobic type) with the lower classes. Next he deduces that because, after World War II, the urban lower classes joined the Muslim Brotherhood *en masse*, their true aspirations had always been those of conservative Islam, and had been only temporarily channelled into the nationalist movement for want of a more appropriate outlet. By contrast to Safran this chapter proposes that the transference of popular support to the Muslim Brotherhood, and other movements, took place after disappointment with the Wafd and the nationalist movement, and was a result of the very concrete political and social failings of this movement and the political system as a whole.

39.   Copts were active in the nationalist movement in the 1920s, holding seats in parliament and top political positions. Their close links with the Wafd have been well documented. See Carter, B. L., *The Copts in Egyptian Politics, 1918–1952* (London: Croom Helm, 1986), Chapters 2–5. Note that Islam was proclaimed the official religion by the 1923 Constitution thus maintaining the organic link between state and the Muslim religious institutions. The right of apostasy was not recognised, in contravention to the Constitution's guarantee of freedom of belief (ibid., pp. 130–3). Copts began to voice vehement objections against these issues in later years, when strains in the political system started to affect their position as a religious minority. On the relationship between nationalism and women see Badran, M., *Feminists, Islam and Nation: Gender and the Making of Modern Egypt* (Princeton, NJ: Princeton University Press, 1995).

40.   The repressive government of Ismail Sidqi, in power from 1930 to 1933, was in fact the result of the third attempted palace coup against constitutional government. It set a pattern of government coercion to which the populace responded by violence. The Constitution of 1923 was suspended in 1930 and reinstated in 1935 after massive demonstrations. See Al-Sayyid Marsot, *Egypt's Liberal Experiment*, op.cit., pp. 138–78. The king's support of religious conservatives, who became a pawn in the political game as we saw above, contributed to the slowness of reform in the Azhar and also to the failure of Islamic reformism in general.

41. Ibid., pp. 158 and 211–12.

42. Deeb, op.cit., describes how out of the four general elections that took place in the 1920s only the first, of 1923–1924, can be regarded as truly representative. The Wafd suffered further splits after the initial one with the Liberal Constitutionalists of 1922. As a result the Saadist Party was formed in 1938 and the Wafdist Bloc in 1942.

43. Smith, op.cit., Chapter 3.

44. Anderson, J. N. D., 'Law Reform in Egypt: 1850–1950' in Holt (ed.), op.cit., pp. 209–24. The British had also failed to adequately prepare the country for constitutional government.

45. Al-Sayyid Marsot, *Egypt's Liberal Experiment*, op.cit., pp. 122–30. Nevertheless, it must be noted that the student movement overwhelmingly supported the Wafd for most of the 1920s and 1930s, as did the labour movement.

46. Hourani, op.cit., pp. 180–1 and 338–9. This theme runs throughout Haykal's biography by Smith, op.cit. There were exceptions to this trend, a significant one being the socialist Salama Musa.

47. Baer, op.cit., pp. 157–8. This is evident in the study of one prominent family of the Egyptian elite, the Mareis, in Springborg, R., *Family, Power and Politics in Egypt: Sayed Bey Marei, his Clan, Clients and Cohorts* (Philadelphia, PA: University of Pennsylvania Press, 1982).

48. Tignor, R. L., *State, Private Enterprise and Economic Change in Egypt, 1918–1952* (Princeton, NJ: Princeton University Press, 1984).

49. Issawi, C., *Egypt in Revolution: An Economic Analysis* (London: Oxford University Press for the Royal Institute of International Affairs, 1963), pp. 43–5.

50. Middling landowners were those owning between 20 and 200 feddans. The large landowners, mostly absentee, were those in possession of over 200 feddans.

51. Deeb, op.cit., p. 330.

52. Al-Sayyid Marsot, *Egypt's Liberal Experiment*, op.cit., pp. 121–2 and Chapter 7. Deeb, in ibid., is the best source of information for the Wafd's political and social programme which contained, despite its ultimate failure, the aspiration for national economic independence and the ideals of the Bank Misr group. A constant theme running through Deeb's book is the tension between the Wafd as a national, all-inclusive movement and a party representing sections of society. By the 1930s, the Wafd had been transformed into the latter.

53. Reid, D. M., *Lawyers and Politics in the Arab World, 1880–1960* (Minneapolis, MN: Bibliotheca Islamica, 1981). The author notes this, in the

context of a discussion on lawyers, who were vital in the nationalist movement. Although they had implanted the ideals of rule of law, democracy and liberalism, by mid-century they seemed conservative in societies that were moving to the left. Reid argues that the lawyers' emergence had coincided with the peak of Western economic penetration in the Middle East and that their prominence depended on their links with landowning and trading interests, whom they served (see pp. 2–3, 94, 98, 102–4).

54. Botman, S., *Egypt from Independence to Revolution, 1919–1952* (Syracuse, NY: Syracuse University Press, 1991), pp. 61–5.

55. Deeb, M., 'Labour and Politics in Egypt, 1919–1939', in *International Journal of Middle East Studies* (Vol. 10, No. 2, May 1979), pp. 187–203.

56. Baer, op.cit., p. 142. This had been the result of market forces and had occurred already in the nineteenth century. Deeb, *Party Politics in Egypt*, op.cit., p. 162, notes that the peasants did 'not have a class consciousness as such'.

57. Issawi, op.cit., p. 32.

58. Gershoni, I., and Jankowski, J. P., *Redefining the Egyptian Nation, 1930-45* (Cambridge: Cambridge University Press, 1995) have a different argument, that the composition of the middle classes in the cities, from the 1930s onwards, changed because of the influx of traditional groups from rural areas. This static picture of classes and their social and political make-up is what I am trying to dispel here.

59. Deeb, *Party Politics in Egypt*, op.cit., pp. 315–24 and Reid., D. M., 'The Rise of Professions and Professional Organisation in Modern Egypt' in *Comparative Studies in Society and History* (Vol. 16, No. 1, January 1974), pp. 24–57.

60. See Chapter 4 for a re-emergence of a similar pattern in the 1970s to 1990s. On the acting out of this rivalry within the student movement see Abdalla, A., *The Student Movement and National Politics in Egypt, 1923–1973* (London: al-Saqi Books, 1985), Part 1.

61. On Rashid Rida see: Hourani, op.cit., Chapter 9; Kerr, op.cit., especially Chapters 5 and 6, and Enayat, op.cit., especially Chapters 2 and 3.

62. Enayat, op.cit., p. 69.

63. Ibid., p. 76–7.

64. Kerr, op.cit., p. 187.

65. Enayat, op.cit., p. 83. On the Muslim Brothers' ideology see Mitchell, R. P., *The Society of the Muslim Brothers* (Oxford: Oxford University Press, 1969), Part 3.

66. The very notion of Islam as a blueprint for a social order, for example, stemmed 'from modern notions of social and intellectual analysis, in which almost any sort of activity could be treated as forming an autonomous system'.

Hodgson, M., op.cit., p. 389.

67. Mitchell, op.cit., pp. 42–3, 220–2 and 272–82.

68. What these developments meant is debatable. See Smith, C. D., 'The 'Crisis of Orientation': The Shift of Egyptian Intellectuals to Islamic Subjects in the 1930s' in *International Journal of Middle East Studies* (Vol. 4, No. 4, 1973), pp. 382–410. Compare Carter, op.cit., p. 180–1, and Deeb, *Party Politics in Egypt*, op.cit., p. 355.

69. Gamble, A., *An Introduction to Modern Social and Political Thought* (Basingstoke: Macmillan, 1981), Chapters 3 and 6. The author notes the perennial clash between liberalism and democracy and the elitist origins of the former in its Western formulation. In this, as in so many other ways, the Egyptian liberals were not unlike their Western counterparts.

70. Anderson, 'Law Reform in Egypt', op.cit., pp. 216–17.

71. Kerr, op.cit., pp. 15–16.

72. Hill E., *Al-Sanhuri and Islamic Law: The Place and Significance of Islamic Law in the Life and Work of 'Abd al-Razzaq Ahmad al-Sanhuri, Egyptian Jurist and Scholar, 1895–1971* (Cairo Papers in Social Science, Vol. 10, Monograph 1, Spring 1987 / Cairo: American University in Cairo Press). Hill argues that al-Sanhuri's life was devoted to making Islamic law relevant to modern needs and concerns.

73. Al-Sayyid Marsot, *Egypt's Liberal Experiment*, op.cit., pp. 248–50.

4

Egypt, 1970s–1990s

I

The previous chapter looked at the 1920s and 1930s as a self-contained period in the history of Egypt. It made a number of arguments about the connections between Islam and human rights and introduced a historical, socio-political approach in studying the prospects for an Islamic liberalism. This chapter will use the same method, but will concentrate on the 1970s, 1980s and the first half of the 1990s which – for reasons that will be given below – provide a similarly appropriate framework in working out the arguments of the book. This period will be again treated as self-contained, since the principal object of the study is not Egypt or its political development *per se*.

In parallel with many other parts of the Muslim world, and particularly the Middle East, from the early 1970s onwards, Egypt experienced a revival of Islam. This took a variety of forms, from an upsurge in religious observance amongst many sections of the population, to a renewed debate on the public role of Islam. There also occurred a renewed debate on the meaning and interpretation of the concept of authenticity (*asala*). In 1970, upon the death of Gamal Abd al-Nasser, Anwar Sadat became president of the Egyptian Republic. His role was paramount in introducing and reinforcing the new trends in Egyptian politics. An emphasis on religious values was crucially important in his political make-up. Either encouraged by the regime, or in defiance of it, a number of Islamist organisations emerged or reemerged on the political scene – from the moderate (as

114

it became), Muslim Brotherhood to radical groups which employed violent means in the name of Islam, ultimately assassinating Sadat himself and later, in the early 1990s, instigating a violent uprising. The official religious establishment, furthermore, became a more active participant in public and social debates. Islam, in short, in a variety of forms and guises, became progressively important in defining the political and social identity of Egyptians. At the same time secularism, which had to some extent predominated in the Nasser period, declined. For these reasons, the period from the 1970s onwards is useful for examining the manifestations and role of Islam in public life.

A second reason for studying this period is that after the end of the Nasser era, which had witnessed a repression of democratic freedoms, human rights and political liberties once again became a focus of public debate. Sadat's regime initiated a liberal opening and declared, in the early 1970s, that the rule of law and parliamentary democracy would be restored. Throughout the period his regime (and that of Mubarak's after 1981) followed a tortuous course towards enhancing civil and political rights. The gains in that respect were real, albeit limited and falling far short of a fully-fledged liberal polity.

After the lacuna of the Nasser years, then, Islamism and liberalism reemerged simultaneously as determining factors in Egyptian political life. Why was this so? How and why did these two world-views interact and influence one another? How successful was their attempted reconciliation? This chapter will show that the interpretation of Islam which ultimately predominated was not inevitable, but the outcome of competing interpretations and the social and political actors they represented, notably the state as an autonomous or semi-autonomous entity.

The plan of the chapter will be as follows. After a brief overview of the Nasser era, the causes of Islamic revivalism and of political liberalisation in the Sadat and Mubarak periods will be examined. This will be complemented by a more detailed account of the human rights situation from the 1970s onwards. The range of discourses on Islam – of the regime, the religious establishment, the Muslim Brotherhood, the Islamist organisations (*gama'at*), the Islamist militants – and their implications for human rights will then be analysed. The next step will be to concentrate on the main political, social and economic developments of the period, and show that they were principally determined by the role, position and choices of the Egyptian state. The way these developments related to the various interpretations of Islam and conceptions of human rights will then be illustrated. The political landscape will therefore be recast in a different light, and the fluid relationship between the concept of human rights and Islam placed in its concrete political and social context.

II

The failures of the constitutional system in the period prior to 1952, and the impasse which led to its ultimate collapse and the collapse of the social world it represented have already been described. The ease with which the collapse came about suggested that the system and the political values it stood for had rested, in their final years, on brittle foundations. Yet, when the Free Officers came to power in July 1952 they had no particular ideology or detailed plan of action for government and society except for land reform and a final settlement with the British, both long overdue. During the first two years, Nasser consolidated himself in power after the elimination of General Naguib and the Muslim Brotherhood, representing respectively those favouring a democratic political system and political Islam.[1] In the economic sphere, because of the exigencies of the situation, the regime soon became committed to an interventionist state. Land reform was followed, after the war of 1956, by growing regulation of commercial and industrial activities. The process culminated in the July Decrees of 1961 and the official espousal of socialism – a term used to describe what was, in the economic sphere, a 'state capitalist' set of policies.[2]

The discredited institutions of political liberalism were set aside. During 1953 the Revolutionary Council under the leadership of Nasser abolished all existing political parties and postponed elections and parliament indefinitely. Egypt became a one-party state. The Liberation Rally (created in 1953), the National Union (1957) and later the Arab Socialist Union (1962) were mass organisations through which the regime sought to mobilise the people in support of its policies.

Nasser viewed society as an undifferentiated entity which transcended classes and particular groups. In the 1962 Charter for National Action, liberal democracy was condemned as 'bourgeois' and 'real democracy' declared a socio-economic issue.[3] The values which the regime sought to instill in society were still those of civic responsibility, cooperation, equality, free will and rationalism, but within a controlled framework.[4] The priorities of the regime, and the values it championed, were Arab unity and economic development. Individual freedoms were sacrificed in order to achieve them, but Nasser's charisma and his emphasis on social welfare ensured at least the passive acceptance of the regime by the majority of Egyptians.[5]

The shift by the Nasserist regime towards 'socialism' was caused by international factors and foreign policy considerations, namely the conflict with Britain, the difficulties with the United States, and the need for the Soviet Union's political support and financial assistance. The emphasis on economic development as a trade-off for human rights and political freedoms and the appeal of socialism and state interventionism in Egypt also reflected worldwide trends during the 1960s. But the requirements of domestic politics are equally important in explaining the ideological shift.

Two primary – though ultimately contradictory – considerations determined the actions of the regime. Firstly, the need to boost economic development in the context of the growing impasse in the Egyptian economy from the interwar period onwards. The Free Officers continued the policies of import substitution already intimated in the tariff laws of 1930 but with a renewed emphasis on the role of the state. Ultimately, the inability, or unwillingness, of the regime to extract an investable surplus from a repressed labour force, and its reliance on welfare politics financed by external borrowing, led to the failure of the drive to economic development and industrialisation by the mid-1960s.[6] But the issues of 'state capitalism' and the accompanying centralisation and reliance on the state remained with the Egyptian economy thereafter, as we shall see.

The second domestic consideration leading to the adoption of 'socialist' policies was the regime's attempt to acquire a popular base through coopting various social groups. The revolution of 1952 had signalled the collapse of the political and social order *ante*, rather than overwhelming popular support for the Free Officers. The weakening of the large landowning families of the pre-1952 era through land reform led to the emergence, as the dominant rural group, of a middle class of landowners.[7] At the political-bureaucratic level, the old ruling class families were replaced by a new technocratic ruling elite.[8] Through the expansion of the state there emerged a 'state bourgeoisie' whose fortunes were closely tied to those of the regime.[9] State capitalist policies gave prominence to this group but did not result in the expropriation of private property in the agricultural, industrial or commercial sectors which remained important, albeit increasingly dependent on the state. The urban lower middle classes, working classes and the peasantry, moreover, gradually became bound to the state through its regulation of prices, subsidies and wages.[10] In parallel with these economic and social developments, genuine political participation was discouraged and professional organisations, trade unions and cooperative movements were corporatised while other independent associations, for example business or religious groups, were suppressed.[11]

The political, economic and social consequence of these developments was the emergence of an authoritarian state with a populist character and an emphasis on welfare and development rather than political freedoms. In the Nasser era, the state took centre-stage in Egyptian politics as a major, semi-autonomous political actor. Its new position and role provides the key for understanding developments in the sphere of religion, and the connections between Islam and the political process.

Nasser's was a secularising regime. In 1956, all the religious courts of Egypt (Muslim and Christian) were abolished. The government expanded its control over private mosques, abolished the private *waqfs* (religious endowments) and created new Islamic organisations to serve novel goals. Above all, it intensified the process of subjugating Al-Azhar to political authority. Al-Azhar's independence was practically abolished by the reform of 1961, and the ulama employed as legitimating instruments for official policies. At the same time, the regime offered its own interpretation of Islam, which was declared to be the religion of freedom, equality and progress. There were also attempts to promote the idea of 'Islamic Socialism'.[12] Because there was no institutional separation of politics and religion but, rather, an expansion of state control over religious institutions and ideology, 'Islam' became, in effect, a creature of the regime. Arab nationalism and Arab socialism implied a reconceptualisation of religion. Islam became one of many – but not the primary – component of Egyptian identity since Arab nationalism was perceived to unite Muslims and Christians within a context of ethnicity and language, transcending Egyptian borders. Islam was limited to a cultural role and was also used to justify the 'socialist' egalitarian policies of the regime.

Olivier Carré has argued that the suppression of the Muslim Brotherhood by Nasser in the 1950s and 1960s was not dictated by ideological, but by tactical reasons, namely that it constituted a rival mass organisation which appealed to the middle and lower middle classes whose support the Free Officers had to secure in order to consolidate power. Indeed, Nasserist policies echoed the egalitarian spirit of the Muslim Brotherhood of the 1940s and 1950s.[13] Furthermore, the kind of Islam which the regime propagated was heavily influenced by Islamic modernism, the message of Abduh, which had common elements with the world-view of the Muslim Brotherhood (although with significant differences as we saw in Chapter 3). The Brotherhood had not, prior to 1952, stressed the sanctity of individual rights, but the economic and social dimension of Islam, and this was partly adopted by Nasser. Moreover, in the sphere of family law, the regime was unable or unwilling to revise the 1920s codes and thereby further enhance women's rights.[14]

Nasser had not renounced 'Islam', but tried to shape it to serve his regime's ends. He always stressed that Arab socialism did not imply atheism. Religion, once eliminated as a political and ideological rival, was too useful an instrument for the regime to give up. As we shall see, this has been a constant trend in Egypt from Nasser onwards. The second point to note at this stage of the argument is that, because the state under Nasser had become the initiator of social and economic reform (thereby appropriating the radical social message of the Brotherhood), the Muslim Brothers, upon their emergence from the prison cells at the end of the 1960s, were forced into a more politically and socially conservative position. To summarise, in the 1950s and 1960s Islam once again took a form required by political exigencies and social realities. They, not any inherent set of Islamic values, determined its largely negative input in questions of political rights and its emphasis on economic rights, social equality and nationalist unity.

III

With the death of Nasser an era came to a symbolic end for Egypt, although changes had been already set in motion before 1970. The deadlock in economic policy by the mid-1960s, and the defeat in the Arab–Israeli war of 1967 altered the course of events for decades to come. During the last years of Nasser, the seeds of the Sadat period were sown with the first pledges for political liberalisation, the shift away from a command economy, Nasser's appeal to Islam in order to explain away military defeat and his rapprochement with the United States and the conservative Arab regimes.

Instead of Arab unity and socialism, liberalisation and human rights, but also religion and the quest for authenticity, became the pressing concerns of the post-Nasser era. These novel priorities stemmed in part from the widespread perception that the attempt to enhance the country's standing and prosperity through 'foreign' models like socialism had failed, that Arab unity was a sham, and that the only way forward was to revert to Egypt's own resources, traditional and religious. But to point out that Islam and 'authenticity' became a focus of political and social debates after 1970 does not explain very much. If one accepts the arguments of Chapters 2 and 3 – that the cultural essentialist thesis must be rejected, that Islam is determined by the development of the society which espouses it and that in Egypt in particular after the turn of the century many rival interpretations of religion coexisted – then the question must become *which interpretation* of religion became predominant, and why.

The scene must be set by pointing to a number of paradoxes. If it is commonplace to argue that one of the causes of popular religious revivalism are to be found in the profound disillusionment of Egyptians with economic failure and military defeat in the late 1960s, it must immediately be added that the regime of Anwar Sadat promoted an enhanced role of Islam for its own purposes.[15] Islam was to be, firstly, a palliative for a society in crisis and, secondly, a counterbalance to the left – Nasserists, socialists and communists. The regime, therefore, encouraged the formation of Islamist groups in a variety of social settings, especially among the younger generation of students and graduates and recent rural migrants to Egypt's cities. Some of these groups, however, soon became disillusioned with and turned against the regime. In other words, the appeal of Islam grew *both* in defence of the established order *and* in opposition to it.

Similarly with political liberalisation and human rights, where progress was real, albeit slow. The Egyptian elite began to liberalise politically both as a response to international pressures stemming from the shift in Egyptian foreign policy to the West and in particular to the United States, and because liberalism provided Sadat with a legitimating ideology and the means to differentiate himself ideologically from his predecessor. However, once liberalisation was introduced, the activities of civil society began to fill the political space allowed by the regime and popular pressures for further reforms in the area of human rights and democratic freedoms increased. The argument that the regime intended liberalisation as a sop to a small and essentially middle class constituency is a persuasive one.[16] Nevertheless, liberalisation was eventually taken up by a variety of social and political elements (including trade unions and religious groups) and its spirit permeated society as a whole. Human rights, like Islam, was *both* a legitimating instrument for the regime *and* a subversive instrument for the regime's opponents.

The framework for the liberalisation of the economy and the polity was created by the 30 March Programme of 1968, the Constitution of 1971 and the October Paper of 1974, which put in place some of the institutional and legal prerequisites for a democratic and accountable regime.[17] The process of liberalisation was interrupted after the food riots of 1977, and cautiously resumed under Mubarak, until a violent Islamist challenge caused another setback and led to extensive human rights violations from 1992 onwards. Under Sadat and Mubarak, there was a demilitarisation of the cabinet and an effort to ensure that the army be confined to its barracks, even though the presidents of Egypt have all been military men and the role of the military continues to be important in many ways. Nonetheless, during the period as a whole respect for human rights grew, both as a result of governmental initiative and as the outcome of legal and popular challenges against the regime when it backtracked from its pledges of liberalisation (which it often did). Public awareness of human rights issues also increased.[18] In particular, there was some progress in the areas of civil rights, political rights, the rights of association and freedom of expression, and family law.

The protection of civil and political rights was considerably enhanced after 1971. Although respect for the rule of law remained fragile (as the mass arrests of opposition members ordered by Sadat in September 1981 and the anti-fundamentalist campaign in the 1990s showed, to give but two examples), the judiciary took significant steps towards securing some autonomy from the executive and protecting citizens' rights. Indeed, the judiciary, and above all the Supreme Constitutional Court, have emerged as perhaps the principal defenders of democracy and human rights in Egypt.[19]

Egypt became party to the International Covenant on Civil and Political Rights in 1982 and to the United Nations Convention against Torture and Other Cruel, Inhuman or Degrading Treatment or Punishment in 1986. Civil rights were enshrined in the Constitution of 1971 but the use of emergency law – imposed continuously since 1967 except for the period May 1980 to October 1981 – undercut their protection. Under Anwar Sadat, respect for civil rights was somewhat enhanced and the use of torture subsided. Under Mubarak the record was mixed until, in the 1990s, the internal security apparatus came down on the regime's opponents (above all the fundamentalist Islamists) with a heavy hand. Torture and incommunicado detention became, once again, embedded in the system.[20]

Despite Sadat's restricted view of democracy, which will be discussed below, he did represent a step forward from Nasser on the issues of constitutionalism and democratic rule.[21] Egypt ceased to be a one-party state and acquired a (restricted) multi-party system with the emergence of 'platforms' within the dominant Arab Socialist Union (renamed the National Democratic Party in 1978) and their subsequent transformation into political parties. This continued under Mubarak. The opening was used by various forces to challenge the regime whenever possible, primarily through the court system, and to call for press freedoms. Thus, despite the restrictive nature of the Law of May 1977 (Law 40) on political parties and its requirement that a special government committee approve their formation, a number of parties have exercised their right of appeal to the Supreme Constitutional Court and have won their case. Opposition parties have also used the court system to protest against undemocratic behaviour by the government as in 1990 when they joined forces to call for the dissolution of the People's Assembly after it had been declared unconstitutional by the courts.[22] Nevertheless, parties such as the Muslim Brotherhood remain illegal despite their application for permission in the courts. The November 1995 elections were widely condemned as fraudulent by most observers.[23]

The problems with respect to freedom of association, which is regulated by Law 32 of 1964, are many. The law requires all associations to register with the Ministry of Social Affairs and specifies that a precondition for such registration is that the association not be engaged in any 'political activities'. An array of other laws have also been available for the regime to restrict or manipulate associations of all kinds, including professional organisations, trade unions and religious groups.[24] Despite formal restrictions, however, associational life in Egypt has remained considerably active.[25] Two examples would be the activities of the Bar Association in defence of human rights and of non-governmental human rights organisations, principally the Egyptian Organisation for Human Rights (EOHR).[26]

The mixed record in terms of human rights can be seen in two further areas: press censorship (and freedom of expression generally), and labour rights. During the 1970s, Sadat allowed some freedom of expression albeit within the limits of a 'responsible' press. Promises to respect press freedom were undermined by the lack of legal safeguards and the frequent bouts of censorship during which left-wing journalists suffered acutely. Under Mubarak the press had relative freedom (at least until Law 93 of 1995).[27] It is encouraging that, even under the guise of official control, a diversity of voices can exist in the press – the result of balances achieved through compromise and tacit agreements with the authorities.[28] In labour rights, the record is similarly mixed. Despite the prohibition of the right to strike, the 1970s and 1980s were punctuated by labour activism and political involvement.

Corporatist structures have had an negative impact on the promotion of trade union independence and unions are usually tightly controlled; conversely, through the cooptation of the union leadership, some benefits have accrued to the workers although these are being eroded in the 1990s as economic liberalisation proceeds[29]

As regards women's rights, finally, the Sadat period witnessed an end to the stalemate that had existed under Nasser. Law 21 of 1979, guaranteed a proportion of seats for women in the People's Assembly. More importantly, Law 44 of 1979 introduced a number of reforms in family law which partly enhanced women's rights. Women were given the right to divorce should their husband take a second wife and to be informed in the event of divorce and be given alimony; they were also given greater rights of custody. Law 44 was approved by the Assembly as a confirmation of a previous presidential decree. It was challenged in the Supreme Constitutional Court, which indeed declared it unconstitutional on procedural grounds. In 1985, another law, in the same spirit but more restrictive of women's rights, was approved by Parliament. The setbacks were the result of Islamist pressures, and will be discussed further below.[30] Islamists also pressed for making apostasy punishable by death, thereby threatening freedom of conscience. Their campaign, as well as other efforts to introduce Islamic law, was an ominous sign for the country's Coptic minority and contributed to the rise of sectarian violence from the 1970s onwards.[31]

IV

If, during the post-Nasser era, Egypt witnessed an enhanced albeit limited democratisation and respect for human rights, this occurred in parallel to an Islamisation or 're-traditionalisation' of public life.[32] Both developments were seen as alternatives to the hitherto prevalent ideologies. What is less frequently acknowledged is that they were also, *both*, the result of the search for authenticity. This is why there were attempts, more often than not, to combine Islam with the principles of democracy and human rights. This section will outline these attempts, by various key actors in the Egyptian political scene, starting with the two presidents, Sadat and Mubarak.

Anwar Sadat's discourse was a mixture of liberal and authoritarian, modernist and traditionalist ideas. Religion formed an integral part of his political make-up.[33] He projected the image of the 'believing president', the patriarch of the Egyptian 'family'. He frequently used Koranic imagery in the discussion of contemporary issues and alternately argued for the need to be resigned to one's fate (and to Allah) and to take control of one's own destiny. The contradictions in Sadat's thought were many. He claimed, for example, that he was committed to the sovereignty of the people, who were the supreme authority and source of legitimacy in Egypt, but he also argued that the ruler was ordained by God. He asserted that he had reestablished the rule of law, but also implied that he, as the personification of the country as a whole, *conceded* liberties and rights to the people. The corollary was that the president must be on a higher plane than state institutions and immune to criticism. On women he was similarly ambiguous. On the one hand, he argued that true freedom was the fruit of Egypt's indigenous culture and that the woman's place was in the home. Yet on the other hand his regime reformed family law. Regarding the Coptic minority, Sadat always stressed national unity and his sympathy for the Copts. Nevertheless, during instances of conflict with Pope Shenouda and the Coptic community as a whole he emphasised that he was a 'Muslim leader of an Islamic country'.[34]

The 'Islam' to which Sadat appealed was a hybrid of modernism and traditionalism. He lacked an understanding of the major issues surrounding a genuine Islamic liberalism and was content to arbitrarily appeal to whichever element of Islam served his policies. Mubarak, on the other hand, has been much less outspoken on matters of religion. Islamic elements are less part of his image than Sadat's and his appeal to 'traditional' values less pronounced. There have been various cycles in his regime's religious policy. Mubarak continued the liberalisation of political life until 1992. His regime was, until that time, weaker and more permeable by conflicting interests than his predecessor's.[35] Therefore, although its outlook was more secular, it had to appease the powerful Islamic forces in the country.[36] Despite the clampdown on religious extremists after 1992, and on the moderate Muslim Brotherhood after 1995, and although the regime has recently promoted more secularising policies, the conservative tenor in public life under Mubarak continues to prevail.[37]

The official religious establishment has a crucial role to play in the interpretation of religion. In Nasser's Egypt, as we saw, the process of subordination of the ulama to political authority reached its apogee. The religious establishment continued, after 1970, to issue *fatwas* sanctioning government policies as required, papering over the contradictions in its own pronouncements. The most striking example was the Azhar's decision, following the Camp David Accords, to proclaim that peace with the Jews was in agreement with Koranic injunctions, reversing its previous position which forbade it.[38] In domestic politics also the ulama would buttress government policies with elaborate Islamic justifications. Abd al-Halim Mahmud, Shaykh of Al-Azhar, published his 'Fatwas on Communism' in 1976, declaring it heretical and asserting that Islam sanctions private property and individual endeavour, while in 1961 the Mufti of Egypt had sanctioned the socialist decrees. During the reversal of political liberalisation from 1977–81 the Azhar, through the pages of its periodical *Majallat al-Azhar*, argued that the government could wage *jihad* against civil disorder.[39]

There are, however, cracks in the relationship between the regime and the ulama and as a result the ulama have asserted views that are by no means identical to the official line. They have been resentful of regime pressures and arm-twisting and have conversely been accused by the government that they are responsible for the rise of radical Islam.[40] In matters pertaining to human rights and liberalisation, the ulama must be described as more conservative than the regime. Many of them see the *sharia* as a total way of life and consider its imposition imperative – even though they may disagree on what the *sharia* means and on the permissibility of *ijtihad*. Under Sadat some ulama supported the changes in family law of 1979, but under Mubarak they reversed their position. It was partly through the activities of some ulama that family law became more restrictive in 1985. When the Mubarak government demanded that they condemn Sadat's assassins as heretics they retorted that the concept of excommunication was alien to Islam.[41] From 1992 onwards, the Azhar has been even more outspoken and conservative, and seems to have moved closer to the

Islamists' ideas and further away from the official line.[42] There are exceptions to this trend – usually involving the Mufti of Egypt – but, as a general rule, whenever the regime relaxes its grip on the religious establishment the latter reverts to conservative Islamism, rather than a liberal interpretation of the religion.

The ulama in Egypt have, on the whole, rejected Muhammad Abduh's modernist message. So have the Muslim Brothers, for reasons that were discussed in Chapter 3. The same ambivalence on liberal ideas typify their movement from the 1970s onwards – as it did in the 1920s and 1930s – despite the fact that on the surface it became more accommodating to the principles of human rights. One explanation for this superficial accommodation is that the repression suffered by the Society in the 1950s and 1960s made them turn to human rights principles.[43] It is, however, more plausible to explain the shift by the changing nature of their social support and of the political framework in which they operate.

The Society experienced a rift in Nasser's prison camps between the moderate elements represented primarily by the leader of the Brotherhood at the time, Hassan al-Hudaybi, and the radical ideologues, epitomised by Sayyid Qutb. The rift remained a permanent feature of the Islamist movement thereafter. The mainstream of the movement became characterised by a marked reserve in the matter of political ideology and abandoned the egalitarian and social reformist touch of the interwar period and the 1940s and 1950s. Even if *al-Dawa*, the Brotherhood's journal, for example, condemns stark inequalities of income and encourages nationalisations, self-reliance and welfare policies, it does not challenge the fundamentals of the social system. The sanctity of private property is affirmed, *zakat* is considered sufficient for ensuring social welfare and class conflict is denied as un-Islamic.[44] Moderation has also prevailed in political terms. The Brothers have functioned within the letter of the law, avoiding any overt challenges to the regime and have taken part in elections – as independents – in alliance with secular opposition parties.

On human rights specifically, the Muslim Brothers' views have undergone a dramatic transformation. Rights have been incorporated into the organisation's discourse increasingly since the 1970s. *Al-Dawa* virulently criticises the regime's half-hearted democratisation measures. The freedoms of expression and association are not, it argues, a grant bestowed by the ruler, but a birthright stipulated by Islam and exercised by the *umma*. In cooperation with secular opposition figures the Brothers have campaigned in favour of political and civil rights. They claim that the just ruler must rule according to the *sharia* and through the Islamic democratic institution of *shura*.[45]

The Muslim Brothers defend human rights because they are concerned with protecting their own rights, as individuals and as an organisation.[46] They also defend rights because they are intent on presenting a picture of a moderate and respectable movement which espouses the internationally prestigious principles of human rights. However, many students of Egyptian politics and human rights activists, who analyse the day-to-day reaction of the Brotherhood to specific events (like the assassination of the secularist writer Farag Foda in 1992 or the Brotherhood commentary on the policies of the Sudanese regime after 1991), agree that their grasp of the concept of human rights is superficial and pernicious.[47] The compromise of form rather than content (as analysed in Chapter 2), is revealed in the Brotherhood's views on non-Muslims. The rights of non-Muslim minorities within Muslim society, they argue, must be respected; but, in numerous instances, Christians and particularly Jews are pictured in their publications as inherently hostile to Islam and the growth in the Brotherhood's influence has contributed, undeniably, to inter-communal tension between Muslims and Copts.[48] The Brotherhood's ideas on women, although not uniform, tend to converge on the view that there is a fundamental inequality between the sexes which is often explained away as being a 'difference in roles' or about the 'protection of women'.[49]

If the Muslim Brotherhood's synthesis of Islam and human rights is to the detriment of rights, this is even more pronounced among the various Islamic organisations (*gama'at*) which have proliferated in the country since the 1970s. Here, we see the disregard of human rights principles in practice. These groups are informal Muslim voluntary organisations, set up to promote practical 'religious solutions' to social problems. They have functioned on university campuses, where they were encouraged during the 1970s by the regime as a counterweight against leftist students, and in poor urban areas, centering on mosques and local religious leaders. Their behaviour is aggressive and intolerant – particularly in the universities which they dominated until recently – towards those who do not share their views: they promote conservatism on women and the separation of the sexes, attempt to enforce Islamic dress and bully unmarried couples seen together in public. Their activities have also been partially responsible for sectarian strife against the Copts.[50]

The *gama'at* provided one of the pools for the radical, underground organisations of the 1970s, 1980s and 1990s. This extremist element in the Islamist movement – which can be described as fundamentalist proper – draws its inspiration from Sayyid Qutb, the radical Muslim Brother who was hanged by the authorities in 1966. Many of the radicals arrived at their positions after becoming disillusioned with the Brotherhood's moderate views. What distinguishes the fundamentalists from other Islamist organisations is their intransigence, their strict way of life and the view that there is an absolute discrepancy between Islamic ideals and contemporary reality. They are committed to a holy struggle and the overthrow of political authority. They want to rebuild society according to the Islamic ideal, and stress that isolated efforts are not sufficient in accomplishing the transformation. An unjust ruler, according to the radicals, is absolutely unacceptable (they therefore reject the whole corpus of medieval tradition which pronounces unjust authority preferable to disorder). The Islamic polity must be overhauled from its foundation and function on the basis of *shura*. Non-Muslim minorities, the radicals purport, would be respected in Muslim society as would be women – both of course being unequal to Muslims and men respectively.[51] In sum, the radical Islamists totally, and often openly, reject democracy and human rights as being Western and un-Islamic.

Another contribution to the debate on Islam and its political interpretation comes from individual, popular shaykhs who have either a national or localised following. Shaykhs Sharawi and Kishk, for example, present a popularised and simplified interpretation of Islam.[52] It is difficult to ascertain which interpretation of religion these men promote – and impossible to generalise about them because of their wide range of views – but the consensus seems to be that they pander to a simplified and often traditionalist Islam.

It transpires, from the above analysis, that none of the discourses on Islam in Egypt is predominantly liberal. Neither government, nor opposition, are proponents of Islamic liberalism proper. Nevertheless, despite the retraditionalisation of the regime, its interpretation of Islam is less authoritarian and conservative than the Islamists'. Furthermore, within most of the discourses of the major actors outlined above, we can trace *strands* of Islamic liberalism. Within the Muslim Brotherhood, for instance, there exists considerable division and disagreement on the questions of democracy and multi-partyism.[53] Within the broad context of Islamism there are a number of intellectuals – either loosely associated with the Brotherhood or wishing to distance themselves from it – who purport to be Islamic liberals.[54] In a separate category are a number of intellectuals, academics and jurists who assiduously defend a liberal interpretation of Islam or follow Abd al-Raziq's lead in favouring a separation of religion and politics.[55] The modernist tradition of Abduh, in other words, continues to permeate many levels of public life and Islamist discourse.

The 'mix' between liberal and authoritarian interpretations of Islam. in public life is constantly changing. This makes it difficult, sometimes, to separate the views of establishment and those of oppositional groups with regard to religion. Secularism and Islamic fundamentalism are minority positions in Egypt in the 1990s. The main confrontation is between the state and the Muslim Brotherhood.[56] From neither of these two quarters is it likely, in the immediate future, that Islamic liberalism will emerge and predominate in Egyptian public life. The reasons behind this will be explored in the remainder of this chapter.

V

The shift towards economic liberalisation in Egypt was discernible from the late 1960s but became institutionalised under Sadat. As noted above, the 'inclusivist' policies of the Nasser regime – the attempt, that is, to provide for all social groups through a centralised, command economy – had reached an impasse by the mid-1960s. The failure to develop heavy industry and to increase domestic savings led to extensive government borrowing. After the 1967 defeat the regime had to turn to oil-rich Arab countries, its former rivals, to bail it out.

Under Sadat, the abandonment of 'socialism' was reinforced by foreign policy considerations. He judged that Egypt needed support from the West, which also implied some kind of settlement with Israel. From the mid-1970s onwards, a series of laws were enacted opening up the economy and providing incentives to private enterprise. The aim was to reduce state control of the economy and attract foreign capital. But it soon became evident that the policies of *infitah* were not working. The liberalisation of imports led to an influx of luxury consumer goods, inaccessible to the majority of the population; investment levels in productive areas did not rise; foreign capital was not attracted; the economy did not grow, and income gaps widened.[57] The riots of January 1977 were a response to this worsening situation.

Under Mubarak during the 1980s *infitah* continued but was toned down. His governments oscillated between various mixes of the public and the private sector but were unable or unwilling to make a breakthrough in one direction or another.[58] A close identification of interest unites the regime, the state (which is its captive), and a number of social groups, mostly middle class. No class is disadvantaged enough by this state of affairs *and* powerful enough to challenge and ultimately upset the status quo. When the breakthrough came after 1991, in favour of further economic liberalisation, it was not the result of any social force challenging the state but of external pressures.

The bureaucratic establishment in Egypt is huge and has remained so, despite liberalisation and its shrinking economic role.[59] The bureaucracy is not a coherent group with a common set of interests, because considerable internal inequalities make a collective consciousness impossible. Yet, it has the capacity to obstruct reform. The 'state bourgeoisie', initially formed under Nasser, also has an interest in the continuation of a strong role for the public sector whose share in employment and gross output is one of the largest among the developing world.[60]

The private sector industrial and commercial bourgeoisie, having suffered restrictions under Nasser, resurfaced in the 1970s and expanded its role in the economy. But its well-being is dependent on the public sector. It lives off the state, using its connections with the bureaucracy to its own advantage. The state bourgeoisie, also, uses the economic opportunities provided by *infitah* by creating links with the private sector.[61] There are degrees in the corruption involved in this relationship which includes bribery, speeding up the legal process and the blatant embezzlement of public funds for private profit, often with the collusion of civil servants.

Since the International Monetary Fund agreement of 1991, there has been a perceptible shift in economic policy in Egypt towards greater liberalisation and structural adjustment. The result has been positive in terms of economic indicators but negative in terms of the widening gap between rich and poor.[62] This development has been manifestly the result of external factors – the Gulf War, debt relief and IMF pressure on Egypt – rather than of domestic pressures. But is has meant an increased role for a small section of the middle classes, the 'entrepreneurial bourgeoisie', which attempts to survive in the market without assistance from the state. It is possible that at some future stage this group will attempt to promote political as well as economic liberalisation.[63]

Other sections of the middle class which are more independent of the state – those participating in Islamic banks and investment companies; the businessmen who dominate the traditional economy, and those involved in the flourishing black market and other informal sectors, beyond the government's control[64] – have no interest or capacity to demand major revisions of economic structures.

What does all this mean for our argument? Clearly, that the Egyptian bourgeoisie is closely tied to the state, in one way or another, and that the sections that function outside it are either too weak or too corrupt to pose a challenge. The Egyptian bourgeoisie has been formed and nurtured in the shadow of the state, not in opposition to it. This socio-economic development has had, and will continue to have at least in the near future, major implications for political culture and human rights.

Similar observations can be made with regard to other classes. The rural middle class, which has dominated the countryside since Nasser's land reforms, benefits – even more since the inception of *infitah* – from links with the state. The lower classes in both urban and rural settings remained, during the 1970s and 1980s, dependent on the state

– with similar albeit weaker links than had existed under Nasser – through the state's control of prices, subsidies and wages. The welfare aspect of economic policy may have progressively diminished during the 1980s and 1990s, but the state has not given it up altogether.[65] The workers in the public sector depend on the state for obvious reasons and corporatist structures further limit their freedom of action. Their trade unions, as all trade unions in Egypt, are constantly harassed and coopted by the regime.

The picture presented above explains the weakness of both economic and political liberalisation in Egypt. No class, and certainly not the fragmented middle class, can capture the state or challenge it. The working class, until the recent past, was 'given' benefits and did not – with exceptions of course – wrest them from the regime. The state, backed by the army, retains political and ideological domination and controls the pace and depth of liberalisation. But if the above, social and economic reasons, are part of the explanation, the other part involves the shallow roots of political and institutional pluralism in Egypt. Political opposition groups and associations remain weak, both because of the nature of their class support, but also because they lack a tradition of institutional independence and are constantly harassed by the government.

Nasser's regime was the main cause of that. The various mass movements of the Nasser era did not serve as decision-making or participation institutions but as civic associations to mobilise the population for development and as instruments of control and patronage. But by the late 1960s the regime was faced by a participation crisis[66] and soon after Sadat came to power tentative steps towards multi-party democracy began to be taken, as we saw. From the Arab Socialist Union, there emerged in 1976 three 'platforms' which contested the elections of that year which were transformed into political parties in 1977. But if, during the 1980s, democratic life became more institutionalised, no political party was capable of challenging the dominant National Democratic Party (NDP), heir of the ASU.

The secular opposition parties have not really gained mass appeal in the country since their emergence in the late 1970s. The new Wafd – which reemerged briefly in 1978 and then again after 1983 – is in favour of full political and economic liberalisation and is an almost exclusively middle class organisation. Like the old Wafd, its leaders and membership represent the professional bourgeoisie, particularly lawyers, and landowning groups. The large percentage of civil servants in its membership reflects the extent to which the liberal ideology has infiltrated the 'state bourgeoisie'.[67] But its inability to give rise to a vibrant movement also shows the extent to which the liberal spirit of the professional middle class has been weakened, its associations coopted and its interests tied to the state, which is its largest employee.

The constituencies of the other secular parties are also small. The Nationalist Progressive Unionist Party (NPUP) – the legalised left opposition group which emerged out of the 'platforms' of the ASU in 1977 – is a collection of Nasserites, socialists of various hues and Marxists. Its leaders are mostly intellectuals and professionals, workers and trade unionists, and its support – actual or potential – comes from the socially mobile of modest background, the petty bourgeoisie, white-collar employees, lower civil servants and of course working class people. The NPUP has been systematically harassed by the government, one of the reasons being that Nasserism was especially feared by Sadat. A Nasserite party was only legalised in Egypt in 1992 and, before that, the often uneasy coexistence of various ideological groups weakened the NPUP. Furthermore it's electoral support has been abysmally low.[68] The other parties have either been creatures of the regime – like the Socialist Labour Party, created in 1978 by Sadat as a 'loyal opposition' until it eventually escaped the regime's control to align itself with the Muslim Brotherhood – or have tiny constituencies, like the Liberal and the Umma parties. None of them really present a threat to the regime.[69]

The ineptitude of opposition parties has been perpetuated by the constitutional emphasis on a strong executive, the excessive concentration of power in the hands of the president and the inability of the People's Assembly to call the executive to account. The feebleness of constitutional checks and balances and of political parties has a parallel in associational life in general.

Corporatist structures began to be introduced in Egypt from 1940 onwards. With Nasser this process intensified and culminated in an authoritarian brand of corporatism. This was reduced under Sadat and Mubarak under whom the corporatism of Egyptian associational life has been flexible and incoherent, a synthesis of corporatist and pluralist structures.[70] There are two types of associations which have a political impact in Egyptian public life, professional syndicates and trade unions. The former have been active in defending their members' interests and have even had a political voice at times. Since the mid-1980s they have been gradually taken over by the Islamists – a process which culminated in the Muslim Brotherhood victory in the Bar Association's elections in September 1992. They have suffered, thereafter, from a confrontation with the regime.[71] The trade union movement is undergoing a repressive phase in the 1990s.[72]

Rather than formal associations, it is often informal structures that undertake the functions of representation and provide access to the elite and to resources for the population at large in Egypt. Patron-client relations, informal networks like the *shilla* and the *dufaa*, and family and provincial loyalties permeate the bureaucracy, the elite and society as a whole and undermine democratic processes.[73]

VI

It would be simplistic and misleading to take the above analysis as a blanket statement which proves that a repressive state, which is the captive of the regime, controls every aspect of social or political life in Egypt. The reality is much more mixed, nuanced and ambivalent. Egypt has liberalised, to an extent, civil society has not been utterly stultified, and is gradually becoming more robust. A semi-liberal polity does function, in fits and starts.

The Egyptian state is, nevertheless, the key to the analysis of Egyptian politics. The partial success of liberalism is due to the specificity of the Egyptian state: a state which developed, since the nineteenth century, into a relatively centralised and legitimate set of institutions. The failures of this process, conversely, explain the failures of liberalism. Authoritarian political practices have been the norm in Egypt since the 1950s. Furthermore, the massive expansion of state institutions under Nasser meant that the middle classes have been nurtured by the state and are still closely tied to it. This is quite apart from a state bourgeoisie which has a vital interest in perpetuating interventionist economic policies. The state's capabilities have been reduced since 1970 but this has not, as yet, made a full impact. Capitalism in Egypt is still 'state capitalism' and the regime's authoritarian instincts are still unchecked.

Because of the politics of state capitalism, genuine economic liberalisation has no constituency in Egypt. Neither the state nor the middle classes – except for a small segment – will benefit from the collapse of the role of the public sector in the economy. Further, the regime cannot allow full political liberalisation because it fears that this may endanger its hold on power and perhaps the very unity of society. Political and associational opposition has been weakened by cooptation and fragmentation, to the extent that they cannot combine to promote pluralism. This picture of a static economics and politics may be changing – with the emergence of a capitalist class proper and growing signs of life from civil society – but it is too early to assess the prospects. To date, the constituency for liberalism in Egypt has been very small.

It is within this framework that the role of Islam has to be understood. The key position of the state explains the many transmutations of Islam. The Islam that predominates in Egypt since the time of Nasser is Islam as determined by the state, not only because it controls the religious establishment but above all because still, despite the reduction in its capabilities and liberalisation, it also controls the law, the symbols of public life and the means through which they are transmitted.[74] The state has oscillated, since the 1970s, between liberalism and authoritarianism. The Islam for which it stands correspondingly contains a fluid mix of liberal and authoritarian elements.

A number of reasons combine to make state Islam a liberal Islam, to a limited extent. A regime that is committed to liberalisation, at least in name, cannot propound a wholly conservative and traditionalist version of Islam. But the reasons go much deeper, to the modernist values of the regime which came to power in 1952. Despite its many transformations, this regime cannot totally disavow its first principles without losing its legitimacy further. The other major reason why the regime cannot adopt a traditionalist and wholly illiberal interpretation of Islam is the existence of the Coptic minority which it cannot alienate and marginalise.

The forces that work *against* the state adopting a fully liberal interpretation of Islam – symbolised in further reforms of family law for example – are again related to political developments, but in a different fashion. The regime's legitimacy has suffered enormously as a result of its failures in the domestic front (structural economic problems and corruption), and in foreign policy. The ideologies it has successively upheld – socialist of sorts under Nasser, liberal of sorts under Sadat and after – have been discredited in the eyes of the Egyptian people. The regime, therefore, desperate to enhance its moral authority, poses as the defender of authentic values, combined in a haphazard way with its modernist discourse. It brings Islam into the picture, but now as an instrument for its own legitimation. It appeals to what it *perceives* to be a tradition which the people would not lightheartedly reject.[75]

Sadat, because of his troubled presidency, used a traditionalist interpretation of Islam extensively in that way. The contradictions between liberalism and traditionalism in his political discourse can be explained in that he chose to liberalise the economy and society but also sought the means of legitimating himself and holding society together. Under Mubarak, the regime has liberalised further economically and has suffered a more forceful challenge from the Islamists. It has therefore become more vulnerable and responsive to society. Furthermore, because Egyptian society is conservative in its social attitudes the state hesitates to actively promote a progressive interpretation of Islam.[76] Social conservatism explains why Egypt has liberalised and Islamised at the same time. It also provides a comment on the inseparability of the private and the public in questions of liberalism and human rights. A society imbued with hierarchical family values cannot uphold and sustain liberalism in public life.

The Mubarak regime has engaged in a race with the Islamists in which it has felt compelled to defend its Islamic credentials[77] (a strategy that may be changing now as the Islamist threat subsides). Consequently, the question of the *sharia* and its imposition has become central in Egyptian politics. The regime claims that most of the laws of the land are already in accordance with Islamic law, as a way of bypassing constant pressures to introduce the *sharia* penalties on apostasy, adultery and the other *hadd* punishments. It stalls for time and uses procedural devices in the Assembly to avoid debates on the *sharia* without becoming open to charges of being un-Islamic.[78] In the process, the regime participates in a conservative reconceptualisation of Islam and authenticity in Egypt.[79]

VII

The groups that have escaped the state's cooptation and manipulation more than any other in Egypt have been the Islamist groups. Sufi orders, philanthropic and private mosque associations have resisted, more successfully than others, the regime's control.[80] The Muslim Brotherhood is not a legalised opposition party. But it has succeeded in having its candidates elected to the Assembly either as independents or in alliance with the Wafd in 1984 and the Socialist Labour Party in 1987. Its grassroots organisation is superior to the secular opposition parties. In both power political and 'civil society' terms the Islamists seem to be the most robust possible alternative to the present regime.

Why is this so? It is again to the state that we need to turn for an explanation: the delegitimation of the modernist ideologies for which it has stood, since at least 1952, and its policies with regard to the secular opposition parties – mostly of the left – which it has persistently harassed. Islam has emerged, from the 1970s onwards, as the major opposition ideology to the regime, not because it reverberates with the people's authentic self but because the alternatives have been tried and defeated. Even so, as with the Wafd studied in the previous chapter, it can be argued that Nasserism's socialism and modernism had greater support in Egypt than the Brotherhood has had since the 1970s.

The question we need to answer, however, is not whether Islam has been on the rise. Rather we need to ask which interpretation of Islam predominates in Egypt. The state's interpretation is a mixture of modernist and traditionalist elements without, however, a clear emphasis on Islamic liberalism. Why is the interpretation of Islam put forward by the Muslim Brotherhood conservative?

A simple answer is: so that the Brotherhood can differentiate itself from the state. But we need to go further, and look into the social support the Brotherhood commands in Egypt. As a contender for capturing the state, the movement tries to appeal to all classes which explains the all-inclusive nature of its social message. But because of its traditional weakness in the rural constituencies, its limited appeal among the working class and the capture of parts of the impoverished urban sectors by the radical Islamist groups, it focuses its attention mostly on middle and lower middle classes.

The Brotherhood has strong links with Saudi Arabia and is supported by returning migrants who become prosperous there. Advertising in *al-Dawa*, the Brotherhood's publication, is representative of a cross-section of business interests which flourished under *infitah*.[81] This section of the middle class – represented also by the Islamic investment companies – is profiting sufficiently from the present state of affairs and does not seek its structural revision. The Brotherhood has also secured the allegiance of many of the professional middle classes and has gained control of most of their associations as we saw. It has many sympathisers in the lower levels of the bureaucracy.

The Brotherhood, in other words, has become a *largely middle class organisation*, coopted, as its radical Islamic rivals would say, by the system.[82] These middle classes have been nurtured under the state and are tied to it in a multiplicity of ways. The middle classes which are involved in capitalist activities, the professions, the salaried petty bourgeoisie, have not evolved a spirit of independence from the state that would render them defenders of liberal values. The Brotherhood, in their struggle for political supremacy, reflect the values of those middle classes who aspire to either capture or get a better deal from the state, not destroy the political and social system that it represents. Students of Egyptian politics argue that other sections of the middle class who do not support Islamism do not feel particularly threatened by the Brotherhood's toned-down, moderate discourse.[83]

The crux of the argument is this. There is no constituency for liberalism in Egypt and, for this reason, there is no constituency for Islamic liberalism either. As Leonard Binder argues, the space between state Islam and the Islamist alternative, occupied by a few enlightened intellectuals, is too narrow to be a cause for optimism.[84] The Islam propagated by the state and that which is proposed by the Muslim Brotherhood are partly mirrors of this illiberal society. As the state and the Brotherhood make choices in attempting to maintain or increase their legitimacy and support, they contribute to a conservative reconceptualisation of Islam, in a vicious circle.

The lack of a liberal Islam in Egypt today reflects the economic, social and political developments of recent years, not the precepts of 'Islam' as an independent entity. In the Egypt of the 1970s, 1980s and 1990s we can best understand these developments by concentrating on the central role of the state. It is against the state that political actors such as the Brotherhood are defined. It is the state that takes the initiative in proposing the dominant interpretations of religion. As the crisis in the Egyptian economy and society unfolds, the state and the Muslim Brotherhood battle over the allegiance of the middle classes, and over the meaning of Islam and authenticity.

Notes

1. The two ideological forces reemerged after 1970, as I said in the previous section. They will provide the two pillars of the analysis that follows.

2. The term 'state capitalism' means the promotion of capitalist policies by the state, *in lieu* of the private sector. See Waterbury, J., *The Egypt of Nasser and Sadat: The Political Economy of Two Regimes* (Princeton, NJ: Princeton University Press, 1983), Chapters 1 and 4; Cooper, M. N., *The Transformation of Egypt* (London: Croom Helm, 1982), Chapter 2; and Cooper, M. N., 'State Capitalism, Class Structure and Social Transformation in the Third World: The Case of Egypt' in *International Journal of Middle East Studies* (Vol. 15, No. 4, November 1983), pp. 451–69.

3. Dessouki, A. E. H., 'The Transformation of the Party System in Egypt, 1952–1977' in Dessouki, A. E. H. (ed.), *Democracy in Egypt: Problems and Prospects* (Cairo Papers in Social Science, Vol. 1, Monograph 2, 1983 / Cairo: American University in Cairo Press), p. 14.

4. Yadlin, R., 'Militant Islam in Egypt: Some Sociocultural Aspects' in Warburg, G. R. and Kupferschmidt, U. M. (eds), *Islam, Nationalism and Radicalism in Egypt and the Sudan* (New York: Praeger, 1983), p. 161.

5. Baker, R. W., 'Sadat's Open Door: Opposition from Within' in *Social Problems*, (Vol. 28, No. 4, April 1981), p. 381. Baker notes that this popular support was eroded under Sadat, a point to which we will return later.

6. Waterbury, op. cit., Chapters 2 and 5.

7. A debate over this class and its precise relationship to the regime has been raging among various students of Egyptian politics. Binder's thesis, which describes this class (and its urban equivalents) as the 'second stratum' and argues that the regime was its captive, is now deemed unconvincing. See, Binder, L., *In a Moment of Enthusiasm: Political Power and the Second Stratum in Egypt* (Chicago, IL: University of Chicago Press, 1978).

8. Akeel, H. A. and Moore, C. H., 'The Class Origins of Egyptian Engineer-Technocrats' in Nieuwenhuijze, C. A. O. (ed.), *Commoners, Climbers and Notables: A Sampler of Studies on Social Ranking in the Middle East* (Leiden: E. J. Brill, 1977).

9. Waterbury, op. cit., p. 19, defines the 'state bourgeoisie' as comprising the 'upper managerial and technocratic stratum that directs the state capitalist sector'. The fact that the state bourgeoisie promoted capitalist policies did not mean that it was the servant of private capitalist classes: 'suspicion and hostility typified the official attitude' to the private sector. Waterbury argues that the existence of the state bourgeoisie renders the state a semi-autonomous actor in Egyptian society.

10. Cooper, 'State Capitalism, Class Structure and Social Transformation', op. cit., pp. 455–8 and 460–2.

11. Bianchi, R., *Unruly Corporatism: Associational Life in Twentieth Century Egypt* (New York: Oxford University Press, 1989).

12. On Islam under Nasser see, for example, Crecelius, D., 'Al-Azhar in the Revolution' in *Middle East Journal*, (Vol. 20, No. 1, Winter 1966), pp. 31–49 and Berger, M., *Islam in Egypt Today: Social and Political Aspects of Popular Religion*, (Cambridge: Cambridge University Press, 1970).

13. Carré, O., 'The Impact of the Egyptian Muslim Brotherhood's Political Islam Since the 1950s' in Warburg and Kupferschmidt, op. cit., p. 263.

14. Nasser did however give the right to vote (in the 1956 Constitution) and social and economic rights to women. See Hatem, M. F., 'Egyptian Discourses on Gender and Political Liberalisation: Do Secularist and Islamist Views Really Differ?' in *Middle East Journal* (Vol. 48, No. 4, Autumn 1994), p. 664.

15. Transnational Islamist links and material support from abroad, for example Saudi Arabia, also reinforced the revival. Roussillon, A., 'Intellectuels en Crise dans l'Égypte Contemporaine' in Kepel, G. and Richard, Y. (eds), *Intellectuels et militants de l'Islam contemporain* (Paris: Seuil, 1990), p. 247.

16. Cooper, *The Transformation of Egypt*, op. cit., p. 55.

17. On political liberalisation under Sadat generally see Hinnebusch, R. A., *Egyptian Politics Under Sadat: The Post-Populist Development of an*

Authoritarian-Modernizing State (Boulder, CO: Lynne Rienner, 1985), especially Chapter 6.

18.   Mona Makram-Ebeid, political analyst and member of the New Wafd (interview with the author; all interviews were conducted in Cairo, October 1992). Ms Makram-Ebeid argued that the greater number of university graduates from the 1950s onwards has contributed towards a greater awareness of human rights issues and that there have been efforts to introduce the subject in universities and in military and police academies.

19.   *Proceedings of the International Conference on The Role of the Judiciary in the Protection of Human Rights*, 1–3 December 1996, Cairo, Egypt (unpublished); Brown, N. J., *The Rule of Law in the Arab World* (Cambridge: Cambridge University Press, 1997).

20.   Middle East Watch, *Behind Closed Doors: Torture and Detention in Egypt* (New York: Human Rights Watch, 1992); Amnesty International, *Egypt: Arbitrary Detention and Torture under Emergency Powers* (AI Index, MDE 12/ 01/89, May 1989); *Egypt: Ten Years of Torture* (AI Index, MDE 12/18/91, October 1991); *Egypt: Security Police Detentions Undermine the Rule of Law* (AI Index, MDE 12/01/92, January 1992). See also the reports by the Egyptian Organisation for Human Rights which condemns the spiral of violence emanating from the radical Islamist groups and the security forces. For example, EOHR, *Armed Violence in Egypt: Facts and Conclusions*, 14 September 1992; EOHR, *The Campaign to Stop Torture: Rape and Sexual Abuse as Methods of Torture*, 7 January 1992; EOHR, *In Defence of Human Rights: The EOHR May 1993 to December 1994 Press Releases and Reports* (Cairo: EOHR, 1995), Chapters 1–6; EOHR, *Recurrent Detention: Prisoners Without Trial*, 15/1/1993– 30/12/1994; EOHR, *Torture Inside Police Stations Must Be Stopped* (March 10, 1997).

21.   Hinnebusch, op. cit., pp. 117–19.

22.   Al-Sayyid, M. K., 'A Civil Society in Egypt?' in *Middle East Journal* (Vol. 47, No. 2, Spring 1993), p. 238.

23.   EOHR, *Democracy Jeopardised: Nobody 'Passed' the Elections: The EOHR Account of the Egyptian Parliamentary Elections, 1995.*

24.   Al-Sayyid, op. cit., pp. 236–9. Note that in 1993 Law 100, on professional associations, was promulgated. It 'aimed at reducing the likelihood of future electoral victories in these professional bodies by the Muslim Brotherhood'. See, Human Rights Watch, *Egypt: Human Rights Abuses Mount in 1993*, (Vol. 5, Issue 8, October 1993), p. 9.

25.   This is the central argument of Bianchi, op. cit.

26.   Human rights NGOs have proliferated in Egypt since the mid-1990s, but there are many restrictions. The EOHR – and the Arab Organisation for

Human Rights, which is its parent organisation – have repeatedly applied for legal status which has been refused. See, 'Restricting the Human Rights Movement in Egypt: Legal Restrictions on Independent Non-Governmental Organisations' in *Civil Society: Democratic Transformation in the Arab World*, (Cairo: Ibn Khaldun Centre for Development Studies, No. 5, May 1992, pp. 6–9). The article also discusses the dissolution of the Arab Women's Solidarity Association (AWSA) in June 1991 on the basis of Law 32 of 1964. See also the newsletter of the Cairo Institute for Human Rights Studies, *Sawasiah*, which provides analysis of human rights developments in Egypt and the Arab world.

27. 'Egypt' in *Human Rights Watch World Report 1997*, (New York: Human Rights Watch, 1996), p. 279. The confrontation between the government and the journalists about this press law started in 1993 and is still continuing.

28. Interviews with Amina Shafiq, secretary-general of the Journalists' Syndicate and Nabil Zaki, deputy editor of the newspaper *al-Akhbar*.

29. Hinnebusch, op. cit., pp. 244–6 and El Shafei, O., *Workers, Trade Unions and the State in Egypt, 1984–1989* (Cairo Papers in Social Science, Vol. 18, Monograph 2, Summer 1995/Cairo: American University in Cairo Press). Note that, unlike professional associations, the labour movement does not contain a prominent Islamist presence. See, Stork, J., 'Egypt's Factory Privatization Campaign Turns Deadly' in *Middle East Report* (No. 192, Vol. 25, No. 1, January–February 1995), p. 29. In 1995 Law 12 legalised the right to strike (strikes had been banned since 1952), but also provided greater leeway for employers to fire workers and determine wages. See, Pripstein, M., 'Egypt's New Labor Law Removes Worker Provisions' in *Middle East Report* (No. 194/5. Vol. 25, Nos 3 and 4, May–June/July–August 1995, pp. 52–3); EOHR *Annual Report 1995*, pp. 45–53.

30. On the provisions of the Law of 1979, and women generally, see Rugh, A. B., *Family in Contemporary Egypt* (New York: Syracuse University Press, 1984), pp. 271–4 and Sullivan, E. L., *Women in Egyptian Public Life* (Syracuse, NY; Syracuse University Press, 1986), pp. 36–8. See also Nowaihi, M., 'Changing the Law on Personal Status within a Liberal Interpretation of the Sharia' in Nelson, C. and Koch, K. F. (eds), *Law and Social Change: Problems and Challenges in Contemporary Egypt* (Cairo Papers in Social Science, Vol. 2, Monograph 4, July 1983, Cairo: American University in Cairo Press), which discusses the possibility of ensuring women's rights within an Islamic liberal context in Egypt.

31. See *Middle East Contemporary Survey* (Vol. I, 1976–77), pp. 297–8 and (Vol. II, 1977–78), p. 386 for various instances on apostasy bills (and other proposals to introduce Islamic law), in the People's Assembly and the government's efforts to prevent them. On the problems of the Coptic

community in the face of Islamism see EOHR, *Urgent Report on the Sectarian Massacre in Dairout*, 7 May 1992; Ansari, H., 'Sectarian Conflict in Egypt and the Political Expediency of Religion' in *Middle East Journal* (Vol. 38, No. 3, Summer 1984), pp. 397–418; Pennington, J. D., 'The Copts in Modern Egypt' in *Middle Eastern Studies* (Vol. 18, No. 2, April 1982), pp. 158–79; Ibrahim, S. E., et al., *The Copts of Egypt* (Minority Rights Group, 1996).

32. In recent years many formerly secular intellectuals have shifted to Islam; Khaled Muhammad Khaled is one such figure. See Abou el-Magd, N. M. I., *The Political Ideas of Khaled Mohamed Khaled: Islam, Democracy, Socialism and Nationalism* (Cairo: American University in Cairo, Department of Political Science, 1992, unpublished). For an analysis of the debate surrounding the role of Islam in the Egyptian constitution of 1971 and an example of the multiplicity of views on the issue, see O'Kane, J. P., 'Islam in the New Egyptian Constitution: Some Discussions in *al-Ahram*' in *Middle East Journal* (Vol. 26, No. 2, Spring 1972), pp. 137–48. In this constitution the *sharia* was to be 'a principal source of legislation' in Egypt; but it was amended in 1980 to declare the *sharia* 'the' principal source of legislation.

33. The information on Sadat and his understanding of Islam is drawn principally from Israeli, R., *'I Egypt': Aspects of President Anwar al-Sadat's Political Thought* (Jerusalem: Magnes Press, Hebrew University, 1981) and El-Sadat, A., *In Search of Identity: An Autobiography* (New York: Harper and Row, 1977).

34. Pennington, op. cit., p. 174.

35. Springborg, R., *Mubarak's Egypt: Fragmentation of the Political Order* (Boulder, CO: Westview Press, 1989), especially Chapter 2.

36. The government tried to placate the Islamists by promising to revise existing legislation to bring it more in tune with the *sharia*, for example. This is argued by Esposito, J. L., *The Islamic Threat: Myth or Reality?* (New York: Oxford University Press, 1992), pp. 97–100. Esposito also notes Mubarak's attempt (until 1992), to divide and rule the Islamist movements by appeasing the moderate Islamists and providing them with 'public outlets for their opposition: they could compete in parliamentary elections, publish newspapers, voice criticism in the media.' After that time this policy was reversed in favour of repression against all Islamists, moderate and extremists.

37. Azzam M., 'Egypt: The Islamists and the State under Mubarak' in Sidahmed, A. S. and Ehteshami, A., (eds), *Islamic Fundamentalism* (Boulder, CO: Westview Press, 1996), p. 119.

38. *Middle East Contemporary Survey* (Vol. III, 1978–79), pp. 400–1.

39. Rahman, H. R., 'The Concept of *Jihad* in Egypt – A Study of *Majallat al-Azhar* (1936–1982)', in Warburg and Kupferschmidt, op. cit. p. 257 and

Ajami, F., 'In the Pharaoh's Shadow: Religion and Authority In Egypt' in Piscatori, J. P. (ed.), *Islam in the Political Process* (Cambridge: Cambridge University Press in association with the Royal Institute of International Affairs, 1983), pp. 14–19.

40. Kepel, G., *The Prophet and Pharaoh: Muslim Extremism in Egypt* (London: al-Saqi Books, 1985, translated by J. Rothschild), pp. 99–101.

41. Rubin, B., *Islamic Fundamentalism in Egyptian Politics* (London: Macmillan, 1990), pp. 81–2 and 86–8.

42. EOHR, *An EOHR Statement on the Assassination of Dr Farag Foda*, 9 June 1992, in which they blame al-Azhar for inciting violence against the writer and *EOHR Demands an End to Clerical Controls on Thought, Literature and Art*, 14 January 1992, in which al-Azhar is again singled out for attempted censorship. See also EOHR, *Freedom of Opinion and Belief: Restrictions and Dilemmas* (Proceedings of the Workshop on the Azhar's Censorship of Audio and Audiovisual Productions, Cairo, 8–9 March 1994). The Islamic Research Academy of the Azhar is playing a growing censorship role in recent years – see EOHR statement, 16/6/1997.

43. Rubin, op. cit., pp. 137–42.

44. Ibrahim, S. E., 'An Islamic Alternative in Egypt: The Muslim Brotherhood and Sadat' in *Arab Studies Quarterly* (Vol. 4, Nos. 1 and 2, Spring 1982), pp. 81–3 and Carré, 'The Impact of the Egyptian Muslim Brotherhood's Political Islam', op. cit., p. 267–9. The Brotherhood's weakness in the trade union movement is probably explained by their conservative views on social and economic issues.

45. Ibrahim, 'An Islamic Alternative in Egypt: The Muslim Brotherhood and Sadat' op. cit. pp. 83–5 and Carré, 'The Impact of the Egyptian Muslim Brotherhood's Political Islam', op. cit., pp. 266–7.

46. Interviews with Egyptian lawyer Kamal Aboulmagd and journalist Fahmi Howaidy; both are Islamists.

47. This is the unequivocal view of Bahey El-Din Hassan, former secretary-general of the Egyptian Organisation of Human Rights. The examples are his. In this context I also interviewed Adel Hussein, a leading figure of the Socialist Labour Party (later renamed the Labour Party), closely associated with the Brotherhood, and editor, in 1992, of its newspaper *al-Sha'b*. He claimed that Islam has its own human rights, which would include the *hadd* punishments and polygamy. Freedom, according to Hussein, is to 'be one's self' and authenticity means to be in conformity with one's history. On the Brotherhood's 'pragmatic' shift towards a support of democracy, see Aly, A. M. S. and Wenner, M. W., 'Modern Islamic Reform Movements: The Muslim Brotherhood in Contemporary Egypt' in *Middle East Journal* (Vol. 36, No. 3,

Summer 1982), pp. 352–4 and Abed-Kotob, S., 'The Accommodationists Speak: Goals and Strategies of the Muslim Brotherhood of Egypt' in *International Journal of Middle East Studies* (Vol. 27, No. 3, August 1995), pp. 321–39.

48. See for example Kepel, op. cit., pp. 110–21. In April 1997 the leader of the Muslim Brotherhood, Mustafa Mashhour, stated that Copts must pay the *jizya* tax and be barred from the army in the event of the institution of an Islamic state. There was uproar and a quick retraction from the Brotherhood. *Al-Ahram Weekly*, 17–23 April 1997.

49. Mitchell, R. P., *The Society of the Muslim Brothers* (Oxford: Oxford University Press, 1969), pp. 254–9. The question of female participation in Islamist movements is, however, extremely complex because the movement in fact empowers many women rather than restricts them. See, el-Guindi, F., 'The Emerging Islamic Order: The Case of Egypt's Contemporary Islamic Movement' in Farah, T. E. (ed.), *Political Behavior in the Arab States* (Boulder, CO: Westview Press, 1983), pp. 61–4.

50. Kepel, op. cit., Chapter 5 and Rubin, op. cit., Chapter 5.

51. Ansari, H. N., 'The Islamic Militants in Egyptian Politics' in *International Journal of Middle East Studies* (Vol. 16, No. 1, March 1984), pp. 136–40 and Ibrahim, S. E., 'Anatomy of Egypt's Militant Islamic Groups: Methodological Note and Preliminary Findings' in *International Journal of Middle East Studies* (Vol. 12, No. 4, December 1980), pp. 423–53.

52. On Shaykh Kishk, see Kepel, G., op. cit., Chapter 6 and Kishk, A. H., *The World of the Angels* (London: Dar al-Taqwa, 1994, translated by A. Bewley); on Sharawi, see Lazarus-Yafeh, H., '*Muhammad Mutawalli al-Sha'Rawi* – A Portrait of a Contemporary *'Alim* in Egypt' in Warburg and Kupferschmidt, op. cit., and al-Sha'rawi, M. M., *The Miracles of the Qur'an* (London: Dar al-Taqwa, translated by M. Alserougii). On the subject generally see Gaffrey, P. D., *The Prophet's Pulpit: Islamic Preaching in Contemporary Egypt* (Berkeley, CA: University of California Press, 1994).

53. Mona Makram-Ebeid (interview), noted that there are profound divisions within the Brotherhood as regards democracy and rights and that many argue that the Brotherhood will develop, in time, in a similar fashion to the Christian Democratic parties of Western Europe. For the divisions and liberal elements in the Brotherhood see, Osman, F., 'Democracy Essential for Ikhwan' in *Arabia: The Islamic World Review* (No. 6, February 1982), pp. 8–10. In 1995 some of the younger generation in the Brotherhood broke away to form the Centre (Wasat) Party but it is too early to judge what the outcome of this will be.

54. Such figures would be the lawyer Kamal Aboulmagd and Muhammad Selim al-Awwa. A different trend is represented by Hassan Hanafi, who is

considered to be part of the Islamic left. For a discussion see Dwyer, K., *Arab Voices: The Human Rights Debate in the Middle East* (London: Routledge, 1991) and Flores, A., 'Egypt: A New Secularism?' in *Middle East Report* (No. 153, Vol. 18, No. 4, July–August 1988), pp. 27–30.

55. One such figure is Muhammad Said al-Ashmawy. See his *L'Islamisme contre l'Islam* (Paris: La Découverte and Cairo: Éditions la Fikr, 1989, translated by R. Jacquemond) and *al-Ahram Weekly* (13–19 May 1993). Farag Foda, assassinated in 1992, was also a prominent liberal figure. For a discussion see Shamir, S., 'Liberalism: From Monarchy to Postrevolution' in Shamir, S. (ed.), *Egypt from Monarchy to Republic: A Reassessment of Revolution and Change* (Boulder, CO: Westview Press, 1995), pp. 195–212.

56. It is impossible to provide figures with regard to popular support for the regime or the Muslim Brotherhood at present. This is because of government repression and also because of frequent electoral fraud in Egyptian elections.

57. See Cooper, *The Transformation of Egypt*, op. cit., Chapter 7, for details of the policies and their failure. See also Springborg, R., 'Egypt' in Niblock, T. and Murphy, E. (eds), *Economic and Political Liberalization in the Middle East* (London: British Academic Press, 1993).

58. See, Springborg, R., *Mubarak's Egypt*, op. cit., pp. 4–7 and Chapter 7, for the causes of this reluctance and the position of the regime as balancer between various interests. On relations between Egypt and the IMF and the 1991 agreement see Niblock, T., 'International and Domestic Factors in the Economic Liberalization Process in Arab Countries' in Niblock and Murphy op. cit., pp. 58–71.

59. Ayubi, N. N., 'Government and the State in Egypt Today' in Tripp, C. and Owen, R. (eds), *Egypt Under Mubarak* (London: Routledge, 1989), pp. 1–2.

60. Economist Intelligence Unit, *Egypt: Country Profile, 1995–96*, p. 20.

61. Waterbury, op. cit., pp. 247–60 and Youssef, S. M., 'The Egyptian Private Sector and the Bureaucracy' in *Middle Eastern Studies* (Vol. 30, No. 2., April 1994), pp. 369–76.

62. Economist Intelligence Unit, *Egypt: Country Profile, 1995–96*. In 1994 Egypt was one of the four countries singled out by the United Nations Development Programme's annual Human Development Report as 'being in danger of joining the world's list of failed states because of wide income gaps' (p. 22).

63. Moore, C. H., *The Mediterranean Debt Crescent: Money and Power in Algeria, Egypt, Morocco, Tunisia and Turkey* (Gainsville, FL: University Press of Florida, 1996).

64. Springborg, *Mubarak's Egypt*, op. cit., Chapter 3.

65. Subsidies and price distortions are pervasive in Egypt even now. See Economist Intelligence Unit, *Egypt: Country Profile, 1995–96*, p. 21.

66. Dessouki, 'The Transformation of the Party System in Egypt', op. cit., p. 16.

67. Hinnebusch, R. A., 'The Reemergence of the Wafd Party: Glimpses of the Liberal Opposition in Egypt' in *International Journal of Middle East Studies* (Vol. 16, No. 1, March 1984), pp. 108–9. The new Wafd secured 15 per cent of the vote in the 1984 elections (58 seats), and 11 per cent of the vote (36 seats), in the 1987 election. It attracted many Copts who were alienated in 1984, however, by the electoral alliance with the Muslim Brotherhood; Makram-Ebeid, M., 'The Role of the Official Opposition' in Tripp and Owen (eds), op. cit., pp. 29–31 and Makram-Ebeid, op. cit. See also Reid, D. M., 'The Return of the Egyptian Wafd, 1978' in *International Journal of African Historical Studies* (Vol. 12, No. 3, 1979), pp. 389–415.

68. On the NPUP's social composition and ideology, see Makram-Ebeid, M., ibid., pp. 36–8 and Hinnebusch, R. A., 'The National Progressive Unionist Party: The Nationalist-Left Opposition in Post-Populist Egypt' in *Arab Studies Quarterly* (Vol. 3, No. 4, Fall 1981), pp. 325–51. The NPUP won 8 per cent of the popular vote in the 1976 elections and 2 per cent eleven years later in the 1987 elections. In 1992 the Nasserist party (ADNP), long opposed by the regime, gained legal approval by the Judicial Court of the State Council. See, 'The Establishment of the Arab Democratic Nasserite Party' in *Civil Society*, op. cit., (No. 5, May 1992), pp. 3–4.

69. Makram-Ebeid, op. cit., pp. 33–5 and 38–40.

70. Bianchi, op. cit., Chapters 1 and 2.

71. On Law 100 of 1993 see note 24 above. On professional associations see Leenders, R., *The Struggle of State and Civil Society in Egypt: Professional Organisations and Egypt's Careful Steps Towards Democracy* (Middle East Research Associates Occasional Paper, No. 26, April 1996).

72. On trade unions and agricultural cooperatives see Bianchi, R., 'The Corporatisation of the Egyptian Labour Movement' in *Middle East Journal* (Vol. 40, No. 3, Summer 1986), pp. 429–44 and note 29 above.

73. Springborg, R., 'Patterns of Association in the Egyptian Political Elite' in Lenczowski, G. (ed.), *Political Elites in the Middle East* (Washington, D.C.: American Enterprise Institute for Public Policy Research, 1975). See also his *Family, Power and Politics in Egypt: Sayed Bey Marei – His Clan, Clients and Cohorts* (Philadelphia, PA: University of Pennsylvania Press, 1982). Contrast Moore, C. H., 'Clientelist Ideology and Political Change: Fictitious Networks in Egypt and Tunisia' in Gellner, E. and Waterbury, J., (eds), *Patrons and Clients*

in Mediterranean Societies (London: Duckworth, 1977). Moore argues that accusations that ideological constituencies are formed only through patronage are not always well-founded and that 'clientelism' is used by governments as a propaganda weapon to discredit opposition groups.

74. The hours devoted to religious programmes on Egyptian television have multiplied and reached 14,500 a year under the government's effort to 'educate' the population on the basis of the 'correct' Islam. See, *Middle East Contemporary Survey* (Vol. IX, 1984–85), p. 351. Given the high level of illiteracy in Egypt the role of television stations is crucial.

75. EOHR, *Freedom of Thought and Belief: Between the State's 'Anvil' and the Islamic Groups 'Hammer'*, 1 May 1992, (a speech by Bahey el-Din Hassan, secretary-general of the EOHR, on 1–2 May 1992).

76. Yadlin, op. cit, pp. 161–3. Sociological research has shown that social attitudes in Egypt are very conservative. Traditional views on and suspicion of authority predominate; social atomism is paramount. The attitudes of the younger generation on the family and the position of women are similarly conservative. Also, authenticity is conceived of as diametrically opposed to Westernisation.

77. Bahey El-Din Hassan (interview) notes that although the government is indeed more liberal than the Islamists in its interpretation of Islam it has entered a competition with the Brotherhood to show that it too respects religion, in order to 'pull the carpet from under their feet' so to speak. Mr Hassan pointed out that some people expect that changes will lead to Islamic rule in a gradual and imperceptible way. The challenge of the Brotherhood, the upsurge of religious values throughout society, and the centrality of the Islamic debate in political life have made their mark on all parties: all now have a religious plank and all (except the NPUP), agree that the *sharia* must be the chief source of law. See, *Middle East Contemporary Survey* (Vol. VIII, 1983–84), p. 368.

78. On the debates on the introduction of *sharia* rules and their implications see; Jacquemond, R., 'Un projet de code pénal islamique égyptien' in *Bulletin du CEDEJ* (Deuxième semestre, 1986), pp. 185–223; Botiveau, B., *Loi islamique et droit dans les sociétés arabes* (Paris: Karthala, 1993); *Bulletin du CEDEJ* (Deuxième semestre, 1985), Special issue on 'Études sur les Droits de l'Homme'; and, for example, *Middle East Contemporary Survey* (Vol. I, 1976–77), pp. 297–8, (Vol. II, 1977–78), p. 386, (Vol. III, 1978–79), p. 401, and (Vol. IX, 1984–85), pp. 349–51.

79. Zubaida, S., 'Islam, the State and Democracy: Contrasting Conceptions of Society in Egypt' in *Middle East Report*, (No. 179, Vol. 22, No. 6, Nov/Dec. 1992), pp. 6–7, points out that many civil servants in Egypt are sympathetic to

political Islam.

80.   The pluralist role of Islam is emphasised by Berger, op. cit., pp. 2–8 and by Bianchi, *Unruly Corporatism*, op. cit., pp. 158–62.

81.   Kepel, *The Prophet and Pharaoh*, op. cit., pp. 107–10 and 127–8. Aly, A. M. S. and Wenner, M. W., op. cit., note that the limited records of Brotherhood membership indicate that 'the activist portion of its support is primarily found among engineers, doctors, and other professionals, i.e., other [sic] elements of the social structure who tend to benefit from a 'capitalist' rather than a 'socialist' economic system' (p. 353). This information is contained in Davis, E., 'Islam and Political Change in Egypt', Paper Presented to the 1980 American Political Science Association Convention, Washington, D.C. The radical groups recruit their members from the deprived urban areas and in Upper Egypt.

82.   Interviews with; Nabil Abdel-Fattah, political analyst in the al-Ahram Institute of Political and Strategic Studies, who argued that the Brotherhood has changed from a petite-bourgeois movement to one supported by the middle classes and the haute bourgeoisie. Saad Eddin Ibrahim, political analyst, expert on the Islamist movement, American University in Cairo, argued that it is the disadvantaged sections of the middle classes – young lawyers, doctors, young professionals generally – who feel that they are in danger of slipping down the social scale and turn to the Brotherhood; and that the Brotherhood's support is greater among the literate. Ibrahim also argued that, with the emergence of provincial universities, the Brotherhood's influence is growing even in the villages where it had traditionally been weak. Hani Shukrallah, journalist and political analyst, argued that the traditional sections of the bourgeoisie are also a major source of support for the Brotherhood.

83.   Shukrallah, interview.

84.   Binder, L., *Islamic Liberalism: A Critique of Development Ideologies* (Chicago, IL: University of Chicago Press, 1988), p. 342.

5

Tunisia, 1970s–1990s

I

I have chosen Tunisia as the third case in this book for a number of reasons. During the 1970s and 1980s – most notably after the removal of Habib Bourguiba in 1987 by Zine El Abidine Ben Ali – Tunisia appeared to be the country in the Arab world with the greatest potential of becoming a polity respectful of human rights and democratic liberties. Furthermore, in Tunisia's case, becoming a democratic state would have been achieved not through discarding Islam altogether – as in modern Turkey for example – but through having institutionalised a modernist interpretation of religion. Tunisia is the only country in the Middle East which has come close to achieving a harmonious relationship between Islam and human rights and becoming a liberal state without being a secular one. The shortcomings and failures of this process, but also its relative successes, will be analysed to shed light on the general questions of this study.

Tunisia has a number of peculiarities, compared to other Arab countries, which make it a fascinating field of study in itself but are also of direct relevance to our subject. First, the absence of army involvement in political life. Ben Ali may have been an army man but it was not the army which came to power in 1987. Second, the existence of a set of laws which go further than any other in the Arab world towards establishing equality between men and women by reinterpreting Islam rather than divorcing it from the domain of the law. Third, a vibrant trade union movement, which had a long and honourable history after the 1920s, at times even rivalling the nationalist and later ruling party in popularity. And, finally, an Islamist movement which has begun, more than any other major political Islamist movement in the Arab world, to incorporate democratic ideals in its political discourse.

The discussion that follows will attempt to show how these four elements connect with one another and, beyond that, what their underlying causation is. The development of liberal and Islamic modernist ideas in Tunisian society from the nineteenth century onwards will provide the common thread for the discussion. The period between the 1970s and 1990s was chosen because it was during that time that human rights became pressing and central demands in public life (before the 1970s human rights *principles* were already being discussed but not explicitly, and pressures for democratisation were not as strong). During the same period a powerful Islamist movement challenged the dominant interpretation of Islam and the regime as a whole. This chapter will consist of an analysis of the social and political developments in Tunisia and their relation to the various discourses on human rights and on Islam. The problem will be approached – as in the case of Egypt in the same period – through highlighting the dialectical relationship between Islam as represented by the state on the one hand and of Islam as a challenge to the state and the regime on the other.

After an overview of the historical background as it relates to the liberal and Islamic traditions of the country, and the vital links between state and society as they developed before independence, a discussion of the major political developments during the 1970s will follow. It will show that these developments, as well as the challenge of secular opposition groups during this decade, contributed to the emergence of human rights as a major issue in Tunisian political debate. The growth and evolution of the Islamist movement during the 1980s will then be analysed. The Islamist movement's conception of human rights will be discussed and accounted for. Finally, the role of the state will be brought in, to highlight the social and political processes underpinning the complex links between Tunisian Islam and the concept of human rights.

II

To understand why Tunisia came closer than any other Arab country to institutionalising a liberal version of Islam and a liberal polity in general, we have to examine the regime that came to power upon independence in 1956 and the foundations of the new state as they were laid in the critical period until 1959. Two major reforms were carried out immediately in 1956: the first was the Personal Status Code. Drawing on a modernist interpretation of Islam, the Code banned polygamy, imposed a minimum age for marriage, made the woman's consent necessary for the marriage to take place and made divorce a right of both spouses, abolishing the practice of unilateral male repudiation. Although complete equality between the sexes was not achieved – the man remained head of the family with extended rights of guardianship over children, and in inheritance the old Islamic practices were not abolished – the Code was a revolutionary change, unparalleled in any other Arab state.[1] At the same time a number of other reforms were carried out to weaken the religious establishment. The *habous* (religious endowments) were abolished, the legal and educational systems were unified, the Zaytouna, the ancient Islamic university and religious centre, was reduced to a mere faculty of theology. Habib Bourguiba carried out a personal campaign against fasting during the month of Ramadan which, he said, sapped the nation's productive energies. He believed that in the process of turning Tunisia into a modern nation, Islam (the official religion of state according to the Constitution), had to be used as a positive force.[2] Indeed, to many observers religion seemed to be a declining force throughout the 1960s.

The second major reform upon independence was the deposition of the bey and the Constitution of 1959. The Constitution guaranteed full civil, political and social rights for all Tunisian citizens regardless of race, religion and sex. This equality was important for the only non-Muslims in the country, the Jews (the discrimination against them that remained, drawing on Islamic law and tradition, was that the head of state had to be a Muslim).[3] But the Constitution was marked by a clear authoritarian bent, primarily in giving enormous powers to the president and a limited role to the legislative assembly. The rights of the press, of association, and social rights became very quickly de facto limited rights despite being guaranteed by the Constitution.[4] The inclination of the regime against full democratisation was soon evident in that, although multi-partyism was officially permitted, no opposition parties functioned after the banning of the Communist Party in 1962. National associations – among them the country's major workers' union, the Union Générale des Travailleurs Tunisiens (UGTT), which was almost as popular as the Neo-Destour at independence – were subordinated to the state. The line between the state and the party apparatus became blurred.[5] In short, although the letter of the Constitution did guarantee human rights, democracy was sacrificed in substance in favour of modernisation, nation-building and to satisfy the regime's power instincts. The Neo-Destour state, however, never reached the heights of authoritarianism of Syria and Iraq. There were many reasons for this, which will be examined below.

To understand the foundations of the new state and its subsequent development, in order to shed light on the relationship between Islam and human rights in Tunisia, we have to look beyond the person of Bourguiba – who did not carry out the reforms single-handedly – to the elite of the Neo-Destour who assumed power in 1956: to their social and ideological make-up and the means at their disposal which enabled them to execute these reforms. Questions surrounding this elite point towards the concept and the political reality of the state and its development in the period prior to independence. The key argument is that the integration between Tunisian state and society, due to the long history and gradual evolution of the former, led to the development of a polity which enjoyed considerable legitimacy. This could have allowed for democracy and human rights reforms.

III

During the nineteenth century Tunisia, faced with a growing European threat to its independence and involvement in the international market, was forced into a process of modernisation. This entailed military and educational reforms and, most importantly, steps towards state-building, in the sense of the growth and consolidation of the state's extractive capacities and administrative control.[6] The small size and traditional homogeneity of the country, built around the nexus of the Sahel, facilitated this process, which laid the groundwork for eventual nation-building in the twentieth century.[7] However, its limitations were also considerable as it was not supported by indigenous social forces: the ruling caste remained Turkish and Mamluk and the local 'bourgeoisie' (the *beldi*) remained traditionally aloof from politics.[8]

This explains why political reforms in the nineteenth century, when they occurred, were not the result of social demands but the outcome of the ruling elite's perceived self-interest and of pressures from the French, whose interest in Tunisia had been growing after their conquest of Algeria in 1830. The Fundamental Pact of 1857 and the Constitution of 1861 were an introduction, albeit superficial, of liberal principles in Tunisia, guaranteeing respect for civil and political liberties, ensuring some government accountability and partially reforming the Islamic penal codes. Society, however, seeing no benefit from its new 'rights' but only sensing a limitation of customary privileges and autonomy (and further taxation), rebelled against them in 1864. This put an end to the drive for reform and the Constitution was suspended, leaving little apparent trace in the legal and political system.[9] Liberal principles did not take root and were even discredited in Tunisian political culture, especially among the population, because they were perceived as instruments for the expansion and consolidation of central authority, which indeed they were.

During the same period, however, and parallel to state and political developments, indigenous political thought introduced the concept of political reform, with the purpose of strengthening Muslim civilisation against European encroachment. The international influences and challenges to Muslim society did not lead to a wholesale adoption of European principles but to a reevaluation of Islam and Islamic law and an attempt to reconcile it with European ideals. The reformists or 'modernists' like Mahmud Qabadu and especially Khayr al-Din, who had also been behind the constitutional innovations described above, pressed for reform against the traditionalists who rejected all foreign ideas.[10] Khayr al-Din was instrumental in establishing the Sadiqi College in 1875 which was to provide Western education for the Tunisian elites for generations to come. The reformists tried, in their writings, to reconcile Islam with liberal principles and institutions through 'reopening the door of *ijtihad*'. However, their ideas were only haphazardly and opportunistically applied, as we saw, and they remained part of a debate confined to the ruling elite. The Zaytouna and the ulama as a whole were not engulfed by religious and political reformism – on the contrary, they acquiesced to an increasingly subordinate role vis-à-vis the central state.

Liberalism and Islamic modernism, in sum, did not become predominant in Tunisia before colonisation by the French in 1881. However, these political and intellectual developments left a 'symbolic capital'[11] that was to be taken up by the nationalist movement later on. In this sense they were important, under very different circumstances, from the beginning of the twentieth century onwards.

IV

France maintained a firm administrative hand in Tunisia until 1955.[12] During this period, no democratic institutions were fostered and, despite the introduction of a parallel French judicial system, Islamic family law was not reformed. Further, the French failed to reform the Zaytouna or weaken the conservative senior ulama.[13] The colonisers, in short, did little to enhance or promote either liberal institutions or Islamic modernism; in fact they arrested the development of both. It was in emulation and later *in reaction* to the French, within the framework of the nationalist movement, that they developed. The French presence did however indirectly encourage them, by accelerating the process of state formation, by setting in motion a number of economic and social changes and by the power of example, that is by upholding certain civilisational ideals in theory even while failing to apply them in practice.

Until the turn of the century, the Tunisian nationalist movement, still embryonic and confined to cultural groups such as al-Hadira and al-Khaldunyia, was composed of contradictory strands of pan-Islamism, Islamic reformism and pro-French ideas. In its early stage, the emerging nationalism seemed inextricably linked with ideas of reformist Islam and the desire to harmonise this with European rationalism and liberalism.[14] But by the first decade of the twentieth century, it was evident that the ground was not fertile for an Islamic reformist movement and the Zaytouna (its major thinkers and senior ulama who remained traditionalist) and the nationalist movement diverged. The Young Tunisians, who were the next nationalist formation, had a different view of Islam to the Islamic reformists. They did not look to the *sharia* but to the French Declaration of the Rights of Man as their ideal, not to the *umma* but to the nation-state as the highest political unit. For them Islam was only one aspect of Tunisian identity.[15]

The Khaldunyia and Young Tunisian activists did not form an organised political party but a small cultural movement among the old Turkish and Mamluk aristocracy. After World War I this traditional elite, discredited by its collaboration with France and the lack of any genuine power in the protectorate regime,[16] was increasingly displaced and the near-assimilationist ideas of the Young Tunisians were abandoned. Once it became evident that Tunisia could no longer adopt wholesale the civilisational ideas of the coloniser, nor be led by men of non-Tunisian extraction, the country entered its first truly nationalist phase. The leading movement during that period was the Destour.

The new nationalist phase was engendered by the evolution of state structures and the transformation of the economy. In contrast to Libya and Algeria, the French in Tunisia consolidated the process of state formation which had begun and was already considerably advanced before 1881. The protectorate established the boundaries of the Tunisian nation-state more clearly and reorganised the Tunisian military and the bureaucracy. The state acquired the resources to intervene in the life of nearly every Tunisian family. Economic changes ensued with the incorporation of Tunisia into the French economic sphere of influence. They accentuated the weakening of tribal solidarities (which had ceased to be a significant political force by the 1930s) and the creation of a rural 'proletarised' mass in the countryside.[17]

The consolidation of state structures, therefore, created the potential for the birth of an integrated modern nation – but the colonisers then blocked its formation. Education had given rise to a potential middle class – trained in part in the Sadiki College – familiar with

French civilisation but obviously not served by French policies, which refused it access to the higher posts in the expanded state bureaucracy. The disruption of the traditional social and economic order placed many social groups (proletarised peasants, artisans, workers), at a disadvantage. After World War I, in which Tunisia participated on the side of France and which shattered the myth of an all-powerful Europe, the Destour sprang as a broadly-based nationalist organisation. It was led by the old indigenous elite of Tunis bourgeois families and its demands included rights of free nationals for all Tunisians, universal suffrage, a responsible government and the separation of powers, freedom of association and the press, equal access to posts and equal pay in the administration. The inspiration was the Constitution of 1861 (Destour means constitution), which had become a symbol for the nationalist movement. Abdelaziz Thaalbi, leader of the Destour until 1923, also tried to incorporate ideas of Islamic reformism into its ideology.[18]

In the 1920s the nationalist movement had entered into its liberal-modernist phase but soon the elitist style of its leaders and their lack of attention to social and economic grievances – exemplified by their failure to support the Confederation Générale des Travailleurs Tunisiens (CGTT), precursor to the UGTT, in 1925 – rendered the organisation inadequate. The Neo-Destour, which broke away from the old party in 1934 under Bourguiba, was by contrast a mass nationalist party. The movement was led mainly by men from the Sahel and Djerba who had entered the liberal professions, having found their way to the bureaucracy blocked. Their provincial origins allowed them to mobilise the peasants and soon the whole of Tunisian society was engulfed by the movement: the urban proletariat, the unemployed, proletarised peasants and petty bourgeoisie. In the 1940s the UGTT was created, joining the nationalist struggle on an equal par with the Neo-Destour.

But the populist style of the Neo-Destour (in a context where democratic traditions had already atrophied under the French), was to lead to authoritarian tendencies. This was coupled with the Neo-Destour's disregard for Islamic reformism and its appeal to the masses through *traditional* Islamic symbols.[19] I mentioned above that an Islamic reformist movement had not acquired momentum in Tunisia. The Old

Destour had perhaps been the last chance for its revival.[20] Consequently, the Neo-Destour's need to appeal to the urban and rural masses (despite the personal liberal-modernist beliefs of its Western educated leaders), led to a disregard of liberalism in favour of a populist rhetoric and a disregard of liberal Islam in favour of a traditional religious discourse.

Upon independence the lack of a democratic tradition in the Neo-Destour left its imprint on the new republic, as we saw above in Section II. The challenge of Salah Ben Youssef,[21] the perceived requirements of state and nation-building, the pressing need for economic development and the lack of democratic traditions led to an authoritarian one-party state. But for many reasons Bourguiba's regime was not a dictatorship. The first was that the nationalist party had enormous legitimacy in the eyes of the people. The second was the nature of the new elite which was broadly-based, with close ties with the population at large. The state that this elite took over was, due to its long development, an apparatus that held the country together effectively. Traditional agents of power such as the bey, the tribes or religious fraternities had already dropped out of the political race.[22] Finally, the ideology of the elite and Bourguiba in particular was inspired by the ideas of liberal and socialist France. The elite and party became a vanguard in transforming a partly traditional society into a modern one with the implicit aim of eventually democratising it.

In this context, and with this aim in mind, Bourguiba tried to transform Islam into a force that would aid the modernisation of society, after easily banishing the discredited ulama to the sidelines. The Personal Status Code was the pinnacle of this policy.[23] The man who had used traditional religious symbols in the confrontation with France now assumed, through the state, the role of religious reformer. He built on the enormous capital of Khayr al-Din, the Young Tunisians and the Old Destour. This historical continuity was the most important symbolic capital of the official ideology. It was, of course, not only Bourguiba but the whole context of state and society at the time of independence which allowed this reform – unique in the Arab world – to take place, and provided the impetus for Islamic reformism, even though it did not have strong social roots.[24] Tunisia seemed, in 1956 and in the years immediately afterwards, a country with the real potential to become not only a democratic state but also one in which a liberal Islam would take root in society and promote, rather than hinder, the evolution of democratic institutions. This potential was only partly realised for reasons which the remainder of this chapter will analyse.

V

After the failure of the private sector between 1956 and 1960 to become the engine of economic development, as the regime wished it to be, the Tunisian leadership opted for 'socialism' (which was in reality a 'state capitalist' solution).[25] Under Ahmed Ben Salah, minister for planning and the national economy in the 1960s, the state attempted to collectivise agriculture and nationalise trade and industry. The trade union movement was manipulated into docility, ostensibly so as not to hinder the development process, and workers' wages were kept under strict control. The feminist and Islamic modernist movements were judged incapable of spearheading social change (and were also probably seen as a threat by the regime), so they were taken over and directed by the state. The cost of these policies – whatever their rationale, legitimate or not – was that the institutions and movements that could have led to the development of a pluralist and democratic society were truncated instead of nurtured. The regime stifled the prospects for liberalism and democratisation in the period after independence.

By the late 1960s, however, it became evident that the high hopes invested in the state and the party, and the belief that the state could achieve all economic, political and social goals, were unwarranted. The regime faced a crisis of legitimacy mainly because of the unpopularity of its economic policies, which it quickly started to reverse. Under Prime Minister Hedi Nouira (1970–80), the economy registered impressive growth, albeit one caused mainly by greater oil revenues and the remittances of Tunisian workers from abroad. The 1970s were also marked by growing regional disparities and a widening gap between rich and poor.[26] Nevertheless, the Tunisian middle classes expanded during this period, a development that was to have political consequences (for and against the regime) after the late 1970s, as we shall see.

The relative economic liberalisation was not accompanied by political reform although it is arguable that this was a propitious time for it to take place. From the early 1970s onwards Bourguiba became increasingly authoritarian and intolerant of any opposition. Ageing and in poor health, he lost the contact with his people for which he had been famous. Until his removal in 1987, Tunisia suffered increasingly from his arbitrary interventions in political life, which were not conducive to democracy.[27] Under the authoritarian Hedi Nouira a repressive state took shape which allowed no opposition activities and dealt summarily with any dissidents. Human rights and basic liberties were violated, despite constitutional guarantees; the penal code, the press law and the law of associations were restrictive, and the judiciary was deprived of independence.[28] But the economic boom made a large part of the new, broader middle class acquiesce in this authoritarianism for a time.[29]

By the middle or end of the 1970s, however, civil society had become restless, as the economy started showing signs of faltering. The movements which the state had seemingly coopted – liberals, leftists, the UGTT, Islam and the feminist movement – regrouped. We will examine this opposition bearing in mind that by 1980 a consensus of the majority of politically minded Tunisians had formed in favour of democratisation and respect for human rights.[30] In the 1970s, the challenge to the regime came mainly from the secular opposition, whereas in the 1980s it was the Islamists who took the lead.

VI

The first challenge to the regime came from within. In the 1971 Congress of the Parti Socialiste Destourien (PSD, as the Neo-Destour had been renamed in 1964) it became evident that the majority of party cadres belonged to the liberal current of opinion, headed by Ahmed Mestiri, who wished for the party to reform itself in a liberal direction.[31] Failing to achieve this, and after being expelled from the party in 1974, the liberals organised into the Mouvement des

Démocrates Socialistes (MDS, which is still, in the 1990s, the most important secular opposition party in Tunisia). Their main demands included respect for human rights and political pluralism. The group represented the traditional bourgeoisie of Tunis, who had formed the core of the old Destour. It was not fuelled by the growth of the broad middle classes in the preceding decades. These classses were not in the majority liberal-minded, as they had grown in the shadow of the state in the 1960s and 1970s and were still tied to it for its survival.[32]

In 1977 the Ligue Tunisienne des Droits de l'Homme (LTDH) was formed. It continued to function despite confrontation with the authorities in the mid-1980s and severe harassment in the 1990s. The LTDH was an elite institution, with a leadership of bourgeois and well-known personalities, many of whom were loosely affiliated with the MDS. Its stance was not revolutionary but within the narrow political space in which it was able to function it contributed enormously (and uniquely in the Maghreb), to political liberalisation. The steady rise of its prestige among all social groups testified to the growing awareness of human rights principles in Tunisian society as a whole.[33]

The regime was also challenged by a leftist movement which it considered, in the 1970s, as its primary enemy. There are two main strands in the Tunisian left. First, that which had been present in the nationalist movement and especially in the UGTT and was later represented by Ben Salah in the 1960s. It did not enjoy the widespread support of the working or popular classes themselves, as became evident in the 1960s. The tiny support for the Mouvement de l'Unité Populaire (MUP), the party founded by Ben Salah after he fled to Paris, is a further confirmation of this lack of popular appeal. The second strand in the Tunisian left was more radical, represented by students and workers; but again it did not enjoy widespread support. It started in the late 1960s with the formation of the group 'Perspectives' which later split and gave rise to the 'Parti Ouvrier Communist Tunisien' (POCT, which is still active and persecuted by the regime in the 1990s).

During the 1970s the left felt the full weight of the regime's repression. From the early 1980s onwards, as attention turned to the Islamists, the leftists began leaving the prisons and in 1981 the Communist Party was legalised. What is interesting for our purposes is that, apart from the few who have remained committed to the principles of Marxism-

Leninism, the majority of leftists in Tunisia have undergone a shift in ideology towards a commitment to human rights and democratic principles, thus mirroring a general trend in Tunisian society. They are no longer 'la gauche' but have come to be called and to view themselves as 'démocrates'.[34]

The development in the feminist movement came somewhat later, in the 1980s, and it grew out of the cultural club Tahar Haddad.[35] The 'Femmes Démocrates', who operated illegally until 1989, saw themselves as an alternative feminist movement to the official Union Nationale de Femmes Tunisiennes (UNFT), which had effectively become, since 1956, part of the state bureaucracy. But their movement remained small and was unable to mobilise ordinary women – a role undertaken at a later stage by the Islamists.[36]

However, the greatest challenge to the regime – since both the left and the liberals never really mobilised large constituencies – came from the UGTT. Effectively subdued by the government after independence and an impotent force in the 1960s, the UGTT became increasingly militant from the early 1970s. The UGTT represents all salaried employers in Tunisia, especially the public sector. It does not only represent the working class but a large part of the middle and lower middle classes as well (employers in banks and post offices, teachers, a number of professionals and the salaried in general). In the early 1970s a number of worker-intellectuals entered the union and were crucial in transforming its political discourse.[37] The middle and lower middle class expansion in the 1970s, which had been caused by economic growth and the spread of education on which the regime placed great emphasis, fuelled the movement. If the majority of the middle class did acquiesce to the regime, a small but active opposition channelled their political energies into the UGTT. The union became a umbrella organisation for the expression of all shades of political opinion from the extreme left to the Islamists.

From around 1972, and more so after 1975–76 when the Tunisian economy encountered difficulties, the UGTT, despite restrictive legislation, became involved in increasingly militant strike action. Its demands were economic and social (there is, because of the long trade union history in Tunisia, a great awareness of economic and social rights), but they also became increasingly political. Activists in the organisation gradually realised that union autonomy could only be safeguarded within the context of a properly functioning democracy. Eventually the demands of the UGTT went beyond labour concerns and came to include human rights and liberties in general. The UGTT could at that time be said to have provided the nucleus for a labour party, a real alternative to the PSD.[38]

The increasingly militant base of the UGTT forced its leader, Habib Achour, into confrontation with the regime. But after the bloody riots of 1978 and 1984 the union's organisation was effectively dismantled.[39] The authoritarian tendencies of the regime deprived Tunisia of an opportunity for genuine democratisation. In the 1980s, after the crushing of the UGTT and the left, and the failure of liberal parties to mobilise a large constituency, the way was open for the rise of the Islamists as the principal opposition movement. The key point, however, is that the Islamists entered a political scene in which the secular opposition, liberal, leftist, feminist and trade unionist, had already made human rights a central demand against the regime. The obliteration of this opposition was a setback for democratisation but it did not extinguish the demand for human rights, which dominated Tunisian civil society concerns and inevitably influenced the Islamist movement as well.

VII

The Islamist movement has presented a social and ideological challenge to the dominant elite in Tunisia. Conversely, the state's social and ideological choices explain to a large extent the form the Islamist movement assumed. In this sense the movement can be understood only if its dialectical relationship with the state – its policies and the social groups that the ruling elite represents – is examined.[40] But the state is not everything in Tunisia, it does not coopt and shape all aspects of society. If the initial formation of the Islamist movement can be comprehended in relation to the state primarily, its *subsequent development* can only be understood if we also look at its relationship with society as a whole. We will explore these issues in turn.

The formation of the Islamist movement was influenced by the policies of the regime towards the secular opposition (which it chose to severely restrict, as we have seen), but also by its policies on religion. Responding to the perceived loss of its legitimacy and the challenge by liberals, the left and the UGTT, the ruling elite underwent a 'retraditionalisation' which, together with repressive policies, was aimed at preserving their power.[41] The Personal Status Code was never questioned, but respect for religion was emphasised in the political discourse; education was progressively Arabised, especially under Muhammad Mzali (education minister and then prime minister between 1980 and 1986), and attempts at 'social engineering', especially in women's issues, were abandoned in the 1970s. The Society for the Preservation of the Koran, which inadvertently became one seedbed of the Islamist movement, was created by the government in 1969 for the purposes of exhibiting deference to religion.

Another set of explanations for the rise of the Islamists must be sought in the economic policies of the regime and the reaction to the social groups which the ruling elite represented. Regionalism is central in understanding Tunisian politics. From independence onwards the Bourguiba regime relied extensively on an elite drawn from the Sahel and especially the areas around Monastir, the president's home town and historically the wealthiest in the country.[42] During the 1970s, as we saw, with the abandonment of centralising development policies, the underdeveloped areas of the south and the north-west were further neglected. The rise of the Islamist movement can be seen as one expression of this lopsided development and as a demand by disadvantaged groups for a greater share in the distribution of state benefits. Active support for the Islamist movement has come primarily from educated youth of rural origin, coming into the cities to attend university, or those whose families have recently emigrated into the urban centres. They are mostly science students and include many women activists.[43] They represent the young upwardly mobile middle class frustrated by lack of opportunity, a second generation of 'provincials' which demands, much like the Sahelians of the Neo-Destour at the time of colonisation, the rewards implicitly promised by the expansion of education.[44] The young educated supporters of the Islamists, at lycées and universities, are not from traditional backgrounds. They are a modern, though not modernist social group. They have been deprived of the benefits that the modern world is supposed to provide while never having known the security of the traditional world. It is this group which has most ardently put the yearning for cultural authenticity onto the agenda of Tunisian politics.

Religion is not just a vehicle for the expression of secular needs, and economic deprivation alone does not explain the rise of the Islamist movement – but it is an indispensable part of the explanation. The Islamist discourse seemed to combine, uniquely in the 1980s, the answers to the problems of identity and of social injustice. Furthermore, Islam in the 1980s was the only ideology on offer which was not crushed (like the secular opposition) or appropriated by the state or otherwise discredited; it provided a radically different world-view from that of the regime and that of the left.[45] The causes of the rise of the Islamists, therefore, cannot be comprehended unless we take into account all these factors: political, economic, social and psychological. The evolution of the state and the choices of the regime provide the central nexus of the explanation.

What has been the ideology propagated by the Islamists? How have their views on Islam and human rights evolved since the emergence of the movement? The debate between the Islamists and other social and political groups has centred principally on women's rights and political rights.[46] The analysis of this debate must be placed within the framework of the interaction of the movement with the Tunisian state *and* civil society.

The Islamist movement was formed in the early 1970s initially through contacts with Islamist propagandists coming into Tunisia from abroad.[47] It was later, for a while, fostered by the Association for the Preservation of the Koran. The Mouvement de la Tendance Islamique (MTI, which was established by that name in 1979), had by the middle of the decade emerged as the most important of the organisations, the others being the Dawa, a puritanical but apolitical group, the Progressive Islamists who split in 1977–78 from what was to become the MTI and a number of radical offshoots.[48] Their concerns during those years, however, were cultural and largely apolitical. To the extent that they were interested in politics they rejected all notions of democracy, human rights and equality of the sexes as Western imports, contrary to the Koran and Islamic law.[49] After the 1978 crackdown on the UGTT however and the Iranian revolution of 1979, they were politicised and realised that they could not contest power unless they took a stand on the major concerns of Tunisian society. These included not only economic and social matters but also democracy and human rights.

Until that time the Islamists had enjoyed the toleration, even the support, of the regime which used them as a counterbalance to the left. Thereafter they entered into confrontation with the authorities. In June 1981 the MTI applied for a 'visa' (permission to form a political party) and very soon afterwards its leadership was imprisoned. This first period of repression lasted until 1984 when the Islamists were released and entered into negotiations with Mzali. The 1986 bombings targeting tourists led to a second wave of arrests and trials. Bourguiba had by then become obsessed with the Islamist threat. His demand to retry those who had been acquitted for the bombings was the immediate cause for Prime Minister Ben Ali's decision to overthrow him. After the change of the head of state on 7 November 1987, the MTI, together with all other political forces in the country, signed the Social Pact proposed by Ben Ali, which included as one of its basic premises respect for democratic liberties and the Personal Status Code. The Islamists subsequently participated in the elections of 1989, on the Independents' lists, and won 17 per cent of the national vote and in some urban areas up to 30 per cent (the secular left won an overall 3 per cent). The regime took fright and the third wave of repression ensued.[50]

It is understandable, therefore, that the first and perhaps most vital link between the Islamists and the principles of human rights was their evocation for their own protection. The Islamists, by becoming themselves the victims of state repression, appealed to the state's obligation to respect political and civil liberties. *They chose to do so because of the centrality human rights had assumed in the Tunisian political debate by the late 1970s.* They cooperated with the secular opposition issuing, for example, joint communiqués condemning repressive policies. They used the opportunity offered by Amnesty International and other international human rights organisations' reports, to publicise their cause. They entered the UGTT (which they had hitherto scorned as irrelevant to Islam), and as members inevitably became caught up with defending its autonomy.[51] Finally, they participated in the LTDH and sought its good offices in defending their civil rights.[52] Whether the use of human rights principles by the Islamists in this context has been opportunistic is a moot point. What is of relevance to the argument is that, once they entered the contest of power, their interaction with state institutions on the one hand and with civil society and its concerns on the other, made the adoption of human rights principles unavoidable.

A crucial area in which the Islamists' views evolved were women's rights. This evolution was tortuous and ambivalent, characterised by inconsistencies and retractions. But a change can be perceived nevertheless towards acceptance of greater equality between the sexes. Although in the first years of the movement's existence there was outright opposition to the Personal Status Code, by the mid-1980s Rachid Ghannouchi, the leader of the MTI, proclaimed his acceptance of the abolition of polygamy and its other provisions. He also accepted that both men and women have the right to divorce (through the courts) and rejected unilateral male repudiation. [53] In signing the Social Pact of 1988, the MTI conceded the legitimacy of the Code. On the other hand, in 1985, during the debate on the Charter of the LTDH which attempted to concretise a Tunisian bill of human rights, the Islamists had opposed the right of a Muslim woman to marry a non-Muslim. They had also opposed the right of Muslims to renounce Islam. They lost the day even though their views were not far removed from the official position.[54] The Islamists also opposed adoption which had been legalised in the 1960s.[55] As regards the laws on inheritance, there has been less controversy because the Code itself retains the traditional inequality between men and women.

The ambiguity of the Islamist leadership towards women's rights is reflected in the beliefs of many of their many female supporters. The women who are either actively or loosely affiliated with the movement are very clear about why they have chosen to wear the *hijab*.[56] It gives them considerable freedom in what they perceive to be a threatening world. It commands social respect and alleviates practical and psychological strains. But when it comes to translating general Islamic precepts into concrete views on relations between the sexes their answers are extremely vague and disparate.[57]

There is no question that, on the whole, Islamist women tend to be more conservative on the issue of their rights than secular-oriented women,[58] but it would be superficial not to go further than this observation. For many women, Islam is liberating. It allows them to work and circulate in the public sphere without losing their respectability and self-respect, as they understand it, and to participate in political and social affairs, for which other avenues are barred. The Islamist movement has had an impact not only on middle class women but among poorer segments of the population as well. The other opposition feminist movement, the Femmes Démocrates, is too elitist to mobilise large numbers and the UNFT is perceived as an appendage of the state, although it has the resources to touch even the poorest sections of society.[59] The women who sympathise with the MTI have not been confronted with the reforms that its coming to power would entail. It is doubtful that they would easily or willingly accept the curtailment of the rights they already enjoy under the (otherwise illegitimate in their eyes) Tunisian state.[60] Therein lies one cause of the Islamist leadership's vagueness on women's issues.[61]

The Islamists' position on women's rights can therefore be understood only if we focus on their interaction with their own female followers and with society at large; this position changed as the interaction intensified.[62] The fact that the question of women's rights is the cornerstone of the debate between the Islamists and their opponents is a testimony to the widespread acceptance of the Personal Status Code, and hence of Islamic modernism, in Tunisian society. The gradual realisation by the Islamists that their popularity would suffer if they continued to attack the Code is evidence of how Islamic movements are moulded by the societies in which they emerge. Their ambivalence on this and other matters stems from their need to reconcile, on the one hand, the social requirements and views of the particular societies which they seek, ultimately, to govern and, on the other, the requirements of the 'sacred law' (which turns out however to be rather flexible and malleable). Their transformation in Tunisia is evidence of the success of the the Bourguibist state in making Islamic modernist ideas acceptable to society at large.

The MTI's views on civil and political rights underwent a similar evolution. The growing realism of the movement and its politicisation, its stated aim to become a political party and its participation in the election process forced it to show respect for democratic principles. It denounced laws as unconstitutional and spoke of the imperativeness of the freedom of speech and association. In the 1970s it had presented itself as the sole guardian of true Islam against an infidel regime and a secularised society. It renounced this claim by the 1980s and implicitly accepted that its version of Islam was one choice among many. This view tied in well with its claim that it would constitute one party among many in a pluralistic political system and that the final decision on the imposition of Islamic law on society would stem from the popular will, expressed through democratic procedures. Alongside political rights, it demanded respect for worker's rights and trade union autonomy and went as far as qualifying its support for the Iranian revolutionary regime.[63]

A cursory look at the thought of Rachid Ghannouchi, leader of the MTI and later the Nahda (as the MTI was renamed in 1989), is crucially important in evaluating the political stance of the Islamists, although his views do not go unchallenged and as a result the movement's message is often confused. We can perceive in his writings a change from strict traditionalism to a greater acceptance of modernity and the West. He criticises the West and Westernised intellectuals but does not reject them totally, claiming to recognise their pioneering role in proclaiming the values of freedom and equality. His aim is to preserve Tunisian identity, differentiate it from the West and – an old-standing concern of Muslim reformers – discover the causes of the inferiority of the Islamic world but only through reconciling Islam with modernity and the idea of progress.[64]

Ghannouchi tries, as on the issue of women, to reconcile the requirements of Islamic law with the modern idea of human rights. He argues that the Universal Declaration of Human Rights was a revolutionary and progressive step but that it cannot rest on solid ground unless it is founded on religious principles. The humanistic spirit of Islam is such a foundation. In his view there would be equality in an Islamic state between Muslims and non-Muslims. The Muslim institution of *shura* safeguards democracy and political liberties. The *sharia* law can and should develop through the exercise of *ijtihad* according to the public interest (*maslaha*). The Islamic state would provide general moral safeguards but would not intrude into people's private affairs to force them into compliance (in fasting for example). The *hadd* punishments would be greatly restricted to take into account the extent of the crime and the reasons behind it. There would be no cutting off of thieves' hands if the crime were petty or if the thief was in dire economic need.[65]

Ghannouchi's ideas are similar to Abdelfattah Mourou's, who was the second in command of the movement and is described as a moderate. He broke away from the Nahda in 1991 to distance himself from the violent acts allegedly perpetrated by it. He applied for a 'visa' to form a separate political party and took great pains to emphasise Islam's respect for democracy, his belief that the Koran does not contain all answers to all problems and his insistence on exercising reason in making political and moral decisions.[66]

The pronouncements described above are fine as far as they go. However, they represent a glossing over of the problems, rather than their genuine resolution. This is a view shared by many of the students of the Tunisian Islamists who argue that behind the veneer of a human rights and democratic discourse there exists no profound appreciation of the true meaning of the concepts involved.[67] The term *shura* for example is ripped out of its historical context and transposed to our time in an arbitrary way, while the content of the term remains traditional. The conflict between divine law and the sovereignty of the individual is not resolved. The understanding of citizens' equality and what it entails is superficial. The discourse of the MTI reflects the Islamist ambiguity on human rights. For instance they congratulated the Saudi regime for its executions of those accused for instigating a revolt in Mecca in 1979;[68] they supported, at times, the Sudanese regime and they attacked the Education Minister Muhammad Charfi and his modernist reform of school religious teaching. In at least one of MTI's publications, intended for internal circulation, it is implicit that human rights are viewed as a stick with which to beat the regime, not a genuine principle.[69]

The Islamist movement, having suffered periodic bouts of severe repression, has never had enough time to resolve these contradictions and evolve a coherent programme. This predicament may be one cause of its contradictory language and inconsistencies.[70] But the events surrounding the 1989 elections revealed another cause. During the campaign the Islamist candidates represented three 'currents': traditional Islam, propounded by some Zaytouna shaykhs; a more open and liberal current, and the radical Islam of the underprivileged.[71] In other words the MTI attempted to be all things to all people and to satisfy radically disparate constituencies, of aspiring middle-class educated youth, traditional sectors of the population and militant poor sectors. Each of those constituencies required a different 'language' and set of ideas.

Apart from the MTI, we need in the context of this study to examine the Progressive Islamist movement, whose creative thought is highly interesting in itself and who, given their small size, exert a disproportionate influence in public debate.[72] The Progressive Islamists have struggled to avoid the inconsistencies of their mother party and to genuinely reconcile the principles of human rights with those of Islamic law. They separated themselves in 1977–78 from the mainstream group that was to become the MTI for two main reasons. Firstly, because they disagreed with many of its political views. Secondly, because they believed that Islamic law and doctrine must be reformed before the Islamist movement could undertake political action.[73] The movement comprised of only a few distinguished individuals. The split therefore did not have a debilitating effect on the MTI in terms of numbers but it did contribute to the transformation of its ideological positions and its espousal of some human rights principles through the debate that ensued.

The Progressive Islamists were deeply dissatisfied with the MTI's mode of thought which they found inflexible and anachronistic. They criticised it for being imbued with a Manichean attitude towards all alternative views of Islam. They judged this way of thinking, and its fixation on the time of the Prophet and the first caliphs, as ahistorical. For the Progressive Islamists this period is neither an attainable nor a desirable ideal. They propose a 'historicised' view of Islamic history and expound their belief that future Islamic societies could bring progress, not necessarily decline. They argue for the supremacy of reason over revelation and the need to adapt Islamic principles to the requirements of the times, one example being polygamy which has to be set aside if the welfare of the family (a higher value in Islam than polygamy), is to be preserved. The Progressive Islamists introduced the novel idea that the Islamic *umma* was diverse from the beginning and encouraged the idea of a 'Tunisian Islam', heir of a tolerant and open tradition. They are also keen to situate Islamic thought in the context of a universal civilisation and of humanist thought in general. They do not view the West as a monolithic entity. They draw parallels between the intellectual and moral crisis in the Arab world and its European equivalents.

It is within a context of human and universal values that they situate the question of human rights and democracy. For them the democratic state is Islamic and they contrast their view with that of the MTI for whom democracy would be merely an instrument to an Islamic state, to be discarded perhaps thereafter. In such an Islamic state all political and social freedoms would be respected, including the right not to follow the precepts of Islam (their belief is mirrored in their lifestyle which is not uniform and does not demand of women, for example, to wear the *hijab*). The Progressive Islamists are exceptional in accepting that the concept of human rights is not contained in the Koran and the Sunna and that the principles of human rights are part of a universal humanism of our time, which must be incorporated in the Islamic world-view. A prominent member of the party, Hamid Enneifer, is honest in saying that it was the international evolution of human rights issues which encouraged the Progressive Islamists to consider them and that they see these issues as part of a common human patrimony which must be defended. However, this does not mean in his view that the Islamic conception of human rights can be identical with the Western.[74] For the Progressive Islamists the modern polity requires a solid moral foundation which can only be provided for Muslims by Islam, which is at the same time religion, ethics and cultural heritage.[75]

The Progressive Islamists are accused by other Islamists of being 'too Westernised'[76] and by secularists of being 'too attached to the text'.[77] They lack a large constituency as is typical of many such Islamic thinkers in the Arab world. But it is indicative that only Tunisia, no other Arab country (not even Egypt), has given rise to a group with such original and profound thought on the problems of reconciling Islam and authenticity with democracy and modernity.

Furthermore their impact surpasses their numbers. They have contributed to the evolution of the MTI towards greater acceptance or at least consideration of democratic values, to some of the secular intellectuals' reevaluation of Islam and to the transformation of the government's Islamic policies. It is to these issues that we now must turn.

VIII

The politicisation of the MTI, and after 1989 the Nahda, and the growth of its popular support, which became evident in the 1989 elections, caused a polarisation between the movement and the regime. But it is also Tunisian society as a whole that has been polarised. This has been a result not only of the policies followed by the Islamists but, crucially, of the fundamental *choices* made by the regime.

For Ben Ali, who overthrew Bourguiba in 1987, respect for human rights and democracy was a means of legitimating himself and differentiating his government from that of his predecessor. To this end he carried out his 'coup' with the greatest respect to the letter of the Constitution and initiated a number of democratic reforms upon his accession to power. He abolished the presidency for life, he freed many political prisoners, he abolished the State Security Court, revised the 1975 press code and the law of associations, declared his intention to reform the PSD (which was renamed Rassemblement Constitutionnel Démocratique, RCD), declared his opposition to the death penalty, limited the *garde à vue* period (pre-trial detention) and ratified a number of international human rights conventions.[78] Respect for democratic principles was one of the central principles of the National Pact signed in 1988 by all political forces, including the Islamists.

But the process of reform and democratisation was sharply reversed after the elections of 1989 and even more after the electoral victory of the Front Islamique du Salut (FIS) in Algeria in 1991. Large-scale arrests began in September 1990 and increased after February 1991. The Islamist movement was crushed through a combination of police methods and other forms of pressure such as the removal of Islamists from jobs in the civil service and the prohibition of the *hijab* in public places. The clampdown did not leave other political forces unaffected. A restrictive party law led to the temporary prohibition of the LTDH in 1992–93 and the press reverted to self-censorship after a period of relative freedom. The presumed fear of Islamism also serves as a means of keeping strict control over organisations such as the UGTT.[79] The Tunisia of Ben Ali in the 1990s is a police state where all free debate is stifled and all opposition – even non-violent – preemptively crushed.[80]

At the same time the regime presents itself as the protector of human rights and takes every opportunity to emphasise its commitment to democracy and the president's pioneering role in it. According to the official Tunisian press, Tunisia is exemplary in fulfilling its human rights obligations. While the LTDH was banned the government set up a 'Higher Committee for Human Rights and Basic Freedoms' to advise the president on human rights issues; the comparison of its report on human rights with the reports by Amnesty International on the same period makes interesting reading.[81] A parallel can be observed between such official pronouncements and the Islamists' claim that their political programme fully guarantees human rights. The concept has in fact been emptied of content by both sides, yet neither would renounce it, because of its widespread prestige in Tunisian and international society. 'Human rights' has become a propaganda bone of contention between the two sides, each vying to prove that it is its best defender and that the 'other' is its greatest enemy.

A similar development has occurred in relation to Islam. Neither side can renounce it and both claim that they are Islam's true defender. The 'retraditionalisation' of the regime and the governing elites which began in the 1970s intensified in the 1980s, especially after 1987; by which time the MTI had become popular enough to further warrant such a policy. Ben Ali condemned the secular excesses of the previous regime and proceeded with a number of reforms: religious programmes filled the audio-visual media, the Zaytouna was reinstated as an autonomous university, the president conspicuously went on a *hadj*, and it became a habit to begin political speeches with invocations of Allah.[82]

But these moves remained at the symbolic level and did not affect the essence of the regime's policies. On the contrary, modernist Islam was strengthened in two major ways: in the sphere of women's rights, the Personal Status Code was further reformed in 1992 and 1993[83] and in the sphere of education all school curricula were revised in 1990–92 to ensure that children were taught an open, tolerant and modernist Islam. This last reform was carried out with the advice, among others, of the Progressive Islamist, Hamid Enneifer, and it revealed the novel configuration in Tunisian politics, with the Islamists pitted against the reform, and the whole secular opposition supporting the government.[84]

This apparent contradiction in the regime's policies – on the one hand respecting the trappings of Islam more conscientiously, on the other reforming it further towards a modernist direction – is not as puzzling as it may initially seem to the outside observer. The first set of policies is the attempt to beat the Islamists on their own ground. But the regime claims that it can be superior to the Islamists by combining their demands with an Islamic modernism. To understand this choice we need to remember the origins of the regime and the fact that it established itself in the newly independent Tunisia as, among other things, a champion of modernising Islam. The regime still perceives itself as the guardian of Islamic modernism which is one of the pillars of Ben Ali's regime, just as it had been for Bourguiba's. It must also be noted that it serves the regime's purpose to exaggerate the obscurantism of Nahda's ideology.

In assessing, therefore, both the Nahda's and the government's interpretations of Islam we must bear in mind that the terms of the debate are eminently political and that neither interpretation is static or more 'authentic' than the other. Furthermore, as this chapter has argued, both sides respond not only to each other but, crucially, to what they perceive to be the demands and attitudes of society at large.

IX

The confrontation between the regime and the Islamists has had major implications for Tunisian politics in general. The regime has reverted in the 1990s to coopting all alternative, pluralist expressions of political life. In this it has been aided by secularist forces which, like the government, now feel threatened by the Islamists. As regards the

UGTT, for example, the Ben Ali period began with promises of trade union autonomy which have not materialised in any substantial way. The MDS has suffered turmoil over the issue of whether it should support the RCD or not and its leadership has been persecuted.[85] In the feminist movement former independent activists claim that the discourse of the 'Femmes Démocrates' has become indistinguishable from that of the UNFT.[86] More generally those anxious about the threat to women's rights have rallied round the regime because they believe it is the best defence against the Islamists. It is as if Tunisia's post-independence history is repeating itself with the state coopting the trade union, liberal and feminist movements in order to defend its modern and progressive social vision against the obscurantism of 'the people' (described, as usual, in contemptuous terms). This must not obscure, however, the differences between the more traditional Islam facing the regime in the 1950s and the very modern Islamist movement of the 1980s.[87]

The prospects for democratisation have worsened due to the failure to reform the RCD, an avowed aim of Ben Ali when he came to power, and the identification of the president of the republic with the party – a precedent which Ben Ali was unable or unwilling to revise.[88] The possibility of the RCD breaking up into a number of groups – the only real avenue for genuine multi-partyism in Tunisia according to some analysts, given that secular opposition parties are bound to remain tiny satellites of the RCD[89] – does not seem realistic at the moment. Neither does the prospect of the UGTT developing into a labour party. The prospects for democratisation and political pluralism in Tunisia at this juncture look grim.

Economic factors and long term processes which have underpinned social and political developments in the 1970s and 1980s have also contributed to the arrest of political liberalisation. The economic strains that Tunisia has faced since the period of 'state capitalism' in the 1960s have contributed to the rise of the Islamist opposition in the 1980s, after the secular opposition – stemming primarily from the UGTT – was crushed. There is indeed a parallel between the rise of opposition to the regime in the 1980s and economic conditions during the same period, which was characterised, in contrast with the 1970s, by slower growth, a deterioration in the balance of payments and rising unemployment. Chronic decline in the agricultural sector – which cannot supply the economy with either enough food or a significant investable surplus – increased migration to urban centres and swelled the ranks of a labour force which was only partly absorbed by industries, tourism, emigration and the informal sector. Poverty in Tunisia has declined but income distribution, from the 1970s onwards, has worsened, and the economy's structural transformation has not led to the creation of self-sustaining new structures.[90] Since the financial crisis of 1986, growing pressures by international donor agencies to liberalise the economy and adopt a broader range of free market policies have inevitably added to social strains, despite the improvement of economic indicators during the 1990s.[91] These strains – as inequalities increase and ordinary people find it more difficult to make ends meet – do not bode well for democratisation, as the regime interprets them as a call for greater political control and repression to contain discontent. In this sense, economic and political liberalisation are on a collision course.

But in other ways economic liberalisation may enhance the prospects of its political equivalent. In Tunisia, 'structural adjustment' was introduced in the absence of a strong, self-assured private sector but the change in economic policy has begun to foster such a sector.[92] A shift towards a less centralised and controlled economy will inevitably mean the state giving up part of the patronage it is able to dispense. It also means that opposition parties could at some later stage seek support from independent financial centres.[93] The industrial bourgeoisie in the post-1970 period has not been altogether parasitic on the state and although it has not shown any inclination towards political activity to date such a development cannot be ruled out in the future.[94] Other processes taking place in tandem with, or as a result of, economic liberalisation could also work in favour of democratisation, through social change. The reduction of the role of the informal sector or family businesses could lead to a more atomised labour market. Economic growth has already transformed the female labour market and allows women greater financial independence.[95]

X

How do the arguments of this chapter connect with the wider arguments of this book? The key term throughout this chapter has been 'Islamic reformism' or 'Islamic modernism'. It is only if Islamic reformism is successfully established in political culture that Islam will not hinder the development of a liberal polity in a Muslim society. The cornerstone of Islamic influence is family law. It is unlikely that human rights norms can become established in a Muslim country unless a liberal and modernist interpretation of religion in this sphere becomes the accepted norm. The first assumption here is that, for the majority of Muslims, discarding Islam altogether and establishing a secular polity is not an option at this particular moment in history. The second assumption (argued in Chapter 2) is that a harmonious relationship between Islam and human rights, or an 'Islamic liberalism', can be worked out in theoretical and doctrinal terms, and that its success or failure in becoming the predominant view in a given society is the result of social and political developments and not of it being more or less 'authentic' than other interpretations of Islam.

The purpose of this chapter has been to show that the above assumptions and arguments can stand. From the nineteenth century the Tunisian state evolved into a modern set of institutions. By 1956 it had become closely integrated with society and was controlling it effectively. This crucial development, as well as the way in which the nationalist struggle against the French was waged, the type of leadership which emerged during that struggle and its relationship with other social groups, explain the legitimacy of the post-independence state in Tunisia.

A full liberalisation at that time would have come about if the modernist religious policies of 1956 and thereafter had been the outcome of a social movement. As we saw this did not happen; neither did Tunisian society express a demand for a liberal system at large. In the nineteenth century, Islamic reformism was an elite affair, connected in popular conscience with an increasingly extracting and centralising state. The ulama fought against it. The early nationalist movement did attempt to incorporate some of these reformist ideas but the Neo-Destour adopted a traditionalist religious symbolism. This was essential not because the people would not otherwise be mobilised – the people did not oppose the protectorate for the sake of Islam but for Tunisian nationalism – but because of the need to emphasise the differences between colonised and colonisers. At independence, the Neo-Destour reversed its position and sought to reform Islam. Islamic reformism may not have sprung from a broad social movement but the legitimacy of the state and of the elite made it acceptable in the eyes of the people.

State development and the regime's legitimacy would have allowed the creation of a liberal polity at the time of independence but this did not happen to any great extent because of the choices of the regime. However, in the 1970s and 1980s, especially after Bourguiba's removal in 1987, the mixture of liberal and illiberal elements in Tunisia could have tilted the country towards democratisation. Education and economic development had led to the creation of a broad middle class.[96] Islamic modernist ideas had become inculcated into social consciousness – especially through the Code – to a sufficient degree for an Islamic liberalism to flourish. This liberal potential however was only partly realised.[97]

The identification of state and government had grown too close since independence. In the 1960s the Tunisian state became an 'overbearing' set of institutions especially in its pursuit of a command economy. But the problem was, above all, the practices of the regime with regard to the liberal opposition and later the UGTT which it chose to severely repress. An opportunity for liberalisation and democracy was lost. The choices of the regime and the handicapping of secular opposition forces, explain the rise of Islamism as a powerful movement in the 1980s. There was nothing inevitable about the rise of Islamism in Tunisia. The movement was not an expression of the people's 'authentic' self.[98] It was a political phenomenon, to be explained by tracing its interaction with the state and the policies of the regime. It was also a social phenomenon, representing a 'second generation of provincials' who demand a better deal from the state. If, furthermore, the Islamists adopted a fairly illiberal interpretation of Islam it was in order to differentiate themselves from the Islamic modernism for which the regime has stood since independence.

The failures of liberalisation and democracy in Tunisia, however, must not totally obscure the partial successes in that direction. These partial successes point again to the primacy of a political and social analysis of Islamism. Once the movement began interacting with civil society at large it underwent a further transformation, in particular on matters regarding the concept of human rights. The change in Islamist views on women and political rights was the result of their decision to contest power and win over the allegiance of the majority of the electorate. Tunisian society and its concerns transformed the Islamist movement and forced it to begin to incorporate the principles of human rights into its ideology. This was the result, as was noted, of the success of the Bourguibist state in inculcating Islamic modernism in the collective consciousness. In its turn this was possible for two reasons. Firstly because of the fundamental legitimacy of the state and the legacy running from Khayr al-Din to Bourguiba which it represents. Secondly because of the manner in which the Tunisian state developed from the nineteenth century onwards, nurturing, not crushing civil society.[99] But it was also the result of the concern of Tunisian society with human rights and the demand for democratisation, *against* the government, which has preoccupied the country since the late 1970s.

In the case of Tunisia the rise of Islamism can be explained by focusing on the state. Its subsequent development and the interpretation of Islam which the movement advocated can be explained by tracing its interaction with Tunisian society at large. It is not easy to separate the two – state and society – because the former shapes the latter and vice-versa. Nevertheless, the conceptual distinction has it analytic uses. Tunisian Islamism, has gone further than any other such movement in the Arab world towards a liberal interpretation of Islam (without necessarily achieving it). This along with the existence of the Progressive Islamist thought in Tunisia reflects the evolution of the Tunisian state and society. It is evident that the success or failure of a liberal interpretation of Islam and its conciliation with the concept of human rights is not determined by any immutable precepts of the religion but by the political and social development of any given society at any given historical time.

The present human rights situation in Tunisia is, as I stressed above, very grim. This is the result of government choice but also of the situation in neighbouring Algeria. However, the potential of Tunisian society for democratisation and of Tunisian Islamism for an Islamic liberalism may still not have completely dissipated.

Notes

1.Chamari, A. C., *La Femme et la loi en Tunisie* (Casablanca: Éditions le Fennec, 1991); Charfi, M., 'Le Droit tunisien de la famille entre l'Islam et la modernité' in *Revue Tunisienne de Droit* (1973), pp. 11–37 and 'Droits de l'homme, droit musulman et droit tunisien' in *Revue Tunisienne de Droit* (1983), pp. 405–23.

2. Moore, C. H., *Tunisia since Independence: The Dynamics of One-Party Government* (Berkeley, CA: University of California Press, 1965), pp. 48–60. The author argues that Bourguiba saw himself as a great Muslim reformer, in the tradition of Muhammad Abduh.

3. Sebag, P., *Histoire des Juifs de Tunisie* (Paris: L'Harmattan, 1991), especially Chapter 11. With the unification of the legal system the Jews lost their autonomy in family law. The Code, however, although partly inspired by Islamic law, was an improvement on the rabbinical law which accorded women inferior status. Note that Bourguiba was keen on safeguarding the rights of the Jews and emphasising that they are protected in Tunisia. Laskier, M. M., *North African Jewry in the Twentieth Century: The Jews of Morocco, Tunisia and Algeria* (New York: New York University Press, 1994), Chapters 8 and 9.

4. Moore, op.cit., pp. 71–82. Moore describes the Tunisian political system as a 'presidential monarchy' because, in his view, Bourguiba's style of leadership was reminiscent of a traditional autocrat.

5. Rudebeck, L., *Party and People: A Study of Political Change in Tunisia* (London: C. Hurst, 1967), pp. 35–42.

6. The modernisation process began under the reign of Ahmad Bey (1837–55), who established the Military Academy of Bardo and some local industries to support military reforms. By the end of his reign, however, despite these initiatives, economic and political structures had remained largely unchanged. Ahmad Bey had refused to apply the Tanzimat (in order to underline Tunisian autonomy from the Ottoman empire), except for the abolition of slavery in 1846. Brown, L. C., *The Tunisia of Ahmad Bey, 1837–1855* (Princeton, NJ: Princeton University Press, 1974).

7. Other factors too contributed to state-building. Virtually all of Tunisia's inhabitants were Arabic speakers. There was no Christian minority and very few Berbers although a Jewish community did exist. Furthermore, there was a long urban tradition in the area of the Sahel which had always been open to

Mediterranean influences and was populated by a middle class living on the production of olive oil. Government had already had a tradition of relative stability and centralisation and the traditional tribal areas of dissidence were weak. See, Moore, *Tunisia since Independence*, op.cit., pp. 14–15. For a discussion of the development of the Tunisian state, see Anderson, L., *The State and Social Transformation in Tunisia and Libya* (Princeton, NJ: Princeton University Press, 1986) and Hermassi, E., *Leadership and National Development in North Africa* (Berkeley, CA: University of California Press, 1972). The analysis of this section and subsequent ones has been strongly influenced by both Anderson's and Hermassi's works.

8. Brown, *The Tunisia of Ahmad Bey*, op.cit., pp. 194–5.

9. Perkins, K. J., *Tunisia: Crossroads of the Islamic and European Worlds* (Boulder, CO: Westview Press, 1986), pp. 72–80 and Fitoussi, E., *L'État tunisien: Son origine, son développement et son organisation actuelle, 1525–1901* (Tunis: J. Picard, 1901), pp. 61–129. The Fundamental Pact guaranteed respect of the person and of property, civil and religious equality, liberties of conscience and of commerce (including the abolition of government monopolies) and the right of foreigners to own property in Tunisia. The Constitution of 1861 limited the authority of the bey, introduced a Grand Council of high functionaries and notables, established the principle of ministerial responsibility and the separation of powers (including the independence of the judiciary) and reduced the applicability of Islamic penal laws except in the case of the death penalty.

10. Tlili, B., *Les rapports culturels et idéologiques entre l'orient et l'occident en Tunisie au XIXème siècle* (Tunis: Publications de l'Université de Tunis, 1974), especially Chapters 10 and 11. See also Khayr ol-Din, *Essai sur les réformes nécessaires aux états musulmans* (Aix-en-Provence: Édisud, 1987). Khayr al-Din was not of course a democrat in our contemporary sense, but he did advocate the limitation of arbitrary and despotic government. He was also critical of the ulama's failure to remain in touch with society's needs and interpret the religious law accordingly.

11. Zghal, A., 'Le Retour du sacré et la nouvelle demande idéologique des jeunes scholarisés' in Souriau, C. (ed.), *Le Maghreb Musulman en 1979* (Paris: CNRS, 1981), pp. 44–8.

12. The treaty of La Marsa (1883) obliged the Tunisian government to undertake reforms which were deemed essential by the French but it did not challenge – in theory – the bey's domestic jurisdiction. Moore argues that the type of French rule established in Tunisia gave rise to the perfect conditions for its overthrow. Moore, op.cit., pp. 15–17.

13. Ling, D. L., *Tunisia: From Protectorate to Republic* (Bloomington, IN:

Indiana University Press, 1967), Chapters 2 and 3. The discrediting of the ulama because of their collaboration with the French led to the weakening of their official status after independence. See: Green, A. H., *The Tunisian Ulama, 1873–1915: Social Structure and Response to Ideological Currents* (Leiden: E. J. Brill, 1978); Green, A. H., 'A Comparative Historical Analysis of the Ulama and the State in Egypt and Tunisia' in *Revue de l'Occident Musulman et de la Mediterranée* (No. 29, Premier Semestre, 1980), pp. 31–54.

14.   Muhammad Abduh visited Tunisia in 1884–5 and again in 1903 and Rida's *Al-Manar* also circulated in Tunisia. See, Ziadeh, N. A., *Origins of Nationalism in Tunisia* (Beirut: American University of Beirut, 1962), Chapter 4 and Abdel Moula, M., *L'Université zaytounienne et la société tunisienne* (Tunis: CNRS, 1971), pp. 95–103. Green, *The Tunisian Ulama*, op.cit. pp. 185–7, discusses Abdelaziz Thaalbi (a Zaytounian, later to become leader of the Destour) and his book 'L'Esprit libéral du Coran', which was attacked for being extremely pro-French.

15.   Green, ibid., p. 208.

16.   Anderson, op.cit., p. 149.

17.   These are central arguments in Anderson, ibid. and Hermassi, E., op.cit

18.   For a classic document of the Tunisian nationalist struggle see Thaalbi, A., *La Tunisie martyre* (Dar al-Gharb al-Islami, 1985, deuxième édition tirée de l'édition originale de 1920).

19.   Salem, N., *Habib Bourguiba, Islam and the Creation of Tunisia* (London: Croom Helm,1984).

20.   Hermassi, op.cit., pp. 94–5.

21.   Salah Ben Youssef had been the leader of the Neo-Destour while Bourguiba was in exile in the 1940s. Just before independence Ben Youssef mounted a challenge to Bourguiba which was subsequently defeated. Anderson, L., op.cit., pp. 232–3.

22.   An exception to this was Moncef Bey who gained popularity in 1942 upon acceding to the throne; but he was subsequently deposed by the French for his alleged Axis sympathies.

23.   Zghal, A., 'The Reactivaton of Tradition in a Post-Traditional Society' in *Daedalus* (Vol. 102, No. 1, Winter 1973), pp. 228–9, suggests that the modernist intelligentsia, being aware that they were not a majority in country, introduced the Code as a modernist interpretation of religious texts, rather than a secular proposition.

24.   The feminist movement before independence was quite active but would not have been sufficiently strong in itself to press for such reforms. See Labidi, L., *Les Origines des mouvements féministes en Tunisie* (Tunis, 1987); 'L'Émergence du sentiment politique chez les intellectuelles musulmanes dans

le Monde Arabe dans la premier moitié du XXème siècle: Le Cas de la Tunisie' (unpublished) and 'Circulation des femmes musulmanes dans l'espace public et politique formel: Le Cas de la Tunisie' (unpublished, used with the author's permission), and Bakalti, S., *La Femme tunisienne au temps de la colonisation, 1881–1956* (Paris: L'Harmattan, 1996), Chapter 2.

25. For a discussion of state capitalism see Chapter 4 above.

26. Moudoud, E., *Modernisation, the State, and Regional Disparity in Developing Countries: Tunisia in Historical Perspective*, (Boulder, CO: Westview Press, 1989), Chapter 5.

27. See Bessis, S. and Belhassen, S., *Bourguiba: Un si long régne (1957–89)* (Paris: Japress/Jeune Afrique Livres, 1989), Vol. 2, Chapters 4–7, for a vivid description of Bourguiba's decline and its effect on public life. The authors describe how his reliance upon a few 'courtiers' fostered faction-fighting and personality clashes. In 1974 Bourguiba had the Constitution amended to make him president for life.

28. Belaid, S., 'La Justice politique en Tunisie' in *Revue Tunisienne de Droit* (1983), pp. 361–404.

29. Bessis and Belhassen, op.cit, p. 114.

30. Ibid., p.175. In 1980 there was an attempted insurrection in Gafsa which shook the regime and led to a partial revision of policy towards greater pluralism; but this political opening was superficial. See, Toumi, M., *La Tunisie de Bourguiba à Ben Ali* (Paris: PUF, 1989), Chapter 5.

31. Moore, C. H., 'Clientelist Ideology and Political Change: Fictitious Networks in Egypt and Tunisia' in Gellner, E. and Waterbury, J. (eds), *Patrons and Clients in Mediterranean Societies* (London: Duckworth, 1977), p. 267.

32. Interview with Khemais Chamari, former MDS and LTDH activist, who argued that the assumption that a middle class would necessarily cherish liberal sentiments is not correct. All interviews were conducted in Tunisia in April 1993, unless otherwise stated.

33. On the LTDH see: Dwyer, K., *Arab Voices: The Human Rights Debate in the Middle East* (London: Routledge, 1991), Chapters 8 and 10; Waltz, S., 'Tunisia's League and the Pursuit of Human Rights' in *The Maghreb Review* (Vol. 14, Nos. 3–4, 1989), pp. 214–25, and Waltz, S., *Human Rights and Reform: Changing the Face of North African Politics* (Berkeley, CA: University of California Press, 1995); and Charfi, S., *La Ligue Tunisienne pour la Défense des Droits de l'Hommes*, (Unpublished Mémoire, Université de Tunis, Faculté de Droit et des Sciences Politiques, Juin 1987).

34. Bessis and Belhassen, op.cit., pp. 174–5, on how the left in Tunisia began to respect 'formal liberties'; Zghal, 'Retour du sacré', op.cit., pp. 52–5; and interview with Hishem Gribaa, vice-president of the LTDH and former political

activist.

35. Dwyer, op.cit., Chapters 8 and 11. The views of the club were expressed in the pages of their publication *Nissa* during 1985–86.

36. Interviews with: Saïda Bhiri, lawyer, Islamist feminist and former MTI activist and Lilia Labidi, researcher on women's issues.

37. Interview with Taïeb Baccouche, former UGTT activist and one such intellectual.

38. The above information on the UGTT was drawn from Taïeb Baccouche, interview; an extended interview with Christopher Alexander, researcher on the Tunisian trade union movement; Ben Romdhane, M. B., *Mutations économiques et sociales et mouvement ouvrier en Tunisie, de 1956 à 1980*; Karoui, H. and Messaoudi, M., 'Le discours syndical en Tunisie à la veille du 26 janvier 1978: L'Élan suspendu' and Toumi, M., 'Le discours 'ouvrier' en Tunisie: usages syndicaux et usages politiques' in Sraieb, N. et al., *Le Mouvement ouvrier maghrébin*, (Paris: CNRS, 1985).

39. According to one author the riots of 1984 revealed the existence of a 'second Tunisia' of those who had been left behind by the 1970s boom. Adda, S., 'Enjeux: Le Possible et le probable' in Camau, M., (ed.), *Tunisie au present: Une modernité au-dessus de tout soupçon?* (Paris: CNRS, 1987), p. 404.

40. Zubaida, S.,*Islam, the People and the State: Political Ideas and Movements in the Middle East* (London: I. B. Tauris, 1993). Zubaida emphasises that the state, and the way in which its political choices interact with the Islamists, is central for a proper understanding of these movements.

41. Zghal, 'The Reactivation of Tradition', op.cit., and Tessler, M., 'Political Change and the Islamic Revival in Tunisia' in the *Maghreb Review* (Vol. 5, No. 1, January–February 1980), pp. 8–19.

42. On the Tunisian elites see: Stone, R. A., 'Tunisia: A Single Party System Holds Change in Abeyance' in Zartman, I. W., et al. (eds), *Political Elites in Arab North Africa* (New York: Longman, 1982); Larif-Béatrix, A., *Édification étatique et environment culturel: Le personnel politico-administratif dans la Tunisie contemporaine* (Paris: Publisud – O.P.U., 1988); Zghal, A., 'L'Élite administrative et la paysannerie en Tunisie' in Debbasch, C., et al., *Pouvoir et administration au Maghreb: Études sur les élites maghrébines* (Paris: CNRS, 1970) and Berrady, L., et al., *La formation des élites politiques maghrébines* (Paris: CNRS, 1973).

43. Hermassi, E., 'La société tunisienne au miroir Islamiste' in *Maghreb-Machrek* (No. 103, janvier–fevrier 1984), pp. 39–56.

44. Waltz S., 'Islamist Appeal in Tunisia' in *Middle East Journal*, (Vol. 40, No. 4, Autumn 1986). In a footnote on p. 661, Waltz points out that the students who have rallied to the MTI come from the very middle class which for the

past fifty years yielded loyal nationalists. She also notes that the traditional bazaar sector has not visibly supported the MTI, thus reinforcing the argument that the MTI is a traditionalist but it not a traditional movement. Zghal, A., in 'The New Strategy of the Movement of the Islamic Way: Manipulation or Expression of Political Culture?' in Zartman, I. W. (ed.), *Tunisia: The Political Economy of Reform* (Boulder, CO: Lynne Rienner, 1991), describes the Islamists as representatives of the 'new social periphery' from the South, Centre and Northwest of the country.

45. Zghal, 'Le retour du sacré', op.cit., pp. 41–64.

46. The question of non-Muslim minorities in Islamic society is not so widely discussed in Tunisia because there are no major religious minorities after the drastic reduction in the numbers of Jews who left progressively since independence (about 2–3,000 remain today). Sebag, op.cit., Chapter 11.

47. Specifically the Pakistan and India based Dawa group. See, Magnuson, D. K., *Islamic Reform in Contemporary Tunisia: A Comparative Ethnographic Study* (PhD thesis, Department of Anthropology at Brown University, May 1987), pp. 77–82.

48. Burgat, F., and Dowell, W., *The Islamic Movement in North Africa*, (Austin, TX: Center for Middle Eastern Studies at the University of Texas, 1993), pp. 200–7.

49. Interview with Saloua Charfi, political analyst at the Arab Human Rights Institute, Tunis.

50. Halliday, F., 'The Politics of Islamic Fundamentalism: Iran, Tunisia and the Challenge to the Secular State' in Ahmed, A. S. and Donnan, H. (eds), *Islam, Globalization and Post-Modernity* (London: Routledge, 1994), p. 104; and Hermassi, A., 'The Rise and Fall of the Islamist Movement in Tunisia' in Guazzone, L., (ed.), *The Islamist Dilemma: The Political Role of Islamist Movements in the Contemporary Arab World* (Berkshire: Ithaca Press, 1995), pp. 105–27.

51. Interviews with Taïeb Baccouche and Christopher Alexander.

52. Dwyer, op.cit., pp. 165–81.

53. Magnuson, op.cit., pp. 201–8 and Bessis S. and Belhassen, S., *Femmes du Maghreb* (Tunis: Cérès Productions – Éditions J. C. Lattès, 1992), pp. 218–9. On the other hand, by making statements to the effect that polygamy is a non-problem because very few men can afford to have many wives, Ghannouchi avoids making his views on the *principle* underlying polygamy explicit. Interview of Rachid Ghannouchi with the author, London, April 1992; interview in *Le Quotidien d'Algérie*, 15 and 16 December 1991; and Mahmoud, M., 'Women and Islamism: The Case of Rashid al-Ghannoushi of Tunisia' in Sidahmed, A. S. and Ehteshami, A. (eds), *Islamic Fundamentalism* (Boulder,

CO: Westview Press, 1996), pp. 249–65.

54.   Although the marriage of a Muslim woman to a non-Muslim is not forbidden by law or the Constitution, there exists a ministry circular of 1973 which does forbid such marriages. See, Chamari, op.cit., p. 43. On the debate on the LTDH Charter see Dwyer, op.cit., pp. 169–81.

55.   'Table ronde: Le statut de la femme en Tunisie' in *Réalités*, (No. 193, 28 April–4 May 1989), pp. 18–23.

56.   Not all those who wear the *hijab* are Islamists though.

57.   Belhassen, S., 'Femmes tunisiennes islamistes' in Souriau, op.cit., and Bessis and Belhassen, *Femmes du Maghreb*, op.cit., pp. 191–275.

58.   Darghouth Medimegh, A., *Droits et vécu de la femme en Tunisie*, (Lyons: L'Hermès-Edilis, 1992), Chapters 4 and 5.

59.   Saïda Bhiri, interview.

60.   Lilia Labidi, interview, and 'Sexualité et politique dans le discours islamiste au féminin: Le cas de la Tunisie' (unpublished, presented at the First International Congress of FRAPPE, Montreal, June 1990 – courtesy of the author).

61.   On other issues, the Islamists have been less ambiguous. They have not opposed, for example, the right to work for women, realising the impossibility of many Tunisian households' surviving on single incomes.

62.   Interview with Saloua Charfi. Mrs Charfi described how Islamist university students were confronted and challenged by their fellow students about their views on women and sexual equality.

63.   Magnuson, D. K., op.cit., Chapter 5.

64.   Hermassi, 'La société tunisienne au miroir islamiste', op.cit., pp. 53–5 and 'The Islamicist Movement and November 7', in Zartman, I. W. (ed.), *Tunisia*, op.cit. See also: Shahin, E. E. A., *The Restitution of Islam: A Comparative Study of the Islamic Movements in Contemporary Tunisia and Morocco*, (PhD thesis, Johns Hopkins University, Baltimore, Maryland, 1989), Chapter 5; interviews with Ghannouchi in *Quotidien d'Algérie*, op.cit., and Ghannouchi, R., *Islam and the West* (publication details unspecified); and Ghannouchi, R., 'Towards Inclusive Strategies for Human Rights Enforcement in the Arab World – A Response' in *Encounters: Journal of Inter-Cultural Perspectives*, (Vol. 2, No. 2, September 1996), pp. 190–4.

65.   Interview with Rachid Ghannouchi.

66.   Interview with Mourou, A., 'L'Islam est pour la démocratie' in *Le Point* (No. 961, 18 Février 1991). See also a series of articles in *Réalités* (No. 290, 15–21 March 1991), pp. 4–9; (No. 292, 29 March 4 April 1991), pp. 4–8; (No. 294, 12–18 April 1991), pp. 4–6; Mourou's 'Communiqué' of 19 November 1991 (courtesy of the Greek Embassy in Tunisia); and Collins Dunn, M., 'The al-

Nahda Movement in Tunisia: From Renaissance to Revolution' in Ruedy, J., (ed.), *Islamism and Secularism in North Africa* (Basingstoke, Hampshire: Macmillan, 1994), pp. 149–65.

67. Interviews with Saloua Charfi and with Abdelkader Zghal, sociologist and political analyst (CERES, Tunis).

68. Ghannouchi in *Quotidien d'Algérie*, op.cit.

69. 'Un Point de vue à propos de notre tactique politique pour l'étape actuel' (MTI) in *Sou'al*, special issue on 'L'Islamisme Ajourd'hui', avril 1985, pp. 180–1 and 196.

70. Saloua Charfi, interview; Hermassi, 'The Islamicist Movement and November 7', op.cit., argues that Tunisia is a suitable case for institutionalising political Islam 'to show that one can be both Muslim and democratic' (p. 204).

71. Belhassen, S., and Soudan, F., 'Élections tunisiennes: Ben Ali face aux islamistes' in *Jeune Afrique* (No. 1475, 12 April 1989), pp. 13–16.

72. This section on the Progressive Islamists is based on interviews with Shaheddine Jourchi, and Hamid Enneifer, the two leading figures of the group; Magnuson, op.cit., Chapter 6; Dwyer, op.cit.; Burgat and Dowell, op.cit., pp. 208–24.

73. Shaheddine Jourchi, op.cit., explained that three issues provided the impetus for their decision to break away. Firstly, the undemocratic structure of the movement, secondly the inferior position of women within the movement and thirdly the lack of relations between the Islamist movement and other intellectual elites in Tunisia.

74. Interview with Hamid Enneifer. Two examples would be the right of conversion for Muslims which should not be allowed, and a rejection of excessive individualism.

75. Their views are not very dissimilar to those expressed by Kolakowski, L., *Religion* (Glasgow: Fontana, 1982). For a discussion see Chapter 1 above.

76. Dwyer, op.cit, pp. 69–84.

77. This is the view of Hishem Gribaa, interview.

78. Zartman, 'The Conduct of Political Reform: The Path Toward Democracy' in Zartman, (ed.),*Tunisia*, op.cit., pp. 16–18.

79. Christopher Alexander, op.lit., who argues that the UGTT's power now depends on the proximity of its leader to the president of the Republic.

80. The list of reports outlining the distressing human rights situation in Tunisia is very extensive. See, for examples: Amnesty International, *Tunisia: Summary of Amnesty International's Concerns*, September 1990; *Tunisia: Prolonged Incommunicado Detention and Torture*, March 1992; *Tunisia: Heavy Sentences after Unfair Trials*, October 1992; *Tunisia: Rhetoric Versus Reality: The Failure of a Human Rights Bureaucracy*, January 1994; *Tunisie: L'Impunité*

favorise le renforcement de la répression, novembre 1995; *Tunisia: A Widening Circle of Repression*, June 1997; and Lawyers Committee for Human Rights, Hicks, N., *Promise Unfulfilled: Human Rights in Tunisia since 1987* (Washington, D.C.: Lawyers Committee for Human Rights, 1993).

81. Republic of Tunisia: Higher Committee for Human Rights and Basic Freedoms, *Report to the President of the Republic on the Implementation of the Recommendations of the Commission of Enquiry* (Tunis, 13 July 1992).

82. Halliday, op.cit., pp. 103–4.

83. Baccouche Bahri, F., 'Discours du 13 août '92: Des décisions qui consacrent une modernité équilibrée et responsable' in *Femme* (No. 69, novembre 1992), pp. 8–10; Mayer, A. E., 'Reform of Personal Status Laws in North Africa: A Problem of Islamic or Mediterranean Laws?' in *Middle East Journal* (Vol. 49, No. 3, Summer 1995), p.441.

84. Saloua Charfi, interview.

85. 'MDS: Le congress de la rupture' in *Réalités* (No. 392, 2–8 April 1993), pp. 12–14; and 'Tunisia' in *Human Rights Watch World Report, 1997*, (New York: Human Rights Watch, 1996), p. 304.

86. Interview with Amel Ben Aba. This former Femme Démocrates activist claims that the independent feminist movement has been taken over by the UNFT.

87. Even though the Nahda comprises among its leaders and militants some elements formed in the Zaytouna and an intellectual connection does exist with the ancient university, it severely criticises the Zaytouna for its lack of contact with the people; on the other hand the Zaytouna shaykhs often point out the ignorance of Islamists as regards Islamic law and theology. See, Ben Achour, Y., 'Islam perdu, Islam retrouvé' in Souriau, (ed.), op.cit., pp. 74–5. Note however that the Zaytouna does not hold as important a position in Tunisian society as the Azhar does in Egypt.

88. Limam, Z., 'Ben Ali a enfin son parti' in *Jeune Afrique* (Nos 1701–2, 12–25 août 1993), pp. 32–4.

89. Zartman, 'The Conduct of Political Reform', op.cit., pp. 26–7.

90. Radwan, S., Jamal, V., and Ghose, A., *Tunisia: Rural Labour and Structural Transformation* (London: Routledge, 1991), pp. 1, 29 and 87–9.

91. In 1988 Tunisia initiated a structural adjustment programme supported by a $150 million World Bank loan which implied privatisation of selected enterprises and the restructuring of others. Pelletrau, P. D., 'Private Sector Development Through Public Sector Restructuring? The Cases of the Gafsa Phosphate Company and the Chemical Group' in Zartman (ed.), op.cit., p. 129. On the politics and economics of economic liberalisation see Pelletreau, P. D., 'Perspectives on Privatisation in Tunisia' in *L'Économiste Maghrébin* (No.

9, 22 août 1990), pp. 9–22; Marks, J., 'Tunisia' in Niblock, T. and Murphy, E. (eds), *Economic and Political Liberalization in the Middle East* (London: British Academic Press, 1993); Economist Intelligence Unit, *Tunisia: Country Profile, 1996–97*; and World Bank Middle East and North Africa Economic Studies, *Tunisia's Global Integration and Sustainable Development: Choices for the 21st Century* (Washington, D.C.: The World Bank, 1996).

92. Richards, A., and Waterbury J., *A Political Economy of the Middle East: State, Class and Economic Development*, (Boulder, CO: Westview Press, 1990), pp. 217 and 244–6.

93. Moore, C. H., *The Mediterranean Debt Crescent: Money and Power in Algeria, Egypt, Morocco, Tunisia and Turkey* (Gainsville, FL: University Press of Florida, 1996), Chapter 6.

94. Bellin, E., 'Tunisian Industrialists and the State' in Zartman (ed.), op.cit.

95. Female labour and its implications are discussed by Ghiles, F., 'Escaping Islam's Past' in *Financial Times Survey: Tunisia* (14 June 1993), p. viii.

96. Zaimeche, S. E., 'Algeria, Morocco and Tunisia: Recent Social Change and Future Prospects' in *Middle Eastern Studies* (Vol. 30, No. 4, Oct. 1994), pp. 944–55.

97. Bellin, E., 'Civil Society in Formation: Tunisia' in Norton, A. R., (ed.), *Civil Society in the Middle East* (Leiden: E. J. Brill, 1995), pp. 120–47.

98. This view on the people and Islam has been influenced by Zubaida's approach. See Zubaida, op.cit. Note also that political analysts in Tunisia agree that the Islamist programme is ultimately unpopular with the majority of Tunisians (although no proof of this can really be produced especially now with the severe repression of Islamism in the country). Hermassi, E., 'The Islamist Movement and November 7', op.cit., p. 195, and interview with Aziz Krichen, prominent journalist and political analyst in Tunisia.

99. This point – namely that a strong, as opposed to an overly oppressive state, gives rise to a strong society and that the key to understanding political developments, including Islam, lies in understanding the role of the state – will be taken up in Chapter 6 below.

6

The Prospects of Islamic Liberalism in the Middle East

I

Chapters 3 to 5 of this book offered detailed studies of Islam and human rights in two countries. This chapter will generalise some of their findings in the Middle East as a whole and also suggest a methodology for assessing the prospects of Islamic liberalism.

Assessing the prospects of an Islamic liberalism is tantamount to assessing the prospects of liberalism in general in the contemporary Middle East. I have argued this point again and again in the preceding chapters and I have shown the reasons why this is so in the three cases studied. I will not, therefore, go into it again here but only spell out its implications. If liberalism and Islamic liberalism are bound together in Middle Eastern societies, the implication is that secularism is not an essential requirement for liberalism.[1] The input of Islamic liberalism in political culture would not be authoritarian, although it would undoubtedly be conservative, as in the case of Christian Democratic parties in the European experience.

Having said that, it is obviously the case that liberalism and Islamic liberalism are two separate phenomena, conceptually, and it is only with the latter that we are concerned in this chapter. In order to assess its prospects we need to look at its agents: governments, opposition groups, social movements and individuals.

Currently, Islamic liberals, as I defined them in Chapter 2, are few and far between in the Middle East. To my knowledge, none of the major Islamist movements can be described as liberal. There are wide variations in the ideologies of the Islamists – the Front Islamique du Salut (FIS) of Algeria occupying one extreme, the Turkish Refah party the other, with the Jordanian Muslim Brotherhood in between, to take a few examples – but the 'moderates' are not liberals, as things stand at present. Similarly, none of the states, as political actors, put forward boldly a liberal interpretation of Islam, with the exception possibly of Tunisia which comes closest to it in the area of family law. Islamic liberalism in the Middle East is confined to individual thinkers and some strands within broader movements. Its prospects are slim indeed. To examine why this is so is important because, as this book has tried to show, Islamic liberalism is a viable proposition. As the ebb and flow of politics continues, its prospects may in the future become brighter. Knowing the reasons for its lack of appeal at the present juncture may help us to reverse its decline.

Our question is the following: Why is it that in a particular country X the interpretation of Islam is extremist, violent or very authoritarian and in country Y it is more open, tolerant or liberal? Already it is clear – by the terms of the question – that to answer it requires a country by country approach. In the modern world of nation-states the parameters for the interpretation of religion are set by the nation-state, not the region, the culture or the religion. Despite the common elements in political culture between Middle Eastern or Arab countries and the transnational links between the Islamists, and even despite the undoubted impact of ideas and norms across state boundaries, the nation-state remains the most important context for analysis. The stark differences between the Islamism of neighbouring countries – compare Algeria and Morocco, for instance – or between Middle Eastern countries generally, means that it is to the history of each country that we must turn in order to assess the interpretation of Islam.

Within the boundaries of each country, as Chapters 3 to 5 have already made clear, we need to focus on the following factors for assessing the interpretation of religion. First, the political decisions of ruling elites with regard to Islam. Have these elites promoted Islam in order to buttress their rule? Have they harassed secular opposition movements? Are these elites illegitimate in the eyes of their people and therefore find religion useful as an instrument of power? The second factor is with regard to the economic structures of the state in question. How have economic systems shaped the social make-up of a country? Wealth here is not the issue – compare Saudi Arabia, a wealthy but illiberal country, with Tunisia which is poorer but less illiberal. The issue is, rather, the kinds of economic elites that a system upholds and the impact of a command economy on the political attitudes of social groups. The third factor, closely connected with the second, is the kind of social support that Islamist movements command. If their supporters are made up of groups which have been nurtured in an authoritarian political system and an economy that has not fostered liberalisation (in both the economic and political sense), or if major social injustices without means of redress exist, then the Islamist movements are bound to be illiberal.

The third of the above points is especially important, and provides us with the link between Islamic liberalism and liberalism in general. If the support of Islamist movements in the Middle East has been predominantly 'middle class', the often obscurantist interpretation of Islam by these classes is best explained by their development: under the tutelage of the state, which has smothered any independent liberal spirit. Islam cannot be liberal if its supporters are not. An explanation of the interpretation of Islam in the Middle East which is firmly anchored in political, economic and social factors is, I suggest, more fruitful than reference to the immutable nature of Islam. Islamism is a political and social phenomenon, not a religious or cultural one, and the role of Islam in political culture is not an independent variable.

However, we can go beyond the above three factors which, although necessary, are not sufficient for our task. The political, economic and social development of Middle Eastern countries becomes intelligible when placed in the wider context of state formation and development. This approach has been implicit in my study of Egypt and Tunisia. Applying it to the Middle East as a whole is a useful way of assessing the interpretation of Islam and therefore the prospects of Islamic liberalism.

The emergence of nation-states in the Middle East was a modern though not exclusively colonial phenomenon.[2] The nuclei of states may have pre-existed in various parts of the region but the phenomenon of the modern state was distinctive, characterised – as I stressed in Chapter 3 – by the following principles: a central administration; served by a bureaucracy; introducing taxation, conscription, planning and schooling, and ; establishing its jurisdiction within territorial boundaries.

The emergence of liberalism presupposes and is inextricably linked with the modern state (I refer here to ideal types). This is because it is the modern state that atomises and individualises society, breaking up traditional bonds and reconstituting subjects as citizens. Liberalism emerges as the process of state formation proceeds.[3] Liberalism presupposes a strong state, capable of upholding the rule of law. If the process is arrested or incomplete, the result is either a very weak or a very repressive state, both inimical to individual rights. (Note the crucial difference: a strong state upholds the rule of law and is subject to it, a repressive state does not. Liberalism flourishes only in the case of the former, of course.) The key question with regard to state formation is: does the state develop into a modern formation in tandem with civil society? Or does it develop perpetually threatened by it or threatening it? State and society must hold a continuous balance if liberalism is to flourish. Otherwise the state is repressive.

There are three types of states in the Middle East – ideal types, which in reality are mixed with one another – and all have had a different impact on human rights. The first type is of states formed on the basis of preexisting central structures, which have been long standing and continuous and which have allowed integral links with society to develop. Some of the reasons for this are geography, tradition, and social factors such as the weakness of tribes. The countries studied in this book, Egypt and Tunisia, fall into this category. Turkey would be another example. In all three cases, constitutional reform began early in the nineteenth century, notably with the *Tanzimat* in the Ottoman Empire. Constitutional reform was part and parcel of centralisation and despite the reactions which it caused it provided the initial impetus for nascent modern state structures by establishing the principle of individual citizen rights.

It is no accident that in the above cases Islamism is less extremist and more closely approximated to a liberal interpretation, than in other cases in the Middle East which we will look at presently. Conversely the failures in the process of state formation explain why a fully-fledged Islamic liberalism did not emerge. The emergence of interventionist states under Nasser, Bourguiba and Ataturk had a deadening effect on social formations. The result was a subjugated middle class which was not always interested in pressing for civil and political rights and a corporatised working class which did not always manage to secure social and economic rights. What could have been a liberal experiment in Islamic politics – through the liberalisation of political culture generally – did not fully emerge.

The second ideal type is what Nazih Ayubi calls 'fierce' states.[4] In these cases central authority has been weak, either because it emerged late or because it has been confronted with strong tribal opposition. This type of state has had to forcibly modernise or otherwise repress society in order to achieve survival within an international and regional system of nation-states. Examples of such states would be Algeria, Syria, Iraq and Iran under the shah.

The third type of state in the Middle East is the 'rentier' type – the rent in the region coming primarily from oil. This type of state authority exists and functions through 'buying off' the acquiescence of large parts of the population. As the example of the Gulf monarchies make clear, liberalism cannot develop if central government is not dependent on taxation.

The second and third types of states described above give rise to an extremist, illiberal type of Islamism. 'Fierce' states give rise to fierce opposition Islamist ideologies. Likewise 'rentier' states, when combined with underdeveloped state structures, have the same effect. Why is this? Without effective state structures developing over a long period of time particularist loyalties – to tribe, kinship group, the extended family – are slow in dissipating. As men continue to dominate over women, older generations over younger ones and the group generally over the individual, a human rights culture cannot develop. Traditionalist attitudes continue to prevail and give rise to illiberal interpretations of Islam.

The example of Algeria is perhaps the most pertinent here. Algeria has had a haphazard and ultimately unsuccessful history of state formation.[5] Weak state structures and the domination of tribes were followed by French colonisation which had an adverse effect on the process of centralisation. In their attempt to subjugate the country the French, as is well known, forcibly uprooted and moved whole sections of the Algerian population and used a policy of 'divide and rule'. This resulted in the hardening of loyalties for tribal and kinship groups rather than their dissolution, as Algerian society tried to defend itself against the French. The bloody war of independence – in which traditional Islam was invoked as a crucial element of identity against the French – and the rentier, authoritarian system of government that was subsequently set up, brutalised Algerian society. It is no coincidence that Algeria is the birthplace of one of the most extremist and illiberal Islamist movements in the Middle East.

I do not claim that the process of state formation can explain everything about Islamism and liberalism in the Middle East. There are special circumstances pertaining to each country – the role of the monarchy in Jordan and Morocco for example – which must, in a state by state approach, be taken into account. But looking at state formation is, I think, most useful as a rough guideline.

Throughout the Middle East state formation has met with mixed success to say the least. Arab nationalism and the artificial nature of state boundaries in the region are often believed to be the causes of this record, but their impact has, I believe, been overestimated. It is within each country that the failures of the process must be accounted for. Overblown, overstaffed and overbearing states are, as Ayubi has shown,[6] ubiquitous in the region, whatever political ideology the ruling elites purport to support. This is not because Middle Eastern elites are exceptionally power-grabbing or because the people are unusually traditionalist but because, in each case, the balance between government and society has not been the right one.

II

The above analysis of liberalism and the interpretation of religion has implications for political and academic debate on civil society and democracy. It allows us to escape a bind which is evident in some of the literature on the Middle East which has been lent credibility and is fed by the claims of the Islamists. The bind arises, firstly, from defining civil society as the space vacated by rolling back the boundaries of the state and, secondly, by equating liberalisation with democratisation. Both these ideas rest on the implicit conception of the state as the villain and society as the locus of freedom, an idea which is both unreal and pernicious.

A strand in the recent literature on civil society describes Islamist or even traditional associations (even tribes) as elements of civil society. Islamist groups are adept in making such claims for themselves. But, as Sami Zubaida has shown in a brief article on Egypt, this is a misrepresentation of the term 'civil society' because such associations are based on hierarchy, control and social repression.[7] They lack the essential elements of freedom and pluralism implied in the term 'civil society'. This is not to say that any Islamic association is inherently illiberal (although traditional 'associations' invariably are, if they are associations at all). It is, however, to deny that any association is an expression of civil society merely by virtue of its being against or independent of the state.

A weak state does not lead to the emergence of a strong civil society. On the contrary, a strong civil society requires a strong state. Here the example of Yemen is pertinent. Yemenis are fiercely independent in the face of a weak central government. Tribal and kinship formations may enjoy a high level of freedom, but the individual is subsumed to the group, a situation which is not conducive to liberalisation.[8]

Democratisation and liberalisation, similarly, are not identical processes. The example of Algeria's 1991 elections and the near assumption of power by an anti-democratic and illiberal Islamist movement are a powerful illustration of the lack of necessary compatibility between the two. The trappings of democracy do not lead to a respect for human rights.

Crucially, we need to recognise that state and society are not two separate entities, alien to one another. Once again Algeria is a pertinent example: the regime which overturned the electoral victory in 1992 is as brutal as the Islamists. Illiberal states exist in illiberal societies and Islamist movements tend to be mirror images of the states in which they emerge.

Notes

1. I am grateful to Fred Halliday for emphasising this point (on which we disagree).

2. On the state in the Middle East generally see Dawisha, A., and Zartman, I. W., (eds), *Beyond Coercion: The Durability of the Arab State* (London: Croom Helm, 1988), Vol. III; Luciani, G., (ed.), *The Arab State* (London: Routledge, 1990); Owen, R., *State, Power and Politics in the Making of the Modern Middle East* (London: Routledge, 1992); and Ayubi, N. N., *Over-stating the Arab State: Politics and Society in the Middle East* (London: I. B. Tauris, 1995).

3. Brown, N. J., *The Rule of Law in the Arab World* (Cambridge: Cambridge University Press, 1997). Brown discusses the intricate links between liberalism and the building of a strong, centralised state. See especially pp. 49–60, with regard to Egypt.

4. Ayubi, op. cit.

5. On state formation in Algeria see especially Hermassi, E., *Leadership and National Development in North Africa* (Berkeley, CA: University of California Press, 1972).

6. Ayubi, op. cit.

7. Zubaida, S., 'Islam, the State and Democracy: Contrasting Conceptions of Society in Egypt' in *Middle East Report* (No. 179, Vol. 22, No. 6, November/ December 1992), pp. 2–10.

8. Carapico, 'Yemen' in Norton (ed.), op. cit. I am grateful to Gerd Nonneman for pointing out the case of Yemen.

Conclusion

The arguments on Islam and human rights in Egyptian and Tunisian society in Chapters 3 to 5 of the book rested on the position worked out in Chapter 2; that it is possible, at an abstract level of ideas, to incorporate the concept of human rights within an Islamic world-view. Chapter 2 argued that such an exercise requires a revision of the traditional understanding of Islam, an emphasis on some elements in the Koran that are conducive to a liberal spirit (and a constructive engagement with those which are not), and a firm acceptance of the historicity of the text. We arrived at this position by shedding the Manichean view of Islam and human rights as irreconcilable absolutes. Islam and human rights cease to be a contradiction if a liberal impulse precedes this intellectual exercise. Similarly, the study of the three cases showed that an Islamic liberalism becomes viable only if liberalism in political culture has already become established. This allowed us to shift attention from the details of Islamic doctrine as they pertain to human rights, to social and political processes.

The book, being about Islam and liberalism, not liberalism *per se*, examined historical instances in which the prospects of Islam being divorced from public life were slim. Egypt and Tunisia are not secular states. During the periods which were studied, Islam in various forms had a considerable input in the political process. This is not to argue that secularisation is not an option in Muslim societies. Two instances of secular or secularising polities in the Middle East are Nasser's Egypt and the Turkey of Atatürk and after. In the Muslim world beyond the Middle East, the examples would multiply. Egypt and Tunisia, and the periods that were studied in the case of each, were chosen precisely because Islam had an input in the political process. But the suggestion was that, given that an Islamic liberalism is a possibility, such an inquiry is useful if we change our question from 'is Islam part of politics or not?' to 'which interpretation of Islam is introduced in the political process and why?'

Human rights and democracy have constituted major concerns in the Muslim societies in question during the twentieth century. This is a testament to the powerfulness of the international influences in these societies and to the power of ideas generally to cross the boundaries of states and civilisations. Islamist groups in Tunisia and Egypt, among other political actors, have been compelled to confront questions of human rights and democracy. In some cases these ideas were rejected (an example being the Muslim Brotherhood in Egypt in the 1920s and 1930s and another the radical *gamaat* in Egypt in the 1970s to 1990s); in others they were only superficially accommodated (as in the case of the Brotherhood in Egypt in the latter period and the Nahda in Tunisia); in others still, a liberal conception of Islam has been worked out (as in the case of the Progressive Islamists in Tunisia). But Chapters 3 to 5 showed that if our analysis stops at oppositional Islam, it is incomplete. They, therefore, centred on the interpretation of Islam that the Egyptian and Tunisian states, as political actors, have put forward. They argued that we need to bring out the dialectical relationship between Islam as a challenge to the state and Islam as part of state and regime ideology in order to understand the variations in the interpretation of religion.

The book also argued that oppositional Islam evolves in interaction with the society it seeks to govern. Here attention focused on the social groups that support the Islamist option. Chapters 3 to 5 showed the direct correlation between the two. The transformation of the Muslim Brotherhood from the radical popular movement of the 1930s and 1940s to the conservative and moderate one from the 1970s onwards, was a prime example. The Brotherhood in the latter period has been forced to tackle questions of democracy and human rights. But the example of the Nahda is even more pertinent. The Nahda has had to modify its ideas on women's rights, political and trade union rights after it entered the political race. The Tunisian Islamists have gone further than their Egyptian counterparts towards incorporating human rights in their understanding of Islam. Tunisian society has given rise to the Progressive Islamist group which, in the opinion of this author, is exceptional in the Middle East in working out a genuinely liberal Islam. No equivalent group exists in Egypt.

What accounts for these developments and the differences between Egypt and Tunisia, I argued, is the societies in question. Different societies give rise to different conceptions of Islam. A liberal Muslim society will give rise to a liberal interpretation of Islam. Tunisia is – or rather had the potential to become – a more liberal society than Egypt.[1] To account for the existence of a liberal impulse in those two societies, Chapters 3 to 5 concentrated on the historical evolution of state structures and the relationship between state and society which they gave rise to. The argument, which was generalised for the Middle East as a whole in Chapter 6, was that strong – as opposed to repressive – states provide the appropriate framework for a respect of rights. The evolution of viable state institutions causes the individualisation of society but also allows for some protection of the individual. In other words, a strong state gives rise to a strong civil society.

Conversely, the limitations in the evolution of state structures explain the limitations and perhaps the ultimate defeat of the liberal impulse: the Egyptian and Tunisian states hover between being effective and being repressive states because many weaknesses remain. Other factors also were brought in to explain the reversal of liberalisation, factors which pertain principally to the economic systems in place. Chapter 3 showed that the political classes in Egypt had an interest in the preservation of semi-feudal economic relations. Chapters 4 and 5 argued that the weakness of a liberal political culture in Egypt and Tunisia was the outcome of the politics of state capitalism, which failed to nurture middle classes independently of the state; and of the inability of 'lower' social groups to press for democratisation. In other words, economic structures are directly relevant to political culture. But the study attempted to eschew deterministic interpretations by showing that an element of choice was nevertheless allowed to the elites or states in question. This leeway was used in a manner which was not conducive to liberalisation.[2]

This analysis gave rise to two interrelated propositions on Islam and liberalism. Firstly, that it was the fate of liberalism in general in Egypt and Tunisia which determined the evolution of Islam. Secondly, that Islam does not have an independent contribution to the political process and *cannot as such explain the reversal of the liberal impulse.*

To connect thus Islamic liberalism with liberalism in general allows us to link the study of Islam with the normative points of the first chapter of the book. Chapter 1 argued that human rights can only be defended within the framework of a 'natural law' tradition of sorts and not on the basis of impartial reason or rationality. To believe that human beings have rights *qua* human beings is a moral value which one either shares or does not. One implication of this argument is that human rights as a value can be incorporated within a religious framework (including an Islamic framework). To break the necessary link between human rights and secularism is to allow for the further universalisation of human rights norms. To break the tradition of natural law with Christianity contributes to this universalisation. The above steps also take us further away from a view that has bedeviled human rights thinking and practice for a long time. A view which identifies 'the West' with liberalism and human rights and places 'other' cultures on the opposite side of the divide.

The normative position outlined in Chapter 1 included a rejection of the division between the private and the public domains. It claimed that the division is superficial and cannot hold; in other words that liberalism cannot be defended or instituted only in public life – on the basis of impartial reason - because the private will inevitably influence the public. Chapters 3 to 5 gave credence to this view by suggesting the impossibility of separating women's rights from human rights in Islam and by implying that illiberal private or family relations inevitably influence the public political sphere.

Once we follow the normative position in Chapter 1 to its logical conclusion and incorporate the private domain in our thinking about liberalism, the depth of the moral dilemma for the liberal becomes apparent. There are no two ways about it. Once human rights and human liberty, which are individual affairs, become the moral priority, other values (such as communal solidarity) will be sacrificed. The liberal will of course retort that the solidarity that arises from free and equal relations is stronger and more genuine than a solidarity based on hierarchy and repression. This may be so but it does not detract from the difficulty of the choice involved.

The moral dilemmas – at a personal and at a societal level – were described in stark outline in Chapter 1. The study of Egypt and Tunisia in the twentieth century however showed that, in those cases at least, the dilemmas are not as hard. This view was integrally linked with the understandings of tradition and modernity which the book contained. Chapters 3 to 5 illustrated that the forces of modernity have transformed the Egyptian and Tunisian societies to the point that there has been a radical break with the traditional world. The argument was *not* that traditional attitudes do not exist at any level or in any segment of society but that those who use Islam as a political force and press for a return to 'cultural authenticity' are not traditional elements but eminently modern ones, part of a world-wide fundamentalist pattern specific to the modern age. I argued that these groups – or those who oppose them – exercise choices in the heritage to which they appeal; in sum, that tradition is not an objective set of ideas and institutions and practices to be retrieved at will, but is reconceptualised and reformulated depending on the goals of political actors.

The search for cultural authenticity is, in other words, a vain one.[3] Authenticity is not an objective standard but is also, like 'tradition', a matter of definition and choice. To accept this view, which has been emphasised time and again in this study, is to counter the cultural essentialist thesis which purports that cultures have immutable and timeless characteristics and that to transpose human rights norms in Muslim societies is impossible. Instead of cultural essentialism, which has bedeviled, in either implicit or explicit form, many strands of international relations thinking and Middle Eastern studies, a 'universal sense of becoming'[4] is posited. This universal sense of becoming emerges from the common concerns of modernity which have two focal points: a break up of society and community to its individual parts; and a practical and psychological concern with the concept of change. It has also arisen from the global spread of state structures of subjugation and control. To those who would argue that human rights are alien to their culture, the liberal would retort that so is the model of the modern state and its mechanisms of control – against which human rights are the *only* possible protection for the individual.

It is thus that the dilemma of the liberal has ceased, in our time, to be an impossible one. In the part of the world examined in this book – and the findings may be applicable elsewhere – authenticity and tradition are not absolutes to be discovered and adhered to. Indeed, they are often pawns in a strictly political game. If this view is taken and the argument is deemed persuasive then it can be further developed. The liberal can argue that a community or society's search for its identity can take place only within a liberal framework. It is only such a framework which allows for the constant reformulation of identity and therefore permits any community to flourish. In other words, whilst the search for personal authenticity can be in clash with authenticity in societal terms, respect for it can allow the emergence of bonds of solidarity between members of the group.

In the three periods in the history of Egypt and Tunisia that were studied, the interpretations of Islam have evolved towards increasing authoritarianism and the potential for a liberalisation of Islam and politics has been almost wholly lost. Nevertheless, the discrediting of cultural essentialism, the rejection of the concept of authenticity and the non-static approach used for the analysis of Islam in society, allow for the possibility that this may again change, if political configurations change. The evolution of Islam is constant. Such a position therefore encourages action – by liberals, including Islamist liberals, and defenders of human rights within Muslim societies and outside them.

The arguments developed in this book have a number of implications for the study of international relations. The first pertains to the debate on communitarianism in the discipline.[5] The book has suggested that the understanding of community cannot be a static one. Communities do not evolve in isolation and it is vain, in the modern world especially which revolutionises human societies and binds them together in common concerns, to search for authenticity. The findings, therefore, can be taken to imply that a communitarian position does not provide a sound analytic basis for the study of international relations.[6]

The second point relates to the study of culture in international relations. Culture has been neglected as an issue in a discipline which has been state-centric (and, patently, Eurocentric too). It has also been neglected because culture as an analytic tool is hopelessly vague, especially as it pertains to the global level. Attempts to discuss international relations in terms of culture inhere the danger of reverting to stereotype.[7] This book, however, has proposed that we can – and must – incorporate culture in the discipline, not as an objective element with immutable characteristics, but through focusing on the role of political agency and the use to which political agents put cultural elements.

The third point pertains to the universalisation of human rights principles which many would see as part of a process of globalisation. The framework of this book has been the enormous international impact of human rights as a norm and value. This impact, as Chapter 3 showed, is longstanding although in recent times it has been even greater. Two points can be made in this context: the first is that globalisation does not bypass the state – it is, indeed, often the state which is the connecting link between universal norms and domestic societies. The second is that the spread of human rights norms is not a unilinear process. It is, on the contrary, a process which by its very forcefulness creates extreme reactions. Thus, in Egypt and Tunisia in the 1970s, 1980s and 1990s, oppositional Islamists may have felt compelled to adopt human rights principles but have also, in appropriating them, emptied the concept of human rights of any substance.[8] This was a reaction both to international norms which are identified with a dominant culture – a supposed 'Western' culture – and a reaction to the state *per se* which in part represented these norms. The comment arising from this study is, in other words, that globalisation and the universalisation of human rights norms may ultimately be reversed.

A fourth point pertains to the understanding of the state in international relations. Implicit in this book has been the belief that, despite the impact of international norms and values onto disparate societies, ultimately the role of human rights and liberalism can be worked out only within societies. In this sense the book reinforces the state-centric model, by implying that the framework provided by the state continues to be the dominant institutional framework in international relations, the context in which norms and values will be worked out.[9] Chapters 3 to 5 have also shown that the state – as an institution of control – is not weakening in our time.

Because of the way in which the discipline of international relations developed – mentioned above – and because international relations theory has the imprint of Western historical experience, it is the state that is taken to be the violator of human rights internationally. The debate on human rights is often seen in terms of state sovereignty. In other words, it is believed that as the state weakens so human rights and international norms will be more respected. This view is incongruent with the picture presented in this book which suggested that it is often states that undertake liberalisation under the impact of international forces;[10] that in many instances it is the state that defends human rights against society or plays a pioneering role in promoting those rights; and that a strong (as opposed to a repressive), state may be a guarantee for the respect of rights and contribute to the emergence of a liberal society. The profound ambiguity of the state and the impossibility of assuming, before detailed study, whether a state is a violator or guarantor of human rights must inform the study of human rights in international relations.

The book, finally, has suggested ways in which we can approach the concept of human rights in the study of international relations. It has also proposed that such questions – which require acceptance of solid links between the domestic and international contexts – must be of primary importance in the discipline. The implication of this study has also been that human rights principles can be a binding international norm in the modern world and that many of the normative objections to the concept of rights rest on shaky foundations. This study, therefore, encourages the defence of human rights across societies and cultures without, however, underestimating the costs that such a defence inevitably entails.

Notes

1. This is of course a speculative point.
2. This fine line between a deterministic and voluntarist explanation of developments in Egypt came into play in the discussion of dependency links between the international capitalist and domestic economic systems. Chapters 3 and 4 showed that the former played a part in the formation of the domestic

situation but that it did not fully constrain elite or state decision-making.

3. Authenticity can only be meaningful at a personal level. In that sense, as Chapter 1 argued, there is an inevitable clash between the search for personal and societal authenticity, for if the latter takes precedence the former is bound to be restricted.

4. For a discussion of this term see Windsor, P., 'Cultural Dialogue in Human Rights' in Desai, M., and Redfern, P., (eds), *Global Governance: Ethics and Economics of the World Order* (London: Pinter, 1995).

5. On this question contrast Frost, M., *Towards a Normative Theory of International Relations: A Critical Analysis of the Philosophical and Methodological Assumptions in the Discipline with Proposals towards a Substantive Normative Theory* (Cambridge: Cambridge University Press, 1986) with Beitz, C. R., *Political Theory and International Relations* (Princeton, NJ: Princeton University Press, 1979).

6. The study has also commented on the post-modernist concerns in the discipline of international relations. See Chapter 1.

7. Huntington, S. P., 'The Clash of Civilizations?' in *Foreign Affairs* (Vol. 72, No. 3, Summer 1993), pp. 22–49.

8. A similar development occurred in the United Nations Conference on Human Rights in June 1993, in which a number of Asian states – such as Singapore, Indonesia, Malaysia and Thailand, with China behind the scenes – proposed a specifically 'Asian' conception of rights. Interview with Pierre Robert, Researcher on the Asia and Pacific Region, Amnesty International, February 1996. See the Bangkok Declaration, April 1993, by the Asia intergovernmental meeting in preparation for the Conference in *Our Voice: The Bangkok NGO Declaration on Human Rights* (Bangkok: Asian Cultural Forum on Development, 1993) and the *Bangkok NGO Declaration on Human Rights* (March 1993; courtesy of Mr Robert). Muslim nations submitted the 'Cairo Declaration on Human Rights in Islam' to the UN Conference; this document had been originally propounded in the 19th Conference of Islamic Foreign Ministers in August 1990. Halliday, F., *Islam and the Myth of Confrontation: Religion and Politics in the Middle East* (London: I. B.Tauris, 1995), p. 134.

9. This view does not imply the morality of the state as such; the state provides the framework for moral relationships. On this point see Vincent, R. J., 'Western Conceptions of a Universal Moral Order', in Pettman, R., (ed.), *Moral Claims in World Affairs* (London: Croom Helm, 1979), discussed in Chapter 1.

10. This does not imply however that the adoption of human rights as an aim in foreign policy is the best way to promote rights. State promotion of

human rights is bound to suffer from double-standards and inconsistencies and creates a cultural reaction which is detrimental to rights, as Chapters 3 to 5 showed. It is arguable that non-governmental organisations are best suited to promote rights.

Bibliography

Books

Abdalla, A., *The Student Movement and National Politics in Egypt, 1923–1973* (London: al-Saqi Books, 1985).

Abdel Moula, M., *L'Université zaytounienne et la société tunisienne* (Tunis: CNRS, 1971).

Abduh, M., *The Theology of Unity* (London: George Allen and Unwin, 1966, translated by I. Musa'ad and K. Cragg).

Ahmad, A., *In Theory: Classes, Nations, Literatures* (London: Verso, 1992).

Ahmed, A. H. M., *The Urgency of Ijtihad* (New Delhi: Kitab Bhavan, 1992).

Al-Alwani, T. J., *Ijtihad* (Herndon, VA: International Institute of Islamic Thought,1993).

Al-Ashmawy, M. S., *L'Islamisme contre L'Islam* (Paris: La Découverte and Cairo: Éditions la Fikr, 1989, translated by R. Jacquemond).

Al-Sayyid-Marsot, A. L., A Short History of Modern Egypt (Cambridge: Cambridge University Press, 1985).

——*Egypt's Liberal Experiment: 1922–1936* (Berkeley, CA: University of California Press, 1977).

——A. L., *Women and Men in late Eighteenth Century Egypt* (Austin,TX: University of Texas Press, 1995).

Al-Sha'rawi, M. M., *The Miracles of the Qur'an* (London: Dar Al-Taqwa, translated by M. Alserougii).

Amin, H., *Le livre du musulman désemparé* (Paris: La Découverte, 1992, translated by R. Jacquemond).

An-Naim, A. A. and Deng, F. M. (eds), *Human Rights in Africa: Cross-Cultural Perspectives* (Washington D. C.: The Brookings Institution, 1990).

——*Towards an Islamic Reformation: Civil Liberties, Human Rights, and*

International Law (Syracuse, NY: Syracuse University Press, 1990).

Anderson, L., *The State and Social Transformation in Tunisia and Libya* (Princeton, NJ: Princeton University Press, 1986).

Ansari, H., *Egypt: The Stalled Society* (Cairo: American University in Cairo Press, 1987).

Arkoun, M., *Rethinking Islam Today* (Washington D. C.: Center for Contemporary Arab Studies, Georgetown University, Occasional Paper Series, 1987).

Avineri, S. and de-Shalit, A. (eds), *Communitarianism and Individualism* (Oxford: Oxford University Press, 1992).

——*Bureaucracy and Politics in Contemporary Egypt* (London: Ithaca Press, for the Middle East Centre, St Anthony's College, Oxford, 1980).

——*Political Islam: Religion and Politics in the Arab World* (London: Routledge, 1991).

——*Over-stating the Arab State: Politics and Society in the Middle East* (London: I. B. Tauris, 1995).

Badran, M., *Feminists, Islam and Nation: Gender and the Making of Modern Egypt* (Princeton, NJ: Princeton University Press, 1995).

Badrawi, M., *Isma'il Sidqi, 1875–1950: Pragmatism and Vision in Twentieth Century Egypt* (Richmond, Surrey: Curzon, 1996).

Bakalti, S., *La Femme tunisienne au temps de la colonisation, 1881–1956* (Paris: L'Harmattan, 1996).

Baker, R. W., *Sadat and After: Struggles for Egypt's Political Soul* (London: I. B. Tauris,1990).

Bani-Sadr, A. A., *Human Rights in Islam* (Arab Encyclopedia House, no date).

Bannerman, P., *Islam in Perspective: A Guide to Muslim Society, Politics and the Law* (London: Routledge for the Royal Institute of International Affairs, 1988).

Beck, L. and Keddie, N. R. (eds), *Women in the Muslim World* (Cambridge, MA: Harvard University Press, 1978).

Beitz, C. R., *Political Theory and International Relations* (Princeton, NJ: Princeton University Press, 1979).

Benedict, R., *Patterns of Culture* (London: Routledge and Kegan Paul, 1935).

Berger, M., *Islam in Egypt Today: Social and Political Aspects of Popular Religion* (Cambridge: Cambridge University Press, 1970).

Berman, M., *All That is Solid Melts into Air: The Experience of Modernity* (London: Verso, 1982).

Berque, J., *Relire le Coran* (Paris: Albin Michel, 1993).

Berrady, L. et al., *La Formation des élites politiques maghrébines* (Paris: CNRS, 1973).

Bessis S. and Belhassen, S., *Femmes du Maghreb* (Tunis: Cérès Productions – J. C. Lattès, 1992).

——*Bourguiba: Un si long regne* (Paris: Japress/Jeune Afrique Livres, 1989).

Bianchi, R., *Unruly Corporatism: Associational Life in Twentieth Century Egypt* (NewYork: Oxford University Press, 1989).

Binder, L., *In a Moment of Enthusiasm: Political Power and the Second Stratum in Egypt* (Chicago, IL: University of Chicago Press, 1978).

——*Islamic Liberalism: A Critique of Development Ideologies* (Chicago, IL: University of Chicago Press, 1988).

Botiveau, B., *Loi islamique et droit dans les sociétés arabes* (Paris: Karthala, 1993).

Botman, S., *Egypt from Independence to Revolution, 1919–1952* (Syracuse, NY: Syracuse University Press, 1991).

Boullata, I. J., *Trends and Issues in Contemporary Arab Thought* (Albany, NY: State University of New York Press, 1990).

Bozeman, A., *Conflict in Africa* (Princeton, NJ: Princeton University Press, 1976).

Brown, L. C., *The Tunisia of Ahmad Bey, 1837–1855* (Princeton, NJ: Princeton University Press, 1974).

Brown, N. J., *The Rule of Law in the Arab World* (Cambridge: Cambridge University Press, 1997).

Brownlie, I. (ed.), *Basic Documents on Human Rights* (Oxford: Clarendon Press, 1992).

——*Principles of Public International Law* (Oxford: Clarendon Press, 1979).

Burgat, F. and Dowell, W., *The Islamic Movement in North Africa*, (Austin, TX: Center for Middle Eastern Studies at the University of Texas, 1993).

Carré, O., *Mystique et politique: Lecture revolutionnaire du Coran par Sayyid Qutb, Frère Musulman radical* (Paris: Presses de la Fondation Nationale des Sciences Politiques et Éditions du Cerf, 1984).

Carter, B. L., *The Copts in Egyptian Politics, 1918–1952* (London: Croom Helm, 1986).

Chadwick, O., *The Secularisation of the European Mind in the Nineteenth Century* (Cambridge: Cambridge University Press, 1975).

Chamari, A. C., *La Femme et la loi en Tunisie* (Casablanca: Éditions le Fennec, 1991).

Cherfils, C., *L'Esprit de modernité dans le monotheisme islamique* (Saint-Ouen: Centre Abaad, 1992).

Cohen, B., *Habib Bourguiba: Le Pouvoir d'un seul* (Mesnil-sur-l'Estrée: Flammarion,1986).

Connolly, W. E., *Political Theory and Modernity* (Oxford: Blackwell, 1988).

Cooper, M. N., *The Transformation of Egypt* (London: Croom Helm, 1982).

Coulson, N. J., *A History of Islamic Law* (Edinburgh: Edinburgh University Press, 1964).

Cranston, M., *What Are Human Rights?* (New York: Taplinger, 1973).

Darghouth Medimegh, A., *Droits et vécu de la femme en Tunisie*, (Lyons: L'Hermès – Edilis, 1992).

Dawisha, A. and Zartman, I. W. (eds), *Beyond Coercion: The Durability of the Arab State* (London: Croom Helm, 1988).

De Beauvoir, S., *The Second Sex* (London: Picador-Pan Books, 1988, translated by H. M. Parshley).

Deeb, M., *Party Politics in Egypt: The Wafd and its Rivals, 1919–1939* (London: Ithaca Press, for the Middle East Centre, St Anthony's College Oxford, 1979).

D'Entrèves, A. P., *Aquinas: Selected Political Writings* (Oxford: Basil Blackwell, 1965).

——*Natural Law: An Introduction to Legal Philosophy* (London: Hutchinson University Library, 1970).

Dessouki, A. E. H. (ed.), *Democracy in Egypt: Problems and Prospects*, (Cairo Papers in Social Science, Vol. 1, Monograph 2, 1983 / Cairo: American University in Cairo Press).

Donelan, M., *Elements of International Political Theory* (Oxford: Clarendon Press, 1990).

Donnelly, J., *The Concept of Human Rights* (London: Croom Helm, 1985).

Dwyer, K., *Arab Voices: The Human Rights Debate in the Middle East* (London: Routledge, 1991).

El-Sadat, A., *In Search of Identity: An Autobiography* (New York: Harper and Row, 1977).

El-Shafei, O., *Workers, Trade Unions and the State in Egypt, 1984–1989* (Cairo Papers in Social Science, Vol. 18, Monograph 2, Summer 1995 / Cairo: American University in Cairo Press).

Enayat, H., *Modern Islamic Political Thought: The Response of the Shi'i and Sunni Muslims to the Twentieth Century* (Basingstoke: Macmillan, 1982).

Engineer, A. A., *The Rights of Women in Islam* (London: C. Hurst, 1992).

Esposito, J. L. (ed.), *Voices of Resurgent Islam* (New York: Oxford University Press, 1983).

——*The Islamic Threat: Myth or Reality?* (New York: Oxford University Press, 1992).

——*Islam: The Straight Path* (New York: Oxford University Press, 1988).

Fahmi, H., *Divorcer en Egypte* (Le Caire: CEDEJ, 1987, Dossier 3, 1986).

Farah, T. E. (ed.), *Political Behaviour in the Arab States* (Boulder, CO: Westview Press, 1983).

Ferdinand, K. and Mozaffari, M. (eds), *Islam: State and Society* (London and

Riverdale, MD: Curzon Press and the Riverdale Company, 1988).

Ferjani, M. C., *Islamisme, laïcité et droits de l'homme* (Paris: L'Harmattan, 1991).

Finnis, J., *Natural Law and Natural Rights* (Oxford: Clarendon Press, 1980).

Fitoussi, E., *L'État tunisien: Son origine, son developpement et son organisation actuelle, 1525–1901* (Tunis: J. Picard, 1901).

Forsythe, D. P. (ed.), *Human Rights and Development: International Views* (Basingstoke: Macmillan, 1989).

Frost, M., *Towards a Normative Theory of International Relations: A Critical Analysis of the Philosophical and Methodological Assumptions in the Discipline with Proposals towards a Substantive Normative Theory* (Cambridge: Cambridge University Press, 1986).

Gaffrey, P. D., *The Prophet's Pulpit: Islamic Preaching in Contemporary Egypt* (Berkeley, CA: University of California Press, 1994).

Gamble, A., *An Introduction to Modern Social and Political Thought* (Basingstoke: Macmillan, 1981).

Geertz, C., *Islam Observed: Religious Development in Morocco and Indonesia* (Chicago, IL: University of Chicago Press, 1968).

Gellner, E. and Waterbury, J. (eds), *Patrons and Clients in Mediterranean Societies* (London: Duckworth, 1977).

——*Legitimation of Belief* (London: Cambridge University Press, 1974).

——*Reason and Culture* (Oxford: Blackwell, 1992).

——*Relativism and the Social Sciences* (Cambridge: Cambridge University Press, 1985).

Gershoni, I. and Jankowski, J. P., *Redefining the Egyptian Nation, 1930–45* (Cambridge: Cambridge University Press, 1995).

Ghannouchi, R., *Islam and the West* (publication details unspecified).

Goldberg, E., Kasaba, R. and Migdal, J. S. (eds), *Rules and Rights in the Middle East: Democracy, Law, and Society* (Seattle, WA: University of Washington Press, 1993).

Goldschmidt, A., *Modern Egypt: The Formation of a Nation-State* (Boulder, CO: Westview Press, 1988).

Gran, P., *Islamic Roots of Capitalism: Egypt, 1760–1840* (Austin, TX: University of Texas Press, 1979).

Green, A. H. (ed.), *In Quest of an Islamic Humanism: Arabic and Islamic Studies in Memory of Mohamed al-Nowaihi* (Cairo: American University in Cairo Press, 1984).

——*The Tunisian Ulama, 1873–1915: Social Structure and Response to Ideological Currents* (Leiden: E. J. Brill, 1978).

Guazzone, L. (ed.), *The Islamist Dilemma: The Political Role of Islamist Movements in the Contemporary Arab World* (Reading, Berkshire: Ithaca

Press, 1995).

Guen, M., *Les Défis de la Tunisie: Une analyse économique* (Paris: L'Harmattan, 1988).

Halliday, F. and Alavi, H. (eds), *State and Ideology in the Middle East and Pakistan* (Basingstoke: Macmillan Education, 1988).

——*Islam and the Myth of Confrontation: Religion and Politics in the MiddleEast* (London: I. B. Tauris, 1995).

Heikal, M., *Autumn of Fury: The Assassination of Sadat* (London: André Deutsch, 1983).

Hermassi, E., *Leadership and National Development in North Africa* (Berkeley, CA: University of California Press, 1972).

Higgins, R., *Problems and Processes: International Law and How We Use It* (Oxford: Oxford University Press, 1994).

Hijab, N., *Womanpower: The Arab Debate on Women at Work* (Cambridge: Cambridge University Press, 1988).

Hill, E., *Al-Sanhuri and Islamic Law: The Place and Significance of Islamic Law in the Life and Work of 'Abd al-Razzaq Ahmad al-Sanhuri, Egyptian Jurist and Scholar, 1895–1971* (Cairo Papers in Social Science, Vol. 10, Monograph 1, Spring 1987 / Cairo: American University in Cairo Press).

——*Makhama! Studies in the Egyptian Legal System* (London: Ithaca Press, 1979).

Hinnebusch, R. A., *Egyptian Politics Under Sadat: The Post-Populist Development of an Authoritarian-Modernizing State* (Boulder, CO: Lynne Rienner, 1985).

Hirsch, E. (ed.), *Islam et droits de l'homme* (Paris: Librairie des Libertés, 1984).

Hodgson, M. G. S., *The Venture of Islam* (Chicago, IL: University of Chicago Press,1974), Vol. 3.

Hollis, M. and Lukes, S. (eds), *Rationality and Relativism* (Oxford: Blackwell, 1982).

Holt, P. M. (ed.), *Political and Social Change in Modern Egypt: Historical Studies from the Ottoman Conquest to the United Arab Republic* (London: Oxford University Press, 1968).

Hopwood, D., *Egypt: Politics and Society, 1945–1984* (Boston, MA: Allen and Unwin, 1985).

Hourani, A., *Arabic Thought in the Liberal Age, 1798–1939* (Cambridge: Cambridge University Press, 1983).

Human Rights in Islam. Report of Seminar Held in Kuwait, 1980 (International Commission of Jurists, 1982).

Hussain, S. S., *Human Rights in Islam* (New Delhi: Kitab Bhavan, 1990).

Hutchinson, J. and Smith, A. (eds), *Nationalism* (Oxford: Oxford University

Press, 1994).

Ibn al-Husayn, Zayn al-Abidin Ali, *The Treatise on Rights* (Qum: Foundation of Islamic Cultural Propagation in the World, 1411 Hijri Year, translated by W. C. Chittick).

Ibrahim, S. E., et al., *The Copts of Egypt* (Minority Rights Group, 1996).

Israeli, R., *'L'Egypt': Aspects of President Anwar Al-Sadat's Political Thought* (Jerusalem: Magnes Press, Hebrew University, 1981).

Issawi, C., *Egypt in Revolution: An Economic Analysis* (London: Oxford University Press for the Royal Institute of International Affairs, 1963).

Kandiyoti, D. (ed.), *Women, Islam and the State* (Basingstoke: Macmillan, 1991).

Keddie, N. R., *An Islamic Response to Imperialism: Political and Religious Writins of Sayyid Jamal ad-Din 'al-Afghani'* (Berkeley, CA: University of California Press, 1983).

Kedourie, E., *Afghani and 'Abduh: An Essay on Religious Unbelief and Political Activism in Modern Islam* (London: Frank Cass, 1966).

——*Politics in the Middle East* (Oxford: Oxford University Press, 1992).

Kepel, G., *The Prophet and Pharaoh: Muslim Extremism in Egypt* (London: al-Saqi Books, 1985, translated by J. Rothschild).

Kerr, M. H., *Islamic Reform: The Political and Legal Theories of Muhammad 'Abduh and Rashid Rida* (Berkeley, CA: University of California Press, 1966).

Khadduri, M., *The Islamic Conception of Justice* (Baltimore, MD: Johns Hopkins University Press, 1984).

Khan, S. M., *Why Two Woman Witnesses?* (London: Ta-Ha Publishers, 1993).

Khayr ed-Din, *Essai sur les réformes nécessaires aux états musulmans* (Aix-en-Provence: Édisud, 1987).

Kishk, A., *The World of the Angels* (London: Dar Al Taqwa, 1994, translated by A. Bewley).

Kolakowski, L., *Religion* (Glasgow: Fontana, 1982).

The Koran, translated with notes by N. J. Dawood (London: Penguin, 1990).

Labidi, L., *Les Origines des mouvements féministes en Tunisie* (Tunis, 1987).

Ladd, J. (ed.), *Ethical Relativism* (Lanham, MD: University Press of America, 1985).

Laqueur, W. and Rubin, B. (eds), *The Human Rights Reader* (Philadelphia, PA: Temple University Press, 1979).

La Non-discrimination a l'égard des femmes entre la convention de copenhague et le discours identitaire (Colloque Tunis 13–16 janvier 1988, UNESCO et CERES, Université de Tunis, 1989).

Largueche, A., *L'Abolition de l'esclavage en Tunisie a travers les archives, 1841–1846* (Tunis: Alif, 1990).

Larif-Béatrix, A., *Édification étatique et environment culturel: Le personnel politico-administratif dans la Tunisie contemporaine* (Paris: Publisud - O. P. U., 1988).

Laroui, A., *Islam et modernité* (Paris: La Découverte, 1987).

Laskier, M. M., *North African Jewry in the Twentieth Century: The Jews of Morocco, Tunisia and Algeria* (New York: New York University Press, 1994).

Lawrence, B., *Defenders of God: The Fundamentalist Revolt Against the Modern Age* (London: I. B. Tauris, 1990).

Leenders, R., *The Struggle of State and Civil Society in Egypt: Professional Organisations and Egypt's Careful Steps Towards Democracy* (Middle East Research Associates Occasional Paper, No. 26, April 1996).

Lewis, B., *The Arabs in History* (London: Hutchinson, 1970).

——*The Political Language of Islam* (Chicago, IL: University of Chicago Press, 1988).

Ling, D. L., *Tunisia: From Protectorate to Republic* (Bloomington, IN: Indiana University Press, 1967).

Little, D., Kelsay, J. and Sachedina, A. A., *Human Rights and the Conflict of Cultures: Western and Islamic Perspectives on Religious Liberty* (Columbia, SC: South Carolina University Press, 1988).

Luciani, G. (ed.), *The Arab State* (London: Routledge, 1990).

Maduagwu, M. O., *Ethical Relativism versus Human Rights* (London: Third World Centre, 1987).

Marcus, G. E. and Fischer, M. M. J., *Anthropology as Cultural Critique* (Chicago, IL: University of Chicago Press, 1986).

Mawdudi, A. A., *Human Rights in Islam* (Lahore: Islamic Publications, 1977).

Mayer, A. E., *Islam and Human Rights: Tradition and Politics* (London and Boulder, CO: Pinter Publishers and Westview Press, 1991).

Mayer, T., *The Changing Past: Egyptian History and the Urabi Revolt, 1882–1983* (Gainesville, FL: University of Florida Press, 1988).

Mernissi, F., *Islam and Democracy: Fear of the Modern World* (London: Virago Press, 1993, translated by M. J. Lakeland).

Micaud, C. A., Brown, L. K. and Moore, C. H., *Tunisia: The Politics of Modernisation* (London: Pall Mall Press, 1964).

Mitchell, R. P., *The Society of the Muslim Brothers* (Oxford: Oxford University Press, 1969).

Mitchell, T., *Colonising Egypt* (Cambridge: Cambridge University Press, 1988).

Moghadam, V. M., *Modernizing Women: Gender and Social Change in the Middle East* (Boulder, CO: Lynne Rienner, 1993).

Moore, C. H., *Tunisia since Independence: The Dynamics of One-Party Government* (Berkeley, CA: University of California Press, 1965).

——*The Mediterranean Debt Crescent: Money and Power in Algeria, Egypt,*

Morocco, Tunisia and Turkey (Gainsville, FL: University Press of Florida, 1996).

Moudoud, E., *Modernisation, the State, and Regional Disparity in Developing Countries: Tunisia in Historical Perspective*, (Boulder, CO: Westview Press, 1989).

Mulhall, S. and Swift, A., *Liberals and Communitarians* (Oxford: Blackwell, 1992).

Nasr, S. H., *Traditional Islam in the Modern World* (London: Kegan Paul International, 1987).

Nazir-Ali, M., *The Roots of Islamic Tolerance: Origin and Development* (Oxford Project for Peace Studies, Paper No. 26, 1990).

Nelson, C., *Doria Shafi, Egyptian Feminist: A Woman Apart* (Gansville, FL: University Press of Florida, 1996).

Niblock, T. and Murphy, E. (eds), *Economic and Political Liberalization in the Middle East* (London: British Academic Press, 1993).

Norton, A. R. (ed.), *Civil Society in the Middle East* (Leiden: E. J. Brill, 1996), Vols. 1 and 2.

Owen, R., *State, Power and Politics in the Making of the Modern Middle East* (London: Routledge, 1992).

——*The Middle East in the World Economy, 1800–1914* (London: Methuen,1981).

Perkins, K. J., *Tunisia: Crossroads of the Islamic and European Worlds* (Boulder, CO: Westview Press, 1986).

Piscatori, J. P. (ed.), *Islam in the Political Process* (Cambridge: Cambridge University Press in association with the Royal Institute of International Affairs, 1983).

——*Islam in a World of Nation-States* (Cambridge: Cambridge University Press, in association with the Royal Institute of International Affairs, 1986).

Polanyi, K., *The Great Transformation*, (Boston, MA: Beacon Press, 1944).

Pollis, A. and Schwab, P. (eds), *Human Rights: Cultural and Ideological Perspectives* (New York: Praeger, 1979).

Qutb, Sayyid, *Milestones* (International Islamic Federation of Student Organizations, 1978).

Radwan, S., Jamal, V. and Ghose, A., *Tunisia: Rural Labour and Structural Transformation* (London: Routledge, 1991).

Rawls, J. A., *Theory of Justice* (Oxford: Oxford University Press, 1972).

Reid, D. M., *Lawyers and Politics in the Arab World, 1880–1960* (Minneapolis, MN: Bibliotheca Islamica, 1981).

Renteln, A. D., *International Human Rights: Universalism versus Relativism* (Newbury Park, CA: Sage Publications, 1990).

Richards, A. and Waterbury J., *A Political Economy of the Middle East: State, Class and Economic Development*, (Boulder, CO: Westview Press, 1990).

Rodinson, M., *Islam and Capitalism* (London: Allen Lane, 1974, traslated by B. Pearce).

Rorty, R., *Contingency, Irony and Solidarity* (Cambridge: Cambridge University Press,1989).

——*Philosophy and the Mirror of Nature* (Princeton, NJ: Princeton University Press, 1979).

Rosen, L., *The Anthropology of Justice: Law as Culture in Islamic Society* (Cambridge: Cambridge University Press, 1989).

Rubin, B., *Islamic Fundamentalism in Egyptian Politics* (London: Macmillan, 1990).

Rudebeck, L., *Party and People: A Study of Political Change in Tunisia* (London: C. Hurst, 1967).

Ruedy, J. (ed.), *Islamism and Secularism in North Africa* (Basingstoke, Hampshire: Macmillan, 1994).

Rugh, A. B., *Family in Contemporary Egypt* (New York: Syracuse University Press, 1984).

Safran, N., *Egypt in Search of Political Community: An Analysis of the Intellectual and Political Evolution of Egypt, 1804–1952* (Cambridge, MA: Harvard University Press, 1961).

Said, E., *Orientalism* (London: Penguin Books, 1978).

Salem, N., *Habib Bourguiba, Islam and the Creation of Tunisia,* (London: Croom Helm, 1984).

Sandel, M. (ed.), *Liberalism and its Critics* (Oxford: Blackwell, 1984).

Schacht, J., *An Introduction to Islamic Law* (Oxford: Clarendon Press, 1964).

Sebag, P., *Histoire des Juifs de Tunisie* (Paris: L'Harmattan, 1991).

Shamir, S. (ed.), *Egypt from Monarchy to Republic: A Reassessment of Revolution and Change* (Boulder, CO: Westview Press, 1995).

Sharabi, H., *Arab Intellectuals and the West: The Formative Years, 1875–1914* (Baltimore, MD: Johns Hopkins Press, 1970).

Sherif, S., *Women's Rights in Islam* (London: Ta-Ha Publishers, 1989).

Shue, H., *Basic Rights: Subsistence, Affluence and United States Foreign Policy* (Princeton, NJ: Princeton University Press, 1980).

Sidahmed, A. S., and Ehteshami, A. (eds), *Islamic Fundamentalism* (Boulder, CO: Westview Press, 1996).

Smith, C. D., *Islam and the Search for Social Order in Modern Egypt: A Biography of Muhammad Husayn Haykal* (Albany, NY: State University of New York Press, 1983).

Smith, D. E. (ed.), *Religion and Political Modernisation* (New Haven, CT: Yale

University Press, 1974).

Solihin, S. M., *Copts and Muslims in Egypt: A Study on Harmony and Hostility* (Leicester: Islamic Foundation, 1991).

Souriau, C. (ed.), *Le Maghreb musulman en 1979* (Paris: CNRS, 1981).

Springborg, R., *Family, Power and Politics in Egypt: Sayed Bey Marei - His Clan, Clients and Cohorts* (Philadelphia, PA: University of Pennsylvania Press, 1982).

Springborg, R., *Mubarak's Egypt: Fragmentation of the Political Order* (Boulder, CO: Westview Press, 1989).

Sraieb, N. et al., *Le Mouvement ouvrier maghrébin* (Paris: CNRS, 1985).

Stepan, A., *The State and Society: Peru in Comparative Perspective* (Princeton, NJ: Princeton University Press, 1978).

Strauss, L., *Natural Right and History* (Chicago, IL: University of Chicago Press, 1950).

Sullivan, E. L., *Women in Egyptian Public Life* (Syracuse, NY: Syracuse University Press, 1986).

Tabandeh, S., *A Muslim Commentary on the Universal Declaration of Human Rights* (1966, translated by F. J. Goulding).

Tamadonfar, M., *The Islamic Polity and Political Leadership* (Boulder, CO: Westview Press, 1989).

Taylor, C., *The Ethics of Authenticity* (Cambridge, MA: Harvard University Press, 1991).

Thaalbi, A., *La Tunisie martyre* (Dar al-Gharb al-Islami, 1985, deuxième édition tirée de l'édition originale de 1920).

Tignor, R. L., *State, Private Enterprise and Economic Change in Egypt, 1918–1952* (Princeton, NJ: Princeton University Press, 1984).

Tlili, B., *Les Rapports culturels et idéologiques entre l'orient et l'occident en Tunisie au xixème siècle* (Tunis: Publications de l'Université de Tunis, 1974).

Toumi, M., *La Tunisie de Bourguiba à Ben Ali* (Paris: PUF, 1989).

Tripp, C. and Owen, R. (eds), *Egypt Under Mubarak* (London: Routledge, 1989).

Turner, B. S. (ed.), *Citizenship and Social Theory* (London: Sage, 1993).

—— *Citizenship and Capitalism: The Debate over Reformism* (London: Allenand Unwin, 1986).

Vatikiotis, P. J., *The History of Modern Egypt: From Muhammad Ali to Mubarak* (London: Weidenfeld and Nicolson, 1991).

Vincent, R. J., *Human Rights and International Relations* (Cambridge: Cambridge University Press for the Royal Institute of International Affairs, 1986).

Waldron, J. (ed.), *Theories of Rights* (New York: Oxford University Press, 1984).

Waltz, S., *Human Rights and Reform: Changing the Face of North African Politics*

(Berkeley, CA: University of California Press, 1995).

Warburg, G. R. and Kupferschmidt, U. M. (eds), *Islam, Nationalism, and Radicalism in Egypt and the Sudan* (New York: Praeger, 1983).

Waterbury, J., *The Egypt of Nasser and Sadat: The Political Economy of Two Regimes* (Princeton, NJ: Princeton University Press, 1983).

Watt, W. M., *Islamic Philosophy and Theology* (Edinburgh: Edinburgh University Press, 1985).

Ye'or, B., *Juifs et chrétiens sous l'Islam: Les dhimmis face au défi intégriste* (Paris: Berg International, 1994).

Zartman, I. W. (ed.), *Tunisia: The Political Economy of Reform* (Boulder, CO: Lynne Rienner, 1991).

Zebiri, K., *Mahmud Shaltut and Islamic Modernism* (Oxford: Clarendon Press, 1993).

Ziadeh, N. A., *Origins of Nationalism in Tunisia* (Beirut: American University of Beirut, 1962).

Zubaida, S., *Islam, the People and the State: Political Ideas and Movements in the Middle East* (London: I. B. Tauris, 1993).

Articles

Abed-Kotob, S., 'The Accommodationists Speak: Goals and Strategies of the Muslim Brotherhood in Egypt' in *International Journal of Middle East Studies* (Vol. 27, No. 3, August 1995).

Abu Layla, M., 'Islam and the World Religions' in D'Costa, G. (ed.), *Faith Meets Faith: Interfaith Views on Interfaith* (London: BFSS RE Centre, 1988).

Adda, S., 'Enjeux: Le possible et le probable' in Camau, M. (ed.), *Tunisie au présent: Une modernité au-dessus de tout soupçon?* (Paris: CNRS, 1987).

Akeel, H. A. and Moore, C. H., 'The Class Origins of Egyptian Engineer-Technocrats' in Nieuwenhuijze, C. A. O. (ed.), *Commoners, Climbers and Notables: A Sampler of Studies on Social Ranking in the Middle East* (Leiden: E. J. Brill, 1977).

Akehurst, A., 'Humanitarian Intervention' in Bull, H. (ed.), *Intervention in World Politics* (New York: Oxford University Press, 1984).

Al-Sayyid Marsot, A. L. 'Religion or Opposition? Urban Protest Movements in Egypt' in *International Journal of Middle East Studies* (Vol. 16, No. 4, November 1984).

——'The Beginnings of Modernization among the Rectors of al-Azhar, 1798–1879' in Polk, W. R. and Chambers, R. L. (eds), *Beginnings of Modernization in the Middle East: The Nineteenth Century* (Chicago, IL: University of

Chicago Press, 1968).

Al-Sayyid, M. K., 'A Civil Society in Egypt?' in *Middle East Journal* (Vol. 47, No. 2, Spring 1993).

Aly, A. M. S. and Wenner, M. W., 'Modern Islamic Reform Movements: The Muslim Brotherhood in Contemporary Egypt' in *Middle East Journal* (Vol. 36, No. 3, Summer 1982).

An-Naim, A. A., 'A Modern Approach to Human Rights in Islam: Foundations and Implications for Africa' in Welch, C. E. and Meltzer, R. I. (eds), *Human Rights and Development in Africa* (Albany, NY: State University of New York Press, 1984).

——'Religious Minorities under Islamic Law and the Limits of Cultural Relativism' in *Human Rights Quarterly* (Vol. 9, No. 1, February 1987).

Anderson, J. N. D., 'Law Reform in the Middle East' in *International Affairs* (Vol. 32, No. 1, January 1956).

Ansari, H. N., 'Sectarian Conflict in Egypt and the Political Expediency of Religion' in *Middle East Journal* (Vol. 38, No. 3, Summer 1984).

——'The Islamic Militants in Egyptian Politics' in *International Journal of Middle East Studies* (Vol. 16, No. 1, March 1984).

Baker, R. W., 'Sadat's Open Door: Opposition from Within' in *Social Problems*, (Vol. 28, No. 4, April 1981).

Bangkok Declaration, April 1993, by the Asia intergovernmental meeting in preparation for the Conference, in *Our Voice: The Bangkok NGO Declaration on Human Rights* (Bangkok: Asian Cultural Forum on Development, 1993).

Beinin, J., 'Egyptian Women and the Politics of Protest' in *Middle East Report* (No. 176, Vol. 22, No. 3, May–June 1992).

Belaid, S., 'La Justice politique en Tunisie', *Revue Tunisienne de Droit* (1983).

Bianchi, R., 'The Corporatisation of the Egyptian Labour Movement' in *Middle East Journal* (Vol. 40, No. 3, Summer 1986).

Boli-Bennett, J., 'Human Rights or State Expansion? Cross-National Definitions of Constitutional Rights, 1870–1970' in Nanda, V. P., Scarritt, J. R. and Shepherd, G. W. (eds), *Global Human Rights: Public Policies, Comparative Measures and NGO Strategies* (Boulder, CO: Westview Press, 1981).

Borthwick, B. M., 'Religion and Politics in Israel and Egypt' in *Middle East Journal* (Vol. 33, No. 2, Spring 1979).

Brown, C., ''Turtles All the Way Down': Anti-Foundationalism, Critical Theory and International Relations', *Millennium: Journal of International Studies* (Vol. 23, No. 2, Summer 1994).

Brown, L. C., 'Towards a Comparative History of Modernization in the Arab World: Tunisia and Egypt' in *Cahiers du CERES* (Université de Tunis),

Identité culturelle et conscience nationale en Tunisie: Actes du colloque tenu à Tunis, 18–19 mars 1974 (Tunis: CERES, 1974).

Bulletin du CEDEJ (Deuxième semestre, 1985), Special issue on 'Études sur les droits de l'homme'.

Camau, M., 'L'État tunisien: De la tutelle au désengagement' in *Maghreb-Machrek* (No. 103, Janvier–Mars 1984).

——'Religion politique et religion d'état en Tunisie' in Gellner, E., and Vatin, J. – C., (eds), *Islam et Politique au Maghreb* (Paris: CNRS, 1981).

Carré, O., 'L'Ideologie politico–religieuse nasserienne à la lumière des manuels scolaires' in *Politique Étrangère* (No. 4, 37e année, 1972).

Charfi, M., 'Droits de l'homme, droit musulman et droit tunisien' in *Revue Tunisienne de Droit* (1983).

——'Le Droit tunisien de la famille entre l'Islam et la modernité' in *Revue Tunisienne de Droit* (1973).

Cooper, J., 'Human Rights: Towards an Islamic Framework', in *Gulf Report* (No. 34, October 1993).

Cooper, M. N., 'State Capitalism, Class Structure and Social Transformation in the Third World: The Case of Egypt' in *International Journal of Middle East Studies* (Vol. 15, No. 4, November 1983).

Coulson, N. J., 'The State and the Individual in Islamic Law' in *International and Comparative Law Quarterly* (Vol. 6, Part 1, January 1957).

Crecelius, D., 'Al-Azhar in the Revolution' in *Middle East Journal*, (Vol. 20, No. 1, Winter 1966).

——'Nonideological Responses of the Egyptian Ulama to Modernization' in Keddie, N. R. (ed.), *Scholars, Saints and Sufis: Muslim Religious Institutions in the Middle East since 1500* (Berkeley, CA: University of California Press, 1972).

Deeb, M., 'Labour and Politics in Egypt, 1919–1939' in *International Journal of Middle East Studies* (Vol. 10, No. 2, May 1979).

Dessouki, A. E. H., 'The Resurgence of the Islamic Organisations in Egypt: An Interpretation' in Cudsi, A. S., and Dessouki, A. E. H. (eds), *Islam and Power* (London: Croom Helm, 1981).

Donelan, M., 'Reason in War' in *Review of International Studies* (Vol. 8, No. 1, January 1982).

Donnelly, J., 'Cultural Relativism and Universal Human Rights' in *Human Rights Quarterly* (Vol. 6, No. 4, November 1984).

——'Human Rights and Development: Complementary or Competing Concerns?' in *World Politics*, (Vol. 36, No. 2, January 1984).

——'Human Rights and Human Dignity: An Analytic Critique of Non-Western Conceptions of Human Rights' in *American Political Science Review*

(Vol. 76, No. 2, June 1982).

Eliraz, G., 'Egyptian Intellectuals and Women's Emancipation, 1919–1939' in *Asian and African Studies* (Vol. 16, No. 1, March 1982).

Flores, A., 'Egypt: A New Secularism?' in *Middle East Report* (No. 153, Vol. 18, No. 4, July–August 1988).

Geras, N., 'Language, Truth and Justice' in *New Left Review* (No. 209, January / February 1995).

Ghanem, F., 'Profile of a Muslim Militant (Fiction)' in *Jerusalem Quarterly* (No. 34, Winter 1985).

Ghannouchi, R., 'Towards Inclusive Strategies for Human Rights Enforcement in the Arab World – A Response' in *Encounters: Journal of Inter-Cultural Perspectives* (Vol. 2, No. 2, September 1996).

Green, A. H., 'A Comparative Historical Analysis of the Ulama and the State in Egypt and Tunisia' in *Revue de l'Occident Musulman et de la Méditerranée* (No. 29, Premier semestre, 1980).

Guezmir, K., 'Le Mouvement Bach Hamba et la conscience nationale' in *Cahiers du CERES*, (Université de Tunis), *Identité culturelle et conscience nationale en Tunisie: Actes du colloque tenu à Tunis*, 18–19 mars 1974 (Tunis: CERES, 1974).

Haddad, Y. Y., 'Islamic 'Awakening' in Egypt', *Arab Studies Quarterly* (Vol. 9, No. 3, Summer 1987).

Halliday, F., 'The Politics of Islamic Fundamentalism: Iran, Tunisia and the Challenge to the Secular State' in Ahmed, A. S. and Donnan, H. (eds), *Islam, Globalization and Post-Modernity* (London: Routledge, 1994).

Hanafi, H., 'The Relevance of the Islamic Alternative in Egypt' in *Arab Studies Quarterly* (Vol. 4, Nos. 1 and 2, Spring 1982).

Hassan, B. E., 'Towards Human Rights Enforcement in the Arab World: A Comprehensive Strategy' in *Encounters: Journal of Inter-Cultural Perspectives* (Vol. 2, No. 2, September 1996).

Hatem, M. F., 'Egyptian Discourses on Gender and Political Liberalisation: Do Secularist and Islamist Views Really Differ?' in *Middle East Journal* (Vol. 48, No. 4, Autumn 1994).

Hermassi, M. E., 'La Société tunisienne au miroir islamiste' in *Maghreb-Machrek* (No. 103, Janvier–Fèvrier 1984).

Herskovits, M. J., 'Tender- and Tough-Minded Anthropology and the Study of Values in Cultures' in *Southwestern Journal of Anthropology*, (Vol. 7, No. 1, Spring 1951).

——'Some Further Comments on Cultural Relativism' in *American Anthropologist*, (Vol. 60, No. 2, April 1958).

Higgins, R., 'Conceptual Thinking About the Individual in International Law' in *British Journal of International Studies* (Vol. 4, No. 1, April 1978).

Hill, E., 'Courts and the Administration of Justice in the Modern Era' in Hanna, N. (ed.), *The State and its Servants: Administration in Egypt from Ottoman Times to the Present* (Cairo: American University in Cairo Press, 1995).

Hinnebusch, R. A., 'The National Progressive Unionist Party: The Nationalist-Left Opposition in Post-Populist Egypt' in *Arab Studies Quarterly* (Vol. 3, No. 4, Fall 1981).

——'The Reemergence of the Wafd Party: Glimpses of the Liberal Opposition in Egypt' in *International Journal of Middle East Studies* (Vol. 16, No. 1, March 1984).

Hollenbach, D., 'Human Rights and Religious Faith in the Middle East: Reflections of a Christian Theologian' in *Human Rights Quarterly* (Vol. 4, No. 1, Spring 1982).

Homerin, T. E., 'Ibn Arabi in the People's Assembly: Religion, Press and Politics in Sadat's Egypt' in *Middle East Journal* (Vol. 40, No. 3, Summer 1986).

Hoodfar, H., 'A Background to the Feminist Movement in Egypt' in *Women Living Under Muslim Laws* (Dossier 7/8).

Humphreys, R. S., 'Islam and Political Values in Saudi Arabia, Egypt and Syria' in *Middle East Journal* (Vol. 33, No. 1, Winter 1979).

Huntington, S. P., 'The Clash of Civilizations?' in *Foreign Affairs* (Vol. 72, No. 3, Summer 1993).

Ibrahim, S. E., 'An Islamic Alternative in Egypt: The Muslim Brotherhood and Sadat' in *Arab Studies Quarterly* (Vol. 4, Nos. 1 and 2, Spring 1982).

——'Egypt's Islamic Militants' in *Merip Reports* (No. 103, Vol. 12, No. 2, February 1982).

——'Anatomy of Egypt's Militant Islamic Groups: Methodological Note and Preliminary Findings' in *International Journal of Middle East Studies* (Vol. 12, No. 4, December 1980).

Islam, M., 'Human Rights in Islamic Law and International Law: a ComparativeStudy' in *The Iranian Journal* (Vol. 3, No. 4, Winter 1991/2).

Islamic Council: What It Stands For (pamhlet).

Issawi, C., 'Economic and Social Foundations of Democracy in the Middle East', *International Affairs* (Vol. 32, No. 1, January 1956).

Jacquemond, R., 'Un projet de code pénal islamique égyptien' in *Bulletin du CEDEJ* (Deuxième semestre, 1986).

Keddie, N. R., 'The Rights of Women in Contemporary Islam' in Rouner, L. S. (ed.), *Human Rights and the World's Religions* (Notre Dame, IN: University of Notre Dame Press, 1988).

Kupferschmidt, U. M., 'The Muslim Brothers and the Egyptian Village' in *Asian and African Studies* (Vol. 16, No. 1, March 1982).

Lazarus-Yafeh, H., 'Contemporary Religious Thought among the Ulama of Al-Azhar' in *Asian and African Studies*, (Vol. 7, 1971).

Luard, E., 'The Origins of the International Concern over Human Rights' in Luard, E. (ed.), *The International Protection of Human Rights* (London: Thames and Hudson, 1967).

Malik, M. I., 'The Concept of Human Rights in Islamic Jurisprudence' in *Human Rights Quarterly* (Vol. 3, No. 3, Summer 1981).

Mayer, A. E., 'Reform of Personal Status Laws in North Africa: A Problem of Islamic of Mediterranean Laws?' in *Middle East Journal* (Vol. 49, No. 3, Summer 1995).

Mortimer, E., 'Islam and Human Rights' in *Index on Censorship*, 5/83.

MTI, 'Un point de vue à propos de notre tactique politique pour l'étape actuel' in *Sou'al*, Special issue on 'L'Islamisme ajourd'hui', avril 1985.

Mumson, H., 'Islamic Revivalism in Morocco and Tunisia' in *Muslim World*, (Vol. LXXVI, July/October 1986).

Nowaihi, M., 'Changing the Law on Personal Status within a Liberal Interpetation of the Sharia' in Nelson, C. and Koch, K. F. (eds), *Law and Social Change: Problems and Challenges in Contemporary Egypt* (Cairo Papers in Social Science, Vol. 2, Monograph 4, July 1983 / Cairo: American University in Cairo Press).

O'Kane, J. P., 'Islam in the New Egyptian Constitution: Some Discussions in al- Ahram' in *Middle East Journal* (Vol. 26, No. 2, Spring 1972).

Osman, F., 'Democracy Essential for Ikhwan' in *Arabia: The Islamic World Review* (No. 6, February 1982).

Pennington, J. D., 'The Copts in Modern Egypt' in *Middle Eastern Studies* (Vol. 18, No. 2, April 1982).

Pirzada, S., 'Concept of Islamic State and Human Rights in Islam' in *The Iranian Journal* (Vol. 3, No. 4, Winter 1991/2).

Piscatori, J. P., 'Human Rights in Islamic Political Culture' in Thompson, K. W. (ed.), *The Moral Imperatives of Human Rights: A World Survey* (Washington D. C.: University Press of America, 1980).

Pripstein, M., 'Egypt's New Labor Law Removes Worker Provisions' in *Middle East Report* (No. 194/5. Vol. 25, Nos. 3 and 4, May–June/July–August 1995).

Rawls, J., 'The Law of Peoples' in Shute., S. and Hurley, S. (eds) *On Human Rights: The Oxford Amnesty Lectures 1993* (New York: Basic Books, 1993).

Reid, D. M., 'The Return of the Egyptian Wafd, 1978' in *International Journal of African Historical Studies* (Vol. 12, No. 3, 1979).

——'The Rise of Professions and Professional Organisation in Modern Egypt' in *Comparative Studies in Society and History* (Vol. 16, No. 1, January 1974).

Roussillon, A., 'Intellectuels en crise dans l'Égypte contemporaine' in Kepel,

G. and Richard, Y. (eds), *Intellectuels et militants de l'Islam contemporain* (Paris: Seuil, 1990).

Said, A. A., 'Precept and Practice of Human Rights in Islam' in *Universal Human Rights* (Vol. 1, No. 1, January–March 1979).

Sivan, E., 'The Islamic Republic of Egypt' in *Orbis: A Journal of World Affairs* (Vol. 31, No. 1, Spring 1987).

——'The Two Faces of Islamic Fundamentalism' in *Jerusalem Quarterly* (No. 27, Spring 1983).

Smith, C. D., 'The 'Crisis of Orientation': The Shift of Egyptian Intellectuals to Islamic Subjects in the 1930s' in *International Journal of Middle East Studies* (Vol. 4, No. 4, 1973).

Springborg, R., 'Patterns of Association in the Egyptian Political Elite' in Lenczowski, G. (ed.), *Political Elites in the Middle East* (Washington, D. C.: American Enterprise Institute for Public Policy Research, 1975).

Sraieb, N., 'Université et société au Maghreb: Le Qarawiyin de Fes et la Zaytouna de Tunis' in *Revue de l'Occident Musulman et de la Mediterranéee*, (No. 38, Deuxième semestre, 1984).

'Statement on Human Rights'. Submitted to the Commission on Human Rights, United Nations, by the Executive Board, American Anthropological Association in *American Anthropologist* (Vol. 49, No. 4, October–December 1947).

Stone, R. A., 'Tunisia: A Single Party System Holds Change in Abeyance' in Zartman, I. W., et al. (eds), *Political Elites in Arab North Africa* (New York: Longman, 1982).

Stork, J., 'Egypt's Factory Privatization Campaign Turns Deadly' in *Middle East Report* (No. 192, Vol. 25, No. 1, January–February 1995).

Tessler, M., 'Political Change and the Islamic Revival in Tunisia' in the *Maghreb Review* (Vol. 5, No. 1, January–February 1980).

'The 1971 Constitution of the Arab Republic of Egypt' in *Middle East Journal* (Vol. 26, No. 1, Winter 1972).

'Tunisian Constitution' in Blaustein, A. P., and Flanz, G. H., (eds), *Constitutions of the Countries of the World* (Dobbs Ferry, NY: Oceana Publications, 1990).

Vandewalle, D., 'From the New State to the New Era: Toward a Second Republic in Tunisia' in *Middle East Journal* (Vol. 42, No. 4, Autumn 1988).

Vincent, R. J., 'Western Conceptions of a Universal Moral Order' in Pettman, R. (ed.), *Moral Claims in World Affairs* (London: Croom Helm, 1979).

Waltz, S., 'Islamist Appeal in Tunisia' in *Middle East Journal,* (Vol. 40, No. 4, Autumn 1986).

——'Tunisia's League and the Pursuit of Human Rights' in the *Maghreb Review* (Vol. 14, Nos. 3–4, 1989).

Warburg, G. R., 'Islam and Politics in Egypt: 1952–80' in *Middle Eastern Studies* (Vol. 18, No. 2, April 1982).

Ware, L. B., 'Ben Ali's Constitutional Coup in Tunisia', in *Middle East Journal* (Vol. 42, No. 4, Autumn 1988).

Windsor, P. 'Cultural Dialogue in Human Rights', in Desai, M. and Redfern, P. (eds), *Global Governance: Ethics and Economics of the World Order* (London: Pinter,1995).

Yamane, H., 'Asia and Human Rights' in Vasak, K. and Alston, P. (eds), *The International Dimensions of Human Rights* (Westport, CT: Greenwood Press and Paris: Unesco, 1982), Vol. 2.

Youssef, S. M., 'The Egyptian Private Sector and the Bureaucracy' in *Middle Eastern Studies* (Vol. 30, No. 2, April 1994).

Zaimeche, S. E., 'Algeria, Morocco and Tunisia: Recent Social Change and Future Prospects' in *Middle Eastern Studies* (Vol. 30, No. 4, Oct. 1994).

Zghal, A., 'L'Élite administrative et la paysannerie en Tunisie' in Debbasch, C., et al., *Pouvoir et administration au Maghreb: Études sur le élites maghrébines* (Paris: CNRS, 1970).

——'The Reactivaton of Tradition in a Post-Traditional Society' in *Daedalus* (Vol. 102, No. 1, Winter 1973).

Zubaida, S., 'Islam, the State and Democracy: Contrasting Conceptions of Society in Egypt' in *Middle East Report* (No. 179, Vol. 22, No. 6, November/ December 1992).

Newspapers, Journals and Other

Al Ahram Weekly
Bulletin du CEDEJ
Cahiers du CERES
Civil Society: Democratic Transformation in the Arab World (Newsletter issued by Ibn Khaldun Center for Development Studies, Cairo)
Economist Intelligence Unit
Femme
Financial Times Survey, Tunisia, 14 June 1993
Jeune Afrique
L'Economiste Maghrebin
Le Monde Diplomatique
Le Point
Le Quotidien d'Algérie
Middle East Contemporary Survey

Middle East International
Middle East Times: Egypt Edition
Nissa, 1985–86
Réalités
Sawasiah (Newsletter issued by the Cairo Institute for Human Rights Studies)
Summary of World Broadcasts

Human Rights Reports

Amnesty International, *Egypt: Arbitrary Detention and Torture under Emergency Powers* (AI Index, MDE 12/01/89, May 1989).
——*Egypt: Security Police Detentions Undermine the Rule of Law* (AI Index, MDE 12/01/92, January 1992).
——*Egypt: Ten Years of Torture* (AI Index, MDE 12/18/91, October1991).
——*Tunisia: Heavy Sentences after Unfair Trials*, October 1992.
——*Tunisia: Prolonged Incommunicado Detention and Torture*, March 1992.
——*Tunisia: Summary of Amnesty International's Concerns*, September 1990.
——*Tunisia: Rhetoric Versus Reality: The Failure of a Human Rights Bureaucracy*, January 1994.
——*Tunisie: L'Impunité favorise le renforcement de la repression*, Novembre 1995.
——*Tunisia: A Widening Circle of Repression*, June 1997.
Egyptian Organisation of Human Rights (EOHR) Demands an End to Clerical Controls on Thought, Literature and Art, 14 January 1992.
—— *An EOHR Statement on the Assassination of Dr Farag Foda*, 9 June 1992.
——*Armed Violence in Egypt: Facts and Conclusions*, 14 September 1992.
——*Freedom of Thought and Belief: Between the State's 'Anvil' and the Islamic Groups 'Hammer'*, 1 May 1992, (a speech by Bahey El Din Hassan, secretary-general of the EOHR, on May 1–2, 1992).
——*The Campaign to Stop Torture: Rape and Sexual Abuse as Methods of Torture*, 7 January 1992.
——*Urgent Report on the Sectarian Massacre in Dairout*, 7 May 1992.
——*In Defense of Human Rights: The EOHR May 1993 to December 1994 Press Releases and Reports* (Cairo: EOHR, 1995).
——*Recurrent Detention: Prisoners Without Trial*, 15/1/1993 – 30/12/1994.
——*Freedom of Opinion and Belief: Restrictions and Dilemmas* (Proceedings on the Workshop on the Azhar's Censorship of Audio and Audiovisual Productions, Cairo, 8–9 March 1994).
——*Democracy Jeopardised: Nobody 'Passed' the Elections: The EOHR Account*

of the Egyptian Parliamentary Elections, 1995.

——*Annual Report, 1995.*

——*Torture Inside Police Stations Must Be Stopped* (March 10, 1997).

Human Rights Watch World Report, 1997 (New York: Human Rights Watch, 1996).

Human Rights Watch: Middle East, *Egypt: Human Rights Abuses Mount in 1993* (Vol. 5, Issue 8, 22 October, 1993).

Lawyers Committe for Human Rights, Hicks, N., *Promise Unfulfilled: Human Rights in Tunisia since 1987* (Washington, D. C.: Lawyers Committe for Human Rights).

Middle East Watch, *Behind Closed Doors: Torture and Detention in Egypt* (New York: Human Rights Watch, 1992).

Republic of Tunisia: Higher Committe for Human Rights and Basic Freedoms *Report to the President of the Republic on the Implementation of the Recommendations of the Commission of Enquiry* (Tunis, 13 July 1992).

Unpublished Materials

Abou el-Magd, N. M. I., *The Political Ideas of Khaled Mohamed Khaled: Islam, Democracy, Socialism and Nationalism* (Dissertation, American University in Cairo, Department of Political Science, 1992).

Aboulmagd, K., 'Human Rights in Islam: Theory and Practice'.

Bangkok NGO Declaration on Human Rights (March 1993).

Charfi, S., *La Ligue Tunisienne pour la Défense des Droits de l'Hommes,* (Mémoire, Université de Tunis, Faculté de Droit et des Sciences Politiques, Juin 1987).

El-Atrash, S. S., *The Arab Human Rights Position in the Light of International Law,* (LL. M. Dissertation, Glasgow University, June 1986).

Labidi, L., 'Circulation des femmes musulmanes dans l'éspace public et politique formel: Le cas de la Tunisie'.

——'L'Émergence du sentiment politique chez les Intellectuelles Musulmanes dans le Monde Arabe dans la premier moitié du XXème siècle: Le cas de la Tunisie'.

——'Sexualité et politique dans le discours islamiste au féminin: Le cas de la Tunisie' (presented at the 1st International Congress of FRAPPE, Montreal, June 1990).

Magnuson, D. K., *Islamic Reform in Contemporary Tunisia: A Comparative Ethnographic Study* (PhD thesis, Department of Anthropology, Brown University, May 1987).

Proceedings of the International Conference on the Role of the Judiciary in the Protection of Human Rights, 1–3 December 1996, Cairo, Egypt.

Shahin, E. E. A., *The Restitution of Islam: A Comparative Study of the Islamic Movements in Contemporary Tunisia and Morocco*, (PhD thesis, Johns Hopkins University, Baltimore, Maryland, 1989).

Index

232